First World War
and Army of Occupation
War Diary
France, Belgium and Germany

41 DIVISION
Divisional Troops
Machine Gun Corps
41 Battalion
1 March 1918 - 31 October 1919

WO95/2627/4

The Naval & Military Press Ltd
www.nmarchive.com
Published in association with The National Archives

Published by

The Naval & Military Press Ltd

Unit 10 Ridgewood Industrial Park,

Uckfield, East Sussex,

TN22 5QE England

Tel: +44 (0) 1825 749494

www.naval-military-press.com

www.nmarchive.com

This diary has been reprinted in facsimile from the original. Any imperfections are inevitably reproduced and the quality may fall short of modern type and cartographic standards.

© Crown Copyright
Images reproduced by permission of The National Archives, London, England, 2015.

Contents

Document type	Place/Title	Date From	Date To
Heading	WO95/2627/5		
Heading	41 Div Troops 41 Bn Machine Gun Corps 1918 Mar-1919 Oct		
Heading	41st Battalion Machine Gun Corps. March 1918		
War Diary		01/03/1918	31/03/1918
Operation(al) Order(s)	Operation Orders Nos. 1, 3 And 4.		
Operation(al) Order(s)	41st Battalion Machine Gun Corps. Operation Order No 1.	20/03/1918	20/03/1918
Operation(al) Order(s)	41st Machine Gun Battalion Operation Order No. 3.	29/03/1918	29/03/1918
Operation(al) Order(s)	Battalion Orders No 14. By Lieut.-Col. E.M. Beall, D.S.O. Commanding 41st Battalion Machine Gun Corps. Sunday, 31st March, 1918.	31/03/1918	31/03/1918
Heading	41st Battalion M.G.C. April 1918		
Miscellaneous	41st Division "G".	01/05/1918	01/05/1918
War Diary	France	01/04/1918	30/04/1918
Operation(al) Order(s)	41st Battalion Machine Gun Corps Operation Order No. 5.	01/04/1918	01/04/1918
Operation(al) Order(s)	41st Battalion Machine Gun Corps Operation Order No. 6.	02/04/1918	02/04/1918
Operation(al) Order(s)	41st Battalion Machine Gun Corps Operation Order No. 8.	07/04/1918	07/04/1918
Operation(al) Order(s)	41st Battalion Machine Gun Corps Operation Order No. 9.	07/04/1918	07/04/1918
Miscellaneous	O.C. "A" Company.	10/04/1918	10/04/1918
Miscellaneous	O.C. "B" Company.	10/04/1918	10/04/1918
Operation(al) Order(s)	41st Battalion Machine Gun Corps Operation Order No. 16.	13/04/1918	13/04/1918
Operation(al) Order(s)	Operation Order No. 17. By Lieut.-Col. A.W. Tate. Commanding 41st Battalion Machine Gun Corps. 15th April, 1918.	15/04/1918	15/04/1918
Operation(al) Order(s)	Operation Order No. 18. By Lieut.-Col. A.W. Tate. Commanding 41st Battalion Machine Gun Corps. 15th April, 1918.	15/04/1918	15/04/1918
Operation(al) Order(s)	Operation Order No. 19. By Lieut.-Col. A.W. Tate. Commanding 41st Battalion Machine Gun Corps. 16th April, 1918.	16/04/1918	16/04/1918
Operation(al) Order(s)	Operation Order No. 20. By Lieut.-Col. A.W. Tate. Commanding 41st Battalion Machine Gun Corps. 18th April, 1918.	18/04/1918	18/04/1918
Miscellaneous	O.C. "A" Company. O.C. "B" Company. O.C. "C" Company. O.C. "D" Company.	20/04/1918	20/04/1918
Miscellaneous	O.C. "A" Company. O.C. "B" Company. O.C. "C" Company. O.C. "D" Company.	23/04/1918	23/04/1918
Operation(al) Order(s)	Operation Order No. 21. By Lieut.-Col. A.W. Tate. Commanding 41st Battalion Machine Gun Corps. Friday, 26th April, 1918.	26/04/1918	26/04/1918
Heading	Machine Gun Corps 41st Battalion War Diary For May 1918 With Appendices Nos. 1 To 7.		
War Diary		01/05/1918	31/05/1918

Operation(al) Order(s)	Operation Order No. 23. By Lieut.-Col. A.W. Tate. Commanding 41st Battalion Machine Gun Corps. Wednesday, 1st May, 1918.	02/05/1918	02/05/1918
Operation(al) Order(s)	Operation Order No. 24. By Lieut.-Col. A.W. Tate. Commanding 41st Battalion Machine Gun Corps. Monday, 6th May, 1918.	07/05/1918	07/05/1918
Operation(al) Order(s)	Operation Order No. 25. By Lieut.-Col. A.W. Tate. Commanding 41st Battalion Machine Gun Corps. Friday, 10th May, 1918.	10/05/1918	10/05/1918
Operation(al) Order(s)	Operation Order No. 26. By Lieut.-Col. A.W. Tate. Commanding 41st Battalion Machine Gun Corps. Wednesday, 15th May, 1918.	15/05/1918	15/05/1918
Operation(al) Order(s)	Operation Order No. 27. By Lieut.-Col. A.W. Tate. Commanding 41st Battalion Machine Gun Corps. Tuesday, 21st May, 1918.	21/05/1918	21/05/1918
Operation(al) Order(s)	Operation Order No. 28. By Lieut.-Col. A.W. Tate. Commanding 41st Battalion Machine Gun Corps. Monday, 27th May, 1918.	27/05/1918	27/05/1918
Heading	41st Battalion Machine Gun Corps Diary For The Month Of June 1918		
War Diary		01/06/1918	30/06/1918
Miscellaneous	O.C. "A" Company. O.C. "B" Company. O.C. "C" Company. O.C. "D" Company.	01/06/1918	01/06/1918
Miscellaneous	Administrative Orders: By Lieut.-Col. A.W. Tate. Commanding 41st Battalion Machine Gun Corps. Sunday, 2nd June, 1918.	02/06/1918	02/06/1918
Miscellaneous	Administrative Instructions Part II. By Lieut.-Col. A.W. Tate. Commanding 41st Battalion Machine Gun Corps. Sunday, 2nd June, 1918.	03/06/1918	03/06/1918
Miscellaneous	O.C. "A" Company. "B" Company. "C" Company. "D" Company. Transport Officer. Quartermaster. Signal Officer. Medical Officer. R.S.M.	09/06/1918	09/06/1918
Miscellaneous	Training Programme For Week Ending 22nd June, 1918.	22/06/1918	22/06/1918
Miscellaneous	Administrative Order. By Lieut.-Col. A.W. Tate. Commanding 41st Battalion Machine Gun Corps. Tuesday, 25th June, 1918.	25/06/1918	25/06/1918
Miscellaneous	Administrative Order. By Lieut.-Col. A.W. Tate. Commanding 41st Battalion Machine Gun Corps. Monday, 24th June, 1918.	24/06/1918	24/06/1918
Operation(al) Order(s)	Operation Order No. 31. By Lieut.-Col. A.W. Tate. Commanding 41st Battalion Machine Gun Corps. Friday, 28th June, 1918.	29/06/1918	29/06/1918
Miscellaneous	Administrative Instruction No. 1. Issued In Connection With Operation Order No. 31.	29/06/1918	29/06/1918
Miscellaneous	O.C. "A" Company. "B" Company. "C" Company. "D" Company.	29/06/1918	29/06/1918
Heading	41st Battalion Machine Gun Corps War Diary For The Month Of July 1918		
War Diary		01/07/1918	31/07/1918
Miscellaneous	O.C. "A" Company. "B" Company. "C" Company. "D" Company. Quartermaster. Transport Officer. Medical Officer. Signal Officer. R.S.M.	01/07/1918	01/07/1918
Operation(al) Order(s)	Operation Order No. 32. By Lieut.-Col. A.W. Tate. Commanding 41st Battalion Machine Gun Corps. Thursday, 4th July, 1918.	04/07/1918	04/07/1918

Operation(al) Order(s)	Operation Order No. 33. By Lieut.-Col. A.W. Tate. Commanding 41st Battalion Machine Gun Corps. Tuesday, 9th July, 1918.	09/07/1918	09/07/1918
Operation(al) Order(s)	Operation Order No. 34. By Lieut.-Col. A.W. Tate. Commanding 41st Battalion Machine Gun Corps. Sunday, 14th July, 1918.	14/07/1918	14/07/1918
Miscellaneous	O.C. "C" Company. O.C. "D" Company.	14/07/1918	14/07/1918
Operation(al) Order(s)	Operation Order No. 35. By Lieut.-Col. A.W. Tate. Commanding 41st Battalion Machine Gun Corps. Friday, 19th July, 1918.	19/07/1918	19/07/1918
Operation(al) Order(s)	Operation Order No. 36. By Lieut.-Col. A.W. Tate. Commanding 41st Battalion Machine Gun Corps. Wednesday, 24th July, 1918.	24/07/1918	24/07/1918
Operation(al) Order(s)	Operation Order No. 37. By Lieut.-Col. A.W. Tate. Commanding 41st Battalion Machine Gun Corps. Thursday, 25th July, 1918.	25/07/1918	25/07/1918
Miscellaneous	O.C. "A" Company. "B" Company. "C" Company. "D" Company. Quartermaster. Transport Officer. Medical Officer. O.C. No. 5 Section, Divl. Signal Coy.	27/07/1918	27/07/1918
Miscellaneous	O.C. "A" Company. "B" Company. "C" Company. "D" Company. Quartermaster. Transport Officer. Medical Officer. O.C. No. 5 Section, Divl. Signal Coy. O.C. "B" Company, 105th A.M.G. Battn. O.C. "D" Company, 105th A.M.G. Battn.	28/07/1918	28/07/1918
Operation(al) Order(s)	Operation Order No. 38. By Lieut.-Col. A.W. Tate. Commanding 41st Battalion Machine Gun Corps. Monday, 29th July, 1918.	29/07/1918	29/07/1918
Operation(al) Order(s)	Operation Order No. 39. By Lieut.-Col. A.W. Tate. Commanding 41st Battalion Machine Gun Corps. Tuesday, 30th July, 1918.	30/07/1918	30/07/1918
Heading	War Diary For The Month Of August 1918		
War Diary		01/08/1918	07/08/1918
War Diary	Kemmel Sector	08/08/1918	29/08/1918
War Diary	Tilques Area	30/08/1918	31/08/1918
Operation(al) Order(s)	Operation Order No. 40. By Lieut.-Col. A.W. Tate. Commanding 41st Battalion Machine Gun Corps. Thursday, 1st August, 1918.	01/08/1918	01/08/1918
Operation(al) Order(s)	Operation Order No. 41. By Lieut.-Col. A.W. Tate. Commanding 41st Battalion Machine Gun Corps. Saturday 3rd August 1918.	03/08/1918	03/08/1918
Operation(al) Order(s)	Operation Order No. 42. By Lieut.-Col. A.W. Tate. Commanding 41st Battalion Machine Gun Corps.	04/08/1918	04/08/1918
Operation(al) Order(s)	Operation Order No. 43. By Lieut. Col. A.W. Tate. Commanding 41st Battalion Machine Gun Corps. Monday 5th August 1918.	06/08/1918	06/08/1918
Operation(al) Order(s)	Operation Order No. 44. By Lieut.-Col. A.W. Tate. Commanding 41st Battalion Machine Gun Corps. Tuesday August 6th 1918.	07/08/1918	07/08/1918
Operation(al) Order(s)	Operation Order No. 43. By Lieut.-Col. A.W. Tate. Commanding 41st Battalion Machine Gun Corps. Friday 9th August, 1918.	09/08/1918	09/08/1918
Operation(al) Order(s)	Operation Order No. 46 By Lieut.-Col. A.W. Tate. Commanding 41st Battalion Machine Gun Corps. Sunday 11th August 1918.	11/08/1918	11/08/1918

Miscellaneous	Appendix "B" Group Organization Chart. Reference O.O. Nos. 42 & 44 Right Group. Commanded By Major A.S. Hinshelwood.		
Miscellaneous	D.W.		
Operation(al) Order(s)	Operation Order No. 47. By Lieut.-Col. A.W. Tate. Commanding 41st Battalion Machine Gun Corps. Sunday 11th August 1918.	11/08/1918	11/08/1918
Miscellaneous	O.C. "A" Company. O.C. "B" Company. "C" Company. "D" Company. Quartermaster. Transport Officer. Medical Officer. O.C. No. 5. Section Divl. Coy.	13/08/1918	13/08/1918
Miscellaneous	O.C. "A" Company. "B" Company. "C" Company. Reference Operation Order No., 47 Of This Office Dated August 11th.	13/08/1918	13/08/1918
Operation(al) Order(s)	Operation Order No. 48. By Lieut.-Col. A.W. Tate. Commanding 41st Battalion Machine Gun Corps. Wednesday, 14th August 1918.	14/08/1918	14/08/1918
Miscellaneous	O.C. "A" Company. Quartermaster. "B" Company. Transport Officer. "C" Company. Medical Officer. "D" Company. O.C. No 5 Section, Divl. Signal Coy.	15/08/1918	15/08/1918
Operation(al) Order(s)	Operation Order No. 49. By Lieut.-Col. A.W. Tate. Commanding 41st Battalion Machine Gun Corps. Saturday 17th August 1918.	17/08/1918	17/08/1918
Miscellaneous	O.C. "A" Company. Reference 41st Battalion M.G.C. O.C. No. 51 Paras., 1 And 2.	18/08/1918	18/08/1918
Operation(al) Order(s)	Operation Order No. 50. By Lieut.-Col. A.W. Tate. Commanding 41st Battalion Machine Gun Corps. Saturday 17th August 1918	17/08/1918	17/08/1918
Operation(al) Order(s)	Operation Order No. 51. By Lieut.-Col. A.W. Tate. Commanding 41st Battalion Machine Gun Corps. Sunday 18th August 1918.	18/08/1918	18/08/1918
Operation(al) Order(s)	Operation Order No. 52. By Lieut.-Col. A.W. Tate. Commanding 41st Battalion Machine Gun Corps. Monday 19th August 1918.	19/08/1918	19/08/1918
Operation(al) Order(s)	Operation Order No. 53. By Lieut.-Col. A.W. Tate. Commanding 41st Battalion Machine Gun Corps. Friday, 23rd August, 1918.	23/08/1918	23/08/1918
Miscellaneous	O.C. "A" Company. "B" Company. "C" Company. "D" Company.	23/08/1918	23/08/1918
Operation(al) Order(s)	Operation Order No. 55. By Lieut.-Col. A.W. Tate. Commanding 41st Battalion Machine Gun Corps. Tuesday, 27th August, 1918.	28/08/1918	28/08/1918
Operation(al) Order(s)	Operation Order No. 54. By Lieut.-Col. A.W. Tate. Commanding 41st Battalion Machine Gun Corps. Tuesday, 27th August, 1918.	27/08/1918	27/08/1918
Heading	41st Battalion Machine Gun Corps War Diary For The Month Of September 1918 (Original)		
War Diary	Tirques Area	01/09/1918	01/09/1918
War Diary	Dickebusch Sector	02/09/1918	02/09/1918
War Diary	Dickebusch Area	03/09/1918	22/09/1918
War Diary	Dickebusch Sector	23/09/1918	28/09/1918
War Diary	Lock 7 & Spoil Bank Area	29/09/1918	30/09/1918
Operation(al) Order(s)	Operation Order No. 56. By Lieut.-Col. A.W. Tate. Commanding 41st Battalion Machine Gun Corps.	01/09/1918	01/09/1918

Operation(al) Order(s)	Operation Order No. 57. By Lieut.-Col. A.W. Tate. Commanding 41st Battalion Machine Gun Corps. Sunday, 1st September, 1918.	01/09/1918	01/09/1918
Operation(al) Order(s)	Operation Order No. 58. By Lieut.-Col. A.W. Tate. Commanding 41st Battalion Machine Gun Corps. Thursday, 5th September, 1918.	05/09/1918	05/09/1918
Operation(al) Order(s)	Operation Order No. 59. By Lieut.-Col. A.W. Tate. Commanding 41st Battalion Machine Gun Corps. Sunday, 8th September, 1918.	08/09/1918	08/09/1918
Miscellaneous	Reference Operation Order No. 59 Of To-day.	08/09/1918	08/09/1918
Operation(al) Order(s)	Operation Order No. 60. By Lieut.-Col. A.W. Tate. Commanding 41st Battalion Machine Gun Corps. Tuesday, 10th September, 1918.	10/09/1918	10/09/1918
Operation(al) Order(s)	Operation Order No. 61. By Major J. Muhlig, M.C. Commanding 41st Battalion Machine Gun Corps. Thursday, 12th September, 1918.	12/09/1918	12/09/1918
Miscellaneous	O.C. "A" Company. "B" Company. "C" Company. "D" Company.	13/09/1918	13/09/1918
Operation(al) Order(s)	41st Battn. Machine Gun Corps Operation Order No. 62.	25/09/1918	25/09/1918
Operation(al) Order(s)	41st Battalion Machine Gun Corps Instruction No. 1 To Accompany 41st Battalion Machine Gun Corps Operation Order No. 62.	26/09/1918	26/09/1918
Miscellaneous	March Table To Accompany Instruction No. 1		
Miscellaneous	41st Battalion Machine Gun Corps Administrative Instructions Issued In Connection With 41st Battalion Machine Gun Corps Order No. 62	25/09/1918	25/09/1918
Miscellaneous	Amendment No. 1 To 41st Battalion Machine Gun Corps Administrative Instruction Issued In Connection With 41st Battalion Machine Gun Corps Operation Order No. 62.	26/09/1918	26/09/1918
Miscellaneous	Table "A".		
Miscellaneous	Table "B".		
Heading	41st Battalion Machine Gun Corps War Diary For The Month Of October 1918 Original.		
War Diary	Spoil Bank Area	01/10/1918	03/10/1918
War Diary	Ghelevelt	04/10/1918	15/10/1918
War Diary	Dadizeele Area	16/10/1918	18/10/1918
War Diary	Coutrai Area	19/10/1918	28/10/1918
War Diary	Coutrai	28/10/1918	31/10/1918
Operation(al) Order(s)	Operation Order No 63 By Lieut. Col A.W. Tate Comdg 41 Btn Machine Gun Corps.		
Operation(al) Order(s)	Operation Order No. 64 By Lieut.-Col. A.W. Tate. Commanding 41st Battn. Machine Gun Corps. Thursday, 10th October, 1918.	11/10/1918	11/10/1918
Miscellaneous	Administrative Order No. 1 Issued In Connection With 41st Battalion Machine Gun Corps Operation Order No. 64.	11/10/1918	11/10/1918
Miscellaneous	Amendment No. 1 To 41st Battn. Machine Gun Corps Operation Order No. 64.	12/10/1918	12/10/1918
Miscellaneous	Reference 41st Battn. M.G.C. Operation Order No. 64. Para. 6.		
Miscellaneous Map	Part 1 Of 2		
Miscellaneous Map	Part 2 Of 2		

Miscellaneous	O.C. "A" Company. "B" Company. "C" Company. "D" Company. Transport Officer. Signal Officer. O.C. No. 5 Section, Divl. Signal Coy. R.E. Medical Officer.	30/10/1918	30/10/1918
Miscellaneous	O.C. "A" Company. "B" Company "C" Company. "D" Company. Transport Officer. O.C. No. 5 Section, Divl. Signal Coy. R.E. Battn. Signalling Officer. Regimental Sergeant Major.	30/10/1918	30/10/1918
Heading	41st Battalion M.G. Corps War Diary For Month Ending 30th November 1918		
War Diary	Courtrai	01/11/1918	02/11/1918
War Diary	Sweveghem	03/11/1918	03/11/1918
War Diary	Deerlyck Area	04/11/1918	07/11/1918
War Diary	Deerlyck	08/11/1918	09/11/1918
War Diary	Tierghem	10/11/1918	10/11/1918
War Diary	Schoorisse	11/11/1918	11/11/1918
War Diary	Nederbrakel	12/11/1918	18/11/1918
War Diary	Grimminge	19/11/1918	20/11/1918
War Diary	Appleterre	21/11/1918	21/11/1918
War Diary	Santbergen	22/11/1918	30/11/1918
Operation(al) Order(s)	Operation Order No. 65. By Lieut.-Col. A.W. Tate. Commanding 41st Battalion Machine Gun Corps. Thursday, 7th November, 1918.	07/11/1918	07/11/1918
Miscellaneous	O.C. "B" Company, 41st Battn. M.G. Corps. Major J. Muhlig, M.C. Battn. M.G. Corps.	15/11/1918	15/11/1918
Miscellaneous	Reference Attached.	16/11/1918	16/11/1918
Operation(al) Order(s)	Operation Order No. 66. By Lieut.-Col. A.W. Tate. Commanding 41st Battn. Machine Gun Corps. Sunday, 17th November, 1918.	17/11/1918	17/11/1918
Miscellaneous	March Table.		
Miscellaneous	1st Amendment To 41st Battn. Machine Gun Corps Order No. 66.	17/11/1918	17/11/1918
Heading	War Diary For December 1918.		
War Diary	Santbergen	01/12/1918	12/12/1918
War Diary	Enghien	13/12/1918	13/12/1918
War Diary	Hal	14/12/1918	14/12/1918
War Diary	Braine L'Alleud	15/12/1918	17/12/1918
War Diary	Marbais	18/12/1918	18/12/1918
War Diary	Tongrinne	19/12/1918	19/12/1918
War Diary	Dhuy	20/12/1918	20/12/1918
War Diary	Couthain	21/12/1918	21/12/1918
War Diary	Couthin	22/12/1918	28/12/1918
War Diary	Couthuin	29/12/1918	31/12/1918
Heading	41st Battalion Machine Gun Corps War Diary For The Month Ending January 31st 1919		
War Diary	Couthuin	01/01/1919	11/01/1919
War Diary	En Route Cologne	12/01/1919	12/01/1919
War Diary	Cologne	13/01/1919	31/01/1919
Miscellaneous	O.C. "A" Company. "B" Company. "C" Company. "D" Company. Quartermaster. Medical Officer. R.S.M. H.Q. Transport Sergt. Signalling Sergt.	04/01/1919	04/01/1919
Miscellaneous	41st Battalion Machine Gun Corps Administrative Instruction No. 1.	05/01/1919	05/01/1919
Miscellaneous	Programme For Entrainment Of 41st Battalion Machine Gun Corps.		

Miscellaneous	O.C. "A" Company. "B" Company. "C" Company. "D" Company. Quartermaster. R.S.M. Signalling Sergt. H.Q. Transport Sergt.	07/01/1919	07/01/1919
Miscellaneous	O.C. "A" Company. "B" Company. "C" Company. "D" Company. Quartermaster.	10/01/1919	10/01/1919
Heading	41st Batt. Machine Gun Corps. War Diary For The Month Of February 1919		
War Diary	Cologne	08/02/1919	28/02/1919
Heading	41st Battalion Machine Gun Corps. War Diary For The Month Of March 1919		
War Diary	Cologne	01/03/1919	31/03/1919
Miscellaneous	Officers Commanding, "A" Coy. "B" Coy. "C" Coy. "D" Coy.	25/03/1919	25/03/1919
Miscellaneous	41st Battalion Machine Gun Corps. O.O. 66.	26/03/1919	26/03/1919
Heading	41st Battalion Machine Gun Corps War Diary For The Month Of April 1919		
Miscellaneous	O.C. "A" Coy, Q.M. 41st Bn. M.G.C. "B" Coy, Signalling Officer, 41st Bn. M.G.C. "C" Coy, "D" Coy,	21/03/1919	21/03/1919
War Diary	Cologne	01/04/1919	23/05/1919
War Diary	Heumar	24/05/1919	25/05/1919
War Diary	Cologne	26/05/1919	31/05/1919
War Diary	Heumar	31/05/1919	30/06/1919
War Diary	Rath Camp.	01/07/1919	30/09/1919
Heading	Cover For Documents. Nature of Enclosures. 41st Battalion M.G. Corps. War Diary October, 1919.		
War Diary	Cologne	01/10/1919	01/10/1919
War Diary	(Rath Camp.)	02/10/1919	05/10/1919
War Diary	(Wahn.)	06/10/1919	13/10/1919
War Diary	Cologne	14/10/1919	14/10/1919
War Diary	(Wahn.)	15/10/1919	19/10/1919
War Diary	(Rhiel.)	20/10/1919	28/10/1919
War Diary	Cologne Rhiel	28/10/1919	31/10/1919
War Diary	Cologne	01/10/1919	01/10/1919
War Diary	(Rath Camp.)	02/10/1919	05/10/1919
War Diary	(Wahn.)	06/10/1919	13/10/1919
War Diary	Cologne	14/10/1919	14/10/1919
War Diary	(Wahn.)	15/10/1919	19/10/1919
War Diary	(Rhiel.)	20/10/1919	28/10/1919
War Diary	Cologne Rhiel	28/10/1919	31/10/1919

W095/2674/5 Mods

41 DIV TROOPS

41 BN MACHINE GUN CORPS

1918 MAR — 1919 OCT

Battn. returned with
Div. from Italy
3/8.3.18.

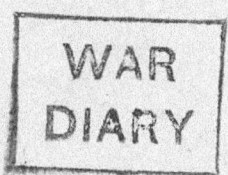

41st BATTALION MACHINE GUN CORPS.

M A R C H

1 9 1 8

Attached:-

Operation Orders Nos.
1, 3 and 4.

Army Form C. 2118.

WAR DIARY
or
INTELLIGENCE SUMMARY
(Erase heading not required.)

41st BATTALION M.G. CORPS
(122, 123, 124 and 199 M.G. Coys.)

MARCH 1918

Place	Date	Hour	Summary of Events and Information	Remarks and references to Appendices
Ref CONEGLIANO Sheet 38., LENS(111) 1/100,000	1st.		Nos. 3 and 4 sections and ½ Transport 122. Coy entrained at FONTANIVA under Capt HARRISON. No 1 section and Transport 123 Coy. Ref: Q95E80 to entrain at PADUA. 124 Coy entrained at POGGIANA.	Apd
	2nd.		No 1 section and Transport under 2/Lt STRINGER. + No 2 section and Transport under 2/Lt HAXFALL of 122 Coy entrained at CARMIGNANO. No1 section 123 Coy entrained at PADOVA. HQ + Nos 2+3 sections 123 Coy entrained at CAMPOSANPIERO 199 Company entrained at CAMPO SAN PIERO.	Apd
	3rd.		In the train	Apd
	4th.		First half 122 M.G Coy detrained at DOULLENS and went into billets at POMMERA. The Train containing Coy HQ. + Nos 2 + 3 sections 123 M G Coy met with an accident near ST MICHIEL, FRANCE, Derailing in 2 men killed, 7men wounded and 4 mules + 1 L.D. Horse killed	Apd
	5th.		Second and third parties (122) detrained at DOULLENS and MONDICOURT respectively and went into billets in POMMERA. 199 Coy. detrained at DOULLENS and went into billets at GRINCOURT LE PAS.	Apd
	6th.		122 Coy commenced training. No 1 + 4 sections 123 Coy detrained at DOULLENS and went into billets at HUMBERCOURT	Apd
	7th.		124 Coy. detrained at MONDICOURT and went into billets at SOMBRIN. 199 Coy spent the day in clearing billets.	Apd
	8th.		Obtaining new billets and straightening up generally.	Apd
	9th.		Remainder of 123 Coy detrained and went into billets at HUMBERCOURT.	Apd
	-16th		During this period the Companies carried out training under their own arrangements. Classes were instituted under selected officers for training of attached men and reinforcements. The 123rd Coy.	Apd

WAR DIARY or INTELLIGENCE SUMMARY

Army Form C. 2118.

2, MARCH 1918.

(Erase heading not required.)

Instructions regarding War Diaries and Intelligence Summaries are contained in F. S. Regs., Part II. and the Staff Manual respectively. Title Pages will be prepared in manuscript.

Place	Date	Hour	Summary of Events and Information	Remarks and references to Appendices
Rd. LENS E.M.2 ¼ AMIENS 1/100,000	17th		Took part in the Tactical schemes of the Brigade. In all cases guns, limbers and equipment were thoroughly overhauled and cleaned. Recreational Training was carried out in the afternoons and the Lewis Gun allotment was increased when the division returned from ITALY. A great deal of attention was paid to Transport: one company had their transport inspected by Lieut Col DOWNING, A.S.C. and pronounced very satisfactory. Much billeted badge in the company Braiding.	Apd
			On this day the 41st Battalion, Machine Gun Corps was formed. The companies concentrated in billets at SOMBRIN. The following officers held appointments in the Battalion — Commanding Officer, Lieut. Col. E.M. BEALL, D.S.O. the King's Liverpool Regt. Second in Command, MAJOR H. SMITH, M.C. The West Riding Regt. a/R.M.T.C. Adjutant Capt. C.N. PORTER, M.S.C. O.C. 'A' Coy Capt. A.S. HINSHELWOOD, O.C. 'B' Cy Capt. A. McKEE REID, M.C., O.C. 'C' Coy. Capt. J.N. LAWSON, M.C., O.C. 'D' Coy Capt. M.F. GADSDON, Transport Officer Capt. R.F. POTTER, M.C. Arisars, Quartermaster Kient. H.E. REINMANN, K.R.R.C. The battalion was made up to strength with men from disbanded supporting battalions.	Apd
	18th -20th		This period was spent in organising the battalion, a considerable amount of work accumulated. Major SMITH went to the Base owing to sickness and Capt. M.F. GADSDON was appointed 2nd in Command. On the morning of the 19th orders were received to be despatched to work at an ARSON astica. On the 20th orders were received that the battalion would move by Tactical Train and march route to billets at FRANVILLERS on the 21st.	VIDE. O.O. No 1. Apd

Army Form C. 2118.

WAR DIARY or INTELLIGENCE SUMMARY

(Erase heading not required.)

3. MARCH 1918.

Ref LENS 1/10,000 57D NE 1/20,000
57 D 1/40,000

Place	Date	Hour	Summary of Events and Information	Remarks and references to Appendices
	21st		The Battalion was divided into various groups, personnel moving by train and transport by road at different times. The distribution was altered and it became apparent that the Battalion was going to take part in operations. HQ, B and D Coys detrained at ACHIET-LE-GRAND and noted for the night in BERKELEY CAMP, BIHUCOURT.	Copy
	22nd		A and C Coys detrained at ACHIET-LE-GRAND and proceeded to FAVREUIL. A Coy went in the line before BEUGNATRE and No 2 section C Coy reported to the 25th M.G. Bn. B Coy relieved guns of the 6th M.G. Bn. N of BAPAUME. D Coy in divisional reserve at BIHUCOURT.	Copy A
	23rd		Enemy attacked at 2.5 a.m and was repulsed after 3 hours fighting. No 2 section A Coy were in the evening sent to take up position before BEUGNY. D Coy was sent up the line. 1 section to 1/22 I. Bde. 1 section to 123 I.Bde. The Company came into action in front of MORY except No 4 section in reserve and No 1 section in front of VAULX-VRAUCOURT. From this section had lost its officer 2/Lt H.H DONKREY who had been killed. Cpl [ ] a Sniper early in the morning.	Copy A
	24th		Enemy again attacked on the whole front. No 2 section A Coy retired after covering infantry retirement, through FREMICOURT, across the BAPAUME road to the high ground in rear of FREMICOURT. The right continued to fall back, and, conforming to the movement of the other section, fell back into BAPAUME finally making a stand on a line to the N.W. of BAPAUME running in front of GREVILLERS. No 3 & 2 sections A Coy resisted the attack till 7.30 p.m. when BEUGNY being captured, and BEUGNATRE having been evacuated, retired to high ground N of FAVREUIL. To the right a line was established in front of BIEFVILLERS. D Coy retired on FAVREUIL and hence to a line S.E of	

Army Form C. 2118.

WAR DIARY or INTELLIGENCE SUMMARY

(Erase heading not required.)

Place	Date	Hour	Summary of Events and Information	Remarks and references to Appendices
Ref. 57D V/40,000 57D N.E. 1/20,000	25th		SAPIGNIES, eventually taking up position about BIHUCOURT under orders of the 122 I. Bde. C + B Coys relied to the BIEFVILLERS line and eventually established themselves in a trench S. of BIHUCOURT. During the day's operations the following casualties were suffered. Capt. J.N. RAWSON, M.C. killed, Capt. M. McK. REID (missing), 2/Lt. N.P. BARKER M.C. wounded and 2/Lt. T. GUYATT suffering Gas. The enemy advanced in the afternoon but was opposed by our Lewis machine gun fire. All the existing guns of the battalion were near in the trench S. of BIHUCOURT under the command of Col. BEALL. Resistance was maintained until the evening of Mch 26th. In the course of the day Lt. LESLIE, U.S. M.O.R.C. the medical officer was wounded.	
	26th		Orders were received to retire at 1.0. a.m. The Bde line was evacuated and the battalion concentrated at BUCQUOY. After a short rest positions were taken up E. of GOMMECOURT. Later in the day orders were received for the battalion to proceed to BIENVILLERS, where the men bivouacked for the night.	
	27th		Day spent in rest.	
	28th		The Battalion was reorganised into 3 Coys under Capts. HINSHELWOOD and HARRISON and "HARTLEY" Coy. Coys moved into support at GOMMECOURT.	Capt. HINSHELWOOD VIDE O.O. No.3.
	29th		Orders received that the 41st Batt. would be relieved by A2nd in the support of BUCQUOY.	Capt. HARRISON VIDE. O.O. No.3.
	30th		Relieved A 2nd Batt. M.G. Coys in the line. Opposite M.A. Squadron came under orders of O.C. Bn.	Capt. HARTLEY VIDE. By Order C No. 4.
	31st		2/Lt. WILLIAMS "B" Coy wounded, died later. Groups carried out harassing fire (direct and indirect) through the night.	

OPERATION ORDERS NOS. 1, 3 and 4.

SECRET.   Copy No......10...

41st Battalion Machine Gun Corps. Operation Order No 1.

Ref. LENS Ed 2 1/100,000.
AMIENS   "   "

1. The Battalion will proceed by rail & march route to FRANVILLERS to be billetted to-morrow the 21st inst.

2. (1) "A" Company & 2 sections "B" Company will entrain at MONDICOURT. Train leaves at 9 a.m. Destination EDGE HILL.
   (2) "B" Company (less two sections) and "C" Company will entrain at SAULTY. Train leaves at 4-30 p.m. Destination ALBERT.
   (3) Battalion Headquarters and "D" Company will entrain at MONDICOURT. Train leaves at 5 p.m. Destination EDGE HILL.

3. The Transport and Riding Horses present with Battalion will entrain as follows:-

   (a) 4 G.S.L. Wagons "A" Company) MONDICOURT
       2   "   "   "B"   "   ) Dep. 12 noon.
       1 Water Cart.   ) EDGE HILL.

   (b) 4 G.S.L. Wagons "C" Company) SAULTY.
       2   "   "   "B"   "   ) Dep. 2-30 p.m.
       1 Water Cart.   ) ALBERT.

   (c) 4 G.S.L. Wagons "D" Company) SAULTY.
       2   "   "   Headquarters) Dep. 8-30 p.m.
       1 Mess Cart.   ) EDGE HILL.
       8 Riders.   )

4. All personnel will report at the station one hour and Transport three hours before advertised departure of the train.

5. "A" Company will arrange a Billeting Party under Capt. HARRISON (with bicycles) for the entire Battalion Billets at FRANVILLERS.

6. The O.C. each Train Party of Machine Gun Battalion Troops will take state in duplicate of strength in personnel, animals and axles and hand to R.T.O.

7. No troops will enter the station yard until the O.C. has reported to the R.T.O. and handed him one copy of this state.

8. Breast ropes for horses must be provided by Units.

9. Dress - Marching Order, packs will be carried on the man.

10. Instructions re lorries will be issued later. Those proceeding by first train must be prepared to carry one blanket.

11. Attention of all is called to the duty of leaving billets and surroundings scrupulously clean.

                                            Capt.
Issued at 9-30 p.m.   Adjutant.
20-3-18.   41st Battn, M.G.Corps.

Copy No. 1. Commanding Officer.   Copy No. 2. Adjutant.
        3. O.C. "A" Company.   4. O.C. "B" Company.
        5. "   "C"   "   6. "   "D"   "
        7. Quartermaster.   8. Transport Officer.
        9. R.S.M.   10. File.

P.110.

Secret.   Copy No...........

41st Machine Gun Battalion Operation Order No. 3.

Ref. Maps. 57 D. 1/40,000.
           57 D. N. E. 1/20,000.

1. The 41st Division will relieve the 42nd Division in the 4th Corps Area, left sector on the night of the 29th/30th.

2. The Machine Guns in the Sector will be relieved to-morrow the 30th instant after 4 p.m.

3. The right sector at present held by 14 guns of the 126th Machine Gun Coy. (Coy Headquarters E.24.d.20.70.) will be relieved by No. 1 Group and 1 Section, No. 3 Group. The whole to under the command of Capt. HINSHELWOOD.
The centre sector at present held by the 125th Machine Gun Coy. (Coy. Headquarters F.28.a.45.20.) with 16 guns will be relieved by No. 2 Group and No. 3 Group (less 1 Section) the whole to be under the Command of Capt. HARRISON.
The left sector at present held by 12 guns of the 268th Machine Gun Coy. will be relieved by the personnel of 12 guns under Lieut. HARTLEY and to be known as No. 4 Group. No. 4 Group will take over the 12 guns complete now in the sector held by the 268th Machine Gun Coy.

4. Brigade Headquarters of the 42nd Division are at E.24.d.8.8.

5. Detailed arrangements for relief to be arranged between Officers concerned.

6. Machine Gun Groups of the 41st Division will start to move to positions to be relieved at 4 p.m. to-morrow the 30th instant.

7. Officers detailed to carry out relief will inform Battalion Headquarters by 12 noon to-morrow the 30th instant if they require Fighting Limbers for the move.

8. Positions of guns at approximate pin points with direction of fire will be prepared as soon as possible.

9. The Divisional Front will also be covered by a Barrage Group of 12 guns of a composite Machine Gun Squadron who will be in position about F.26.D.

Issued at.............   Lieut.-Col.
29-3-18.   Commanding 41st Battn. M.G.Corps.

                    Copies to.   Copy. No. 1. Capt. HINSHELWOOD.
                                    "   " 2. Capt. HARRISON.
                                    "   " 3. Lieut. HARTLEY.

BATTALION ORDERS NO1 4.
by
LIEUT.-COL. E. M. BEALL, D.S.O.
Commanding 41st Battalion Machine Gun Corps.
Sunday, 31st March, 1918.

SECRET.

1. Machine Guns will be active during to-night 31st March/1st April, 1918.

2. The following firing will be carried out by the guns of Nos. 1, 2 and 3 Groups and of the Machine Gun Squadron attached:-

   (a). Bursts of direct fire from forward guns.

   (b). Searching fire from guns in back positions along all lines of approach.

   (c). Searching fire by Machine Gun Batteries of dead ground along the front.

   (d). Between 5-15 p.m. and 5-45 a.m. bursts of barrage fire on S.O.S. lines and on dead ground along the front.

Issued at 2-50 p.m.
31-3-18.

Capt. and Adjutant.
41st Battn. M.G.Corps.

Copies to:-

   Copy No. 1. Capt. HINSHELWOOD.
            2. Capt. HARRISON.
            3. Lieut. HARTLEY.
            4. Major WATERS.
            5. File.
            6. War Diary.

41st Divisional M.G.C.

WAR DIARY

41ST BATTALION M. G. C.

APRIL 1918

41st Division "G".   A/235

        Herewith War Diary for the month of April, 1918.

        Please acknowledge.

                                              Capt. and Adjutant.
1st May, 1918.   41st Battn. M.G.Corps.

WAR DIARY or INTELLIGENCE SUMMARY

Army Form C. 2118.

51st BATTALION THE MACHINE GUN CORPS

APRIL 1918.

Place	Date	Hour	Summary of Events and Information	Remarks and references to Appendices
FRANCE	1st		HAZEBROUCK. Ref: Sheet 57D. 1/40,000. The Battalion, consisting of three groups under the command of Capt. HINSHELWOOD, Capt. HARRISON and Lieut HARTLEY and a Company M.G. Squadron under the command of Major WATERS, was holding the line at BUCQUOY. Orders arrived that the Battalion would be relieved on the night of 1st/2nd by the 42nd Battalion, M.G.C. Owing to an error in the relief, some of the companies were not out of the line until the morning of the 2nd.	Vide A.A. Copy A.O. No.5.
	2nd		After resting at BIENVILLERS, a party under Lieut HARTLEY marched and the remainder rode on lorries to FAMECHON, where billets had been arranged. After considerable difficulty, the billeting also being changed twice during the night. A hot meal was served on arrival and the men A.A. rested during the afternoon and evening.	
	3rd		The Battalion embussed for the PETIT-HOUVIN area, having marched to MONDICOURT. After debussing Copy A on the DOULLENS-ST POL road, the Battalion went into billets at HAUT-COTE. The transport moved Vide A.O. by road and arrived in billets at 6.30.p.m. No. 6.	
	4th		The Battalion spent the morning in overhauling its limbers and motor gun-sit. After dinners the transport moved off to PETIT HOUVIN station and the Battalion followed at 1.30.p.m. It transpired that the train would be impractical in spotting, and the men had teas. Eventually three trains conveyed the Battalion, the first containing the transport, the second, the troops and the third the remainder of the transport. The Battalion detrained at PERNES/HOEK station and was met by lorries to STRETVOORDE after having tea at PERNES/HOEK station. The night was extremely dark and rain fell persistently. Accommodation had been allotted in SMYTHE CAMP.	
	5th		This day was spent in cleaning and overhauling gear. During the morning two Lewis draft arrived A.A. from the base making 5 Officers and 205 men in all. These were posted to different Companies Copy and the Battalion was made over-strength.	

WAR DIARY or INTELLIGENCE SUMMARY

Army Form C. 2118.

Place	Date	Hour	Summary of Events and Information	Remarks and references to Appendices
Ref: HAZEBROUCK 1/150,000	6th		The Battalion was inspected by M Lieut-General SIR AYLMER HUNTER-WESTON K.C.B., D.S.O., C.of the VIII Corps. It was drawn up in Column of Companies in line under the command of Capt. M.F. GADSDON, the C.O. having proceeded to reconnoitre to new sector of the Line. The Corps Commander complimented the Battalion on their cleanliness and smartness. After being inspected the Battalion, following the 123 Brigade, marched past the General. The remainder of the day was spent in preparing for the line.	Rpts.
	7th		Orders were issued for "A" and "B" Companies to relieve two companies of the 29th Battalion in the Left Sector, Right Division, VIII Corps on the right of the 1/8th Transport for these companies left at 12.30 p.m., personnel left in lorries at 4.0 p.m. The relief was carried out satisfactorily.	rDF. O.O. No 5.
	8th		The following reliefs were carried out on the 8th: "A" & "B" Companies were relieved by "C" Company of the 59th M.G. Battalion and proceeded to SUNDERLAND CAMP. "C" Company relieved "C" Company of the 29th M.G. Battalion in the Right Forward area. GOLDBERG NOTE. On this day (9) Lieutenant Colonel A.W. TOTE assumed command of the Battalion, Lieut-Colonel F.I.R. BRYAN having been posted to the 8th E.W.G Battalion.	Apt. rDF. O.O No 9. Apt.
	9th		"D" Company relieved "B" Company of the 29th M.G. Battalion in the Left Forward area. A&D Bk Rfc No 102 and "B" Company relieved "B" Coy 29th M.G. Battalion in support (Coy H.S. GOULDEN) Batt. HQ removed to DEAD END J YPRES. All reliefs were carried out satisfactorily. On this day Capts. H.A. BENTLEY and A.K. LETTS arrived at the Battalion, having been posted to Company Commanders, the officers proceeded to No 47 Batt.	
	10th		Bn. in line. Orders were issued for A Coy. to move to prepared positions around YPRES. Capt. HINSHELWOOD reconnoitred the defences and they company moved in during the night of the 10/11 p.m.	V.DF. oo No. 10. Apt.

Army Form C. 2118.

WAR DIARY
or
INTELLIGENCE SUMMARY
(Erase heading not required.)

Place	Date	Hour	Summary of Events and Information	Remarks and references to Appendices
Reforgeorork R 1/40500 Belgium & France: 28.1/40,000	11th		The 10 guns of B Company in support at GALLIPOLI were withdrawn to PICKLEHAUBE KEEP where positions were occupied in the Army Battle Zone.	Ref. O.O. No 11. Refs
	12th		On withdrawal of the forward troops to the Battle Zone occurred. "B" Coy. occupied positions in the Right Brigade Sub-sector, and B Company moved to positions in the Left Brigade Sub-sector. "A" dusk "D" Coy. withdrew to new positions and "C" Coy. to the Transport lines.	O.O. to 15. Arp.
	13th		Quiet day. Classes of instruction were instituted for details and reserve Coy. under capable officers & N.C.O.s.	Arp. Arp.
	14th		Nothing of importance occurred.	
	15th 16th		A new line was occupied by the Division from WIELTJETERN to a point S.E. & WIELTJE. One section of the 4 forward companies was left forward under the command of the O.C. outposts to give support to the Infantry. The remaining guns, "A" & "B" Coys, were disposed of in depth in the rear Battle Zone. "C" Coy occupied position W. YPRES in Divisional Reserve & D Company moved the Y.P.S. defences. Duties to continue shelling YPRES. "A" Echelon moved forward.	O.O. 16. 17. 18. Arp.
	17th		2 guns each of the forward sections in the Outpost line were withdrawn and placed in Brigade Reserve.	V. O.O. No. 19.
	18th		O.C. Companies made shelter arrangements for barrage fire, and searching dead ground etc. Work was put in on emplacements, accommodation etc.	Cop. OO and Cop. 20.
	19th		Arrangements made for mounting anti-aircraft guns at positions.	Ref.
	20th		Relief operations on outpost work accomplished on the night of the 20th/21st.	Ref.

2449 Wt. W14957/Mg0 750,000 1/16 J.B.C. & A. Forms/C.2118/12.

WAR DIARY
or
INTELLIGENCE SUMMARY

(Erase heading not required.)

Army Form C. 2118.

Instructions regarding War Diaries and Intelligence Summaries are contained in F. S. Regs, Part II. and the Staff Manual respectively. Title Pages will be prepared in manuscript.

Place	Date	Hour	Summary of Events and Information	Remarks and references to Appendices
Belgium; France:	21st		"C" Company relieved "B" Company in the Left Brigade Sector. "B" Coy. relieved "D" Coy in the YPRES defences. "D" Coy. proceeded W. of YPRES to late of positions in Divisional reserve. A considerable number of gas shells were thrown into YPRES and vicinity during the night.	Vide A/157.
S.28. 1/40,000	22nd		Quiet day. Nothing of importance occurred during the day. Several gas casualties in the Bn. Shelling of YPRES with gas shells occurred again at 11.30 p.m. Promotion of O.C. Coy to Major T. Batt is in command of Coy. Captain took effect from this date.	
	23rd		Nothing of importance occurred. An officer & D Coy went forward to reconnoitre the outpost line of the night, with a view to the relief of "D" Coy by "D" Coy. Gas shelling again during the night.	Vide A/163.
	24th		Quiet morning. Arrangements made for visual signalling from left forward company to B. Hq. Greater part of inter-company relief was carried out during the day, as the weather was very misty. Rel of Outposts carried out during the night.	Lists
	25th		Heavy shelling south of FOOTMAEKER from 2.30 a.m - 5 a.m. Several shells of varying cals. also fell in the vicinity of DEAD END during the morning. Batt Hq. moved to ORILLIA CAMP.	Lists
	26th		B Coy withdrew from positions to ORILLIA CAMP. "C" Coy proceeds to VLAMERTINGHE Chateau after being relieved by "D" Coy. 2 Sections B Coy stood to, attached to 122 I. Bde.	V.D.E. 00 21 v 22
	27th		Batt. Hq. moved to 10 Elms Camp School, POPERINGHE.	List
	28th		Outpost line reinforced by 2 section D Coy. B & C Coy took up positions in the 9000 x yellow Bn. Cap Bring harrassing shelling, 2 wounded + 3 wounded N.13. N. Hq.	List
	29th		Batt. Hq. moves to CHATEAU LOVIE.	List
	30th		C.O. & Major GASDON visited positions in the morning.	List

War Diary

Copy No..........

41st Battalion Machine Gun Corps Operation Order No. 5.

Ref. Maps. Sheet 57 D. 1/40,000.
Lens 11, 1/100,000.

1. The 41st Division and the 41st Battalion Machine Gun Corps will be relieved by the 42nd Division and 42nd Battalion Machine Gun Corps on the night of the 1st/2nd April, 1918.

2. Left Group (No.4) under Lieut. HARTLEY (12 guns) will be relieved by "C" Company (127) 42nd M.G. Battalion.
   Central Group (Captain HARRISON) and Right Group No. 1. (Capt. HINSHELWOOD) will be relieved in Front Line by "B" Company (126) 42nd M.G. Battalion, and all barrage and rear positions by "D" Company (268) 42nd M.G. Battalion.
   The composite M.G. Squadron will be relieved by "A" Company (125) 42nd M.G. Battalion.
   All guns, tripods, and belt boxes not required by O.C. Companies of 42nd M.G. Battalion will be brought out.
   All Maps (except LENS No. 11) and ammunition will be handed over.
   O.C. Companies 42nd M.G. Battalion will be supplied with guides by O.C. Companies 41st M.G. Battalion as required.
   Right Group Company H.Q. F.26.a.55.00.
   Squadron H.Q. E.24.d.15.90.
   Left Group Company H.Q. remains at F.21.d.40.75.
   Centre Group Company H.Q. remains at F.21.c.80.35.
   The four guns under Lieut. HANSON under 122nd Brigade will return to BIENVILLERS on relief of 122nd Brigade.
   Relief to be completed by 5 a.m.

3. On relief Groups will march to BIENVILLERS and assemble in Companies, "A", "B", "C", "D". Guides will be stationed at Road Junction E.8.b.9.9.

4. (a). Fighting limbers will be disposed as follows for No. 1 Group Right 8 limbers will be at F.26.c.0.7. at a time to be notified to Battalion Headquarters by Capt. HINSHELWOOD before 6 p.m. this evening.
   (b). Seven limbers for No. 3 Group Centre will be 200 yards North West of Cross Roads in F.20.b.00.95. at a time to be notified to Battalion Headquarters by Capt. HARRISON before 6 p.m. this evening.
   (c). Six limbers for No. 4 Group Left will be at York Roads F.20.b.5.6. at a time to be notified to Battalion Headquarters by Lieut. HARTLEY before 6 p.m. this evening.
   (d). Two limbers for Lieut. HANSON will be at the North West Corner of LE QUESNOY FARM at a time to be notified by him to Battalion Headquarters before 6 p.m. this evening.

5. O.C. Group will report to Battalion Headquarters at BIENVILLERS completion of reliefs and number of men unable to march to PAS after a short rest at BIENVILLERS. The accommodation of lorries is strictly limited for those considered by the Medical Officer unable to march.

6. Two cookers will provide tea and soup at BIENVILLERS and two cookers will proceed to PAS to have dinner ready by 1 p.m. the 2nd instant.
   One water cart will remain at BIENVILLERS and march together with the two cookers and all limbers under Lieut. NYPERT to PAS, starting at 10 a.m. the 2nd instant.

7. Officers riding horses will be at BIENVILLERS by 8 p.m. the 1st instant.

8.   The remainder of Battalion Transport will march under Capt. POTTER to PAS on the evening of the 1st instant.

9.   Acknowledge.

Issued at 1-5 p.m.
1-4-18.

W.J. Gadsdon
Capt.
41st Battn. M.G.Corps.

Copies to:-

Copy No. 1. Capt. HINSHELWOOD.
         2. Capt. HARRISON.
         3. Lieut. HARTLEY.
         4. Lieut. HANSON.
         5. Major WATERS, Composite M.G.Squadron.
         6. 41st Division.
       ✓ 7. File.
         8. War Diary.

SECRET.   Copy No..........

41st Battalion Machine Gun Corps Operation Order No. 6.

Ref. Map. LENS 11. 1/100,000.

1. The Battalion less Transport will embuss for PETIT HOUVIN to-morrow the 3rd instant.

2. The Battalion will be formed up ready to march off in the following order:-
    Headquarters, "B", "C", "D" Companies.
   with head of column at second class road junction half a mile south of S in PAS at 7-30 a.m.
    "A" Company will join column at HURTEBISE FARM at 7-35 a.m.

3. Reveille. 5-30 a.m.
   Breakfast. 6-15 a.m.
    All blankets and kits will be stacked ready for loading outside Battalion and Company Headquarters at 6-45 a.m.

4. The Battalion Transport will proceed by march route to NUNCQ and await further orders.

5. The Battalion will embuss on the PAS - MONDICOURT ROAD at 8-30 a.m. and will join up in rear of 237th Field Company R.E. (each lorry will take 20 and each bus 25 men).
    The Battalion will "debuss" on the main DOULLENS - ST. POL ROAD between NUNCQ and PETIT HOUVIN and await orders.

6. The Battalion complete with supply and baggage wagons will entrain at PETIT HOUVIN in Train 18 after dinner on the 4th instant.
    Further orders will be issued as to this move.

7. On arrival at PETIT HOUVIN Area, O.C. Companies will take immediate steps to:-
   (a). Overhaul guns and repack limbers.
   (b). Render a certificate after inspection by Gas N.C.O.s as to any defects in Box Respirators.
   (c). Make a careful inspection of feet in conjunction with the Medical Officer. He will visit Battalion Headquarters and Companies at times to be arranged after arrival. Every effort must be made to have men's hair cut and clothing and equipment cleaned before entraining.

Issued at 8-30 p.m.
2-4-18.

(Signed) C. Wilfred Porter.
Capt. and Adjutant.
41st Bn. M.G. Corps.

Copies to:-

    Copy No. 1. O.C.
             2. 2nd-in-Command.
             3. Adjutant.
             4. O.C. "A" Company.
             5. "   "B"   "
             6. "   "C"   "
             7. "   "D"   "
             8. Transport Officer.
             9. Quartermaster.
            10. R.S.M.
            11. File.
            12. War Diary.

SECRET.   Copy No. ....

41st Battalion Machine Gun Corps Operation Order No. 8.

Ref. Map. Sheet 28. 1/40,000.

1.   The Machine Guns of the 29th Battalion in Left Sector, Right Division, 8th Corps will be relieved on the night of the 7th/8th April, 1918, by 41st Battalion as follows:-
    "A" Company, 41st Battalion will relieve "B" Company, 29th Battalion with 14 guns.
    "B" Company, 41st Battalion the same with 10 guns under arrangements made with 29th Battalion.
    Each gun will have 10 belt boxes in position.

2.   Lorries will be at STEENVOORDE Square at 4 p.m. and will call at 'DEAD END' to pick up guides and proceed to KASSAS CROSS ROADS for second guides.

    24 guns complete and 10 belt boxes per gun. Rations and Water for 8th instant will be taken in the lorries.

3.   Transport for "A" and "B" Companies to-gether with personnel of "A" and "B" Companies not going into the line will proceed by march route to SUNDERLAND CAMP, I.2.d.4.5. leaving STEENVOORDE at 12-30 p.m. Carrying parties taken by lorries will proceed to that Camp on completion of duty.

4.   Officers Commanding Companies will hand over to the Quartermaster, 29th Battalion, the equivalent of tripods and belt boxes taken over in the line from the 29th Battalion.

5.   Completion of relief will be reported to Division direct by wire.

6.   Battalion Headquarters, "C" and "D" Companies with their Transport will remain at STEENVOORDE. All riders will also remain unless demanded by O.C. Companies.

7.   "A" Company and "B" Company will hand over to the Quartermaster 41st Battalion at STEENVOORDE by noon 7th instant, tripods and belt boxes as follows:-
    "A" Company, all tripods in excess of 14.
    "   "   " belt boxes in excess of 140.
    "B"   "   " tripods in excess of 10.
    "   "   " belt boxes in excess of 100.
    "A" and "B" Companies will each take up in limbers to SUNDERLAND CAMP all their guns in excess of those going into the line.

8.   Officers Commanding "A" and "B" Companies will make necessary arrangements with the Signalling Sergeant for forward Signal Communications and the necessary personnel and equipment will proceed with the lorries.

9.   Acknowledge.

Issued at 12-30 a.m.   Capt. and Adjutant.
7-4-18.   41st Battn. M.G.Corps.

Copies to:-

    Copy No. 1. Commanding Officer.
              2. 2nd-in-Command.
              3. Adjutant.
              4. O.C. "A" Company.
              5.   "   "B"   "
              6.   "   "C"   "
              7.   "   "D"   "
              8. Transport Officer.
              9. Quartermaster.
            10. 29th Battalion M.G.Corps.
            11. 41st Division.
            12. R.S.M.
            13. War Diary.
            14. File.

SECRET.   Copy No........12....

41st Battalion Machine Gun Corps Operation Order No. 9.

Ref. Map Sheet 28. 1/40,000.

1. The following reliefs will take place at times mentioned:-

   (a). "A" Company with 14 guns and "B" Company with 10 guns of the 41st Battalion, will be relieved from the Left Sector, Right Division, 8th Corps, by "C" Company, 59th Battalion on the night of the 8th/9th instant.
   All details to be arranged by O.C. Companies concerned.
   O.C. "C" Company, 59th Battalion will visit O.C. "A" and "B" Companies, 41st Battalion, at TYNE COTTAGE during the morning of the 8th instant.
   On relief "A" and "B" Companies, 41st Battalion, will proceed to SUNDERLAND CAMP, I.8.d.Central.

   (b). "C" Company, 41st Battalion, will relieve "C" Company, 29th Battalion in the Right Forward Area GOUDBERG Sector on the 8th/9th instant, with 16 guns.
   Company Headquarters at LAAMKEEK (D.10.b.Central).
   A box car will call at SMYTHE CAMP (junction of road near Battalion Headquarters, 66 Rue de Poperinghe) at 8 a.m. 8th instant to convey O.C. "C" Company (and 1 N.C.O.) to H.Q. 29th Battalion to DEAD END, YPRES (I.2.c.2.6.) to obtain guides to LAAMKEEK.
   Number ones of "C" Company, 29th Battalion will remain with "C" Company, 41st Battalion, for 24 hours.
   10 lorries for personnel and 16 guns and tripods, and 160 belt boxes of "C" Company, 41st Battalion will be at STEENVOORDE SQUARE at 2 p.m. 8th instant, to proceed to DEAD END and then forward of that point under orders of O.C. "C" Company, 41st Battalion.
   Transport and personnel of "C" Company, 41st Battalion, will proceed by march route to DEAD END at 1 p.m. 8th instant.

   (c). "D" Company of 41st Battalion, will relieve "B" Company, 29th Battalion in Left Forward Area, GOUDBERG SECTOR on the 9th/10th instant, with 16 guns, 16 tripods and 160 belt boxes. Relief to be compelte before midnight.
   Company Headquarters, Pill Box 53.
   O.C. "D" Company will proceed in box car mentioned in sub-para. (b) at 7 a.m. the 8th instant, to reconnoitre this area and return to STEENVOORDE same day.
   Number ones (and N.C.O.s required) of "D" Company, 41st Battalion, will proceed in the lorries leaving STEENVOORDE at 2 p.m. 8th instant, and proceed to Left Forward Area, GOUDBERG SECTOR, and remain there until and after the arrival of "D" Company, 41st Battalion in the line.
   10 lorries for personnel, 16 guns, 16 tripods and 160 belt boxes of "D" Company, 41st Battalion will be at STEENVOORDE SQUARE at 8 a.m. the 9th instant, to convey them to DEAD END and then further as arranged by O.C. "D" Company.
   Transport and personnel of "D" Company not proceeding by lorry will march to DEAD END at 8 a.m. 9th instant.
   "D" Company, 41st Battalion, will pick up four tripods and 140 belt boxes from "A" Company at DEAD END on arrival.

   (d). "B" Company, 41st Battalion, will relieve "A" Company, 29th Battalion, in Support (Company Headquarters GALLIPOLI) on the 9th instant, and place 6 guns in position and be responsible for the remaining gun positions. All details to be arranged between O.C. Companies.

Relief to be completed by 4 p.m.

(e). "A" Company, 41st Battalion, will move into position of Company in Reserve at DEAD END by 12 noon on the 10th instant.

2. Capt. POTTER and a representative of the Quartermasters Stores will proceed to DEAD END by the box car leaving STEENVOORDE at 7 a.m., 8th instant, to reconnoitre Transport Lines and Quartermasters Stores for Battalion at DEAD END, and return same day to STEENVOORDE.

3. Battalion Headquarters will be established at DEAD END on the 10th instant at 10 a.m.
Transport and personnel of Battalion Headquarters will proceed by march route to DEAD END on the 10th instant at a time to be notified later.

4. "A" Company, 41st Battalion, will arrange after arrival at SUNDERLAND CAMP to send to DEAD END by 12 noon, 9th instant, ALL belt boxes and FOUR tripods to be handed over to "D" Company, 41st Battalion, on their arrival there.

5. A Forward Advanced Dressing Station will be established at WILTEJE.

6. Ammunition: Brigade Dump, SEINE. D.16.c.7.3.
Divisional Dump, CAMBRIDGE, C.5.a.4.6.

7. Water Points exist in YPRES and at C.5.a.7.6.
There are wells in the Forward Area at CORDIALE FACTORY, ZONNEBEKE, D.23, central and CREST FARM, D.12.a.1.9.

8. The S.O.S. in the 8th Corps front is rifle grenade signal bursting into coloured stars, red over green over yellow.

9. O.C. Companies taking over should be careful to take over all maps, Defence Schemes and Barrage and S.O.S. programmes, aeroplanes photographs and all other intelligence details connected with the front they are covering.

10. Acknowledge.

Signed. W. F. GADSDON.

Issued at 8 p.m.   Capt.
7-4-18.   41st Battn. M.G.Corps.

Copies to:-

Copy No. 1. Commanding Officer.
         2. O.C. 29th Battn. M.G. Corps.
         3. "   59th   do.
         4. 41st Division.
         5. O.C. "A" Company.
         6. "   "B"   "
         7. "   "C"   "
         8. "   "D"   "
         9. Transport Officer.
        10. Quartermaster.
        11. R.S.M.
        12. War Diary.
        13. C.M.G.O. 8th Corps.
        14. File.

OO10   Copy No. ...7....

O.C. "A" Company.

You will be prepared to move immediately to occupy with 16 guns prepared positions around YPRES. O.C. Sections will indicate these positions to Nos. 1 of guns and will make arrangements for their teams to occupy these positions before dawn. O.C. "A" Company will report immediately to H.Q. Battalion for information as to these positions to be taken up.

Fighting limbers having taken guns into position will return and rejoin "A" Echelon at their Transport Lines.

Two days rations and water will be taken into positions.

Acknowledge.

Issued at 7-45 p.m.
10-4-18.

Lieut.-Col.
Commanding 41st Battn. M.G.C.

Copies to:
Copy No. 1. O.C. "B" Company.
2.   "   "C"   "
3.   "   "D"   "
4. Transport Officer.
5. Quartermaster.
6. O.C. Battalion.
✓ 7. War Diary.
8. R.S.M.
9. File.

SECRET.   Copy No......8......

O.O.11

O.C. "B" Company.

You will withdraw immediately the 10 Reserve Guns (including A.A. Guns) at GALLIPOLI to PICKLEHAUBE KEEP, C.23.c.5.7, and be prepared to occupy Battle Positions in the Army Battle Zone before dawn.

These positions will be indicated to you later.

5 Fighting Limbers of "B" Company will proceed immediately to SOMME DRESSING STATION and will move the 10 Reserve Guns "B" Company to PICKLEHAUBE KEEP. They will then return to Transport Lines and rejoin "A" Echelon.

Acknowledge.

A.W. Tate

Lieut.-Col.
Commanding 41st Battn, M.G.C.

Issued at 7-45 p.m.
10-4-18.

    Copies to:
        Copy No.1. O.C. "A" Company.
              2.   "   "C"   "
              3.   "   "D"   "
              4. Transport Officer.
              5. Quartermaster.
              6. R.S.M.
              7. O.C. Battalion.
        ✓   8. War Diary.
              9. File.

SECRET.   Copy No. 9

41st Battalion Machine Gun Corps Operation Order No. 16.

To O.C. "B" Company,
    41st Battalion Machine Gun Corps.

1.   O.C. "B" Company, 41st Battalion Machine Gun Corps will detail two of the reserve guns under an Officer, at present in position in the Army Battle Zone, to report to O.C. 10th "Queens" R.W.S. Regt. at BELLEVUE, from whom they will receive the necessary orders, as soon as possible after dusk to-day the 13th instant.

2.   These guns will be required for covering the Right Flank of the BELLEVUE line, and for carrying on, as far as possible, with the usual night harassing fire.

3.   On arrival at BELLEVUE, these guns will come under the Command of G.O.C. 124th Infantry Brigade, who will be responsible for issuing orders for their action in case of a withdrawal.

4.   Officer Commanding this half section should report to O.C. "B" Company when these guns are in position.

5.   O.C. "B" Company will make necessary Transport arrangements for moving the guns forward, supply of rations, ammunition and necessary relief.

6.   Acknowledge.

Issued at 12-15 p.m.
13-4-18.

A. W. Tate
Lt.-Colonel.
Commanding 41st Bn. M.G.Corps.

Copies to:-

    Copy No. 1. O.C. "A" Company.
         2.   "   "C"   "
         3.   "   "D"   "
         4.   "   10th "Queens" R.W.S. Regt.
         5. 124th Infantry Brigade.
         6. 41st Division "G".
         7. 2nd Corps "G".
         8. War Diary.
     ✓   9. File.

SECRET.   Copy No......9......

Operation Order No. 17.
By
Lieut.-Col. A. W. TATE.
Commanding 41st Battalion Machine Gun Corps.
15th April, 1918.

Ref. Map Sheet 28 N.W. 1/20,000.

1. The 41st Division are constructing and occupying a line from WITTE CHATEAU, I.10.c. exclusive, to a Point C.28.b.8.6. South East of WIELTJE.

2. The G.O.C. 123rd Infantry Brigade will be in command of the New Battle Zone until the outposts are withdrawn when he will retain command of the Left Brigade Sector and G.O.C. 124th Infantry Brigade will take over command of the Right Brigade Sub-sector.

3. When the garrison of the Army Battle Zone is withdrawn to the New Battle Zone, one Company from each of the Right and Left Battalions of both Brigade Sectors will be left in the Army Battle Zone, disposed as outposts, and keeping touch with the troops of the 6th and 36th Divisions on their Right and Left flanks respectively.

   They will delay any enemy advance, cover all approaches to the Divisional Sector of the New Zone, and will not withdraw, unless forced to do so by a determined hostile attack.

   A Commander has been appointed by G.O.C. 123rd Infantry Brigade.

   One Section each of "A" and "B" Companies, 41st Battalion Machine Gun Corps will be left in position in the Right and Left Brigade Sectors respectively of the Army Battle Zone.

   The Officer Commanding these Sections must get into close touch with the Commander appointed by G.O.C. 123rd Infantry Brigade and the Officers Commanding the Infantry Companies (see para 3, sub-para 1) adjusting their present positions, if necessary, so as to obtain mutual support and the best line of withdrawal, which should be reconnoitred immediately. These two Sections will be under the orders of the Commander appointed by G.O.C. 123rd Infantry Brigade.

   Should these two Sections be forced to withdraw with the Infantry owing to a determined hostile attack, they will withdraw to previously prepared positions in the rear of the New Battle Zone, and Officers Commanding Companies will arrange for guides to conduct them there.

4. The two guns of "B" Company, 41st Battalion Machine Gun Corps, at present in position in advance of the Army Battle Zone, will be withdrawn during the night of 15th/16th April. O.C. "B" Company will arrange for the Officer in Command of these two guns to make arrangements for the withdrawal direct with O.C. Outposts, Headquarters, GALLIPOLI.

   O.C. "B" Company will arrange for necessary Transport and for guides to take these guns to previously prepared positions in the rear of the New Battle Zone.

5. The remaining ten guns of "B" Company and 12 guns of "A" Company, 41st Battalion Machine Gun Corps, will be disposed in depth in the New Battle Zone, in the Right and Left Brigade Sub-sectors respectively.

6. "D" Company, 41st Battalion Machine Gun Corps will occupy positions that have been selected and indicated to them in the YPRES Defences, within the Divisional Boundaries.

7. "C" Company, 41st Battalion Machine Gun Corps, will occupy positions that have been selected and indicated to them in Divisional Reserve West of YPRES.

8. Officers Commanding Companies will arrange so that when their guns are in position in the New Battle Zone, S.O.S. lines can be laid down and dead ground and likely lines of approach searched with direct or indirect fire.

9.   An ample supply of ammunition is to be at each position, and two days extra rations are being arranged for.

10. Machine Gun Battalion Headquarters have moved to old 41st Division Headquarters at DEAD END.

11. "A", Echelon, 41st Battalion Machine Gun Corps, will move to-morrow the 16th instant at 9 a.m. to a position at H.4.central, and will be in signal communication with Battalion Headquarters.

12. ACKNOWLEDGE.

Issued at 8-45 p.m.
15-4-18.

Lt.-Colonel.
Commanding 41st Bn. M.G. Corps.

Copies to:-

    Copy No. 1. O.C. "A" Company.
             2.   "   "B"   "
             3.   "   "C"   "
             4.   "   "D"   "
             5. 2nd Corps "G".
             6. 41st Division "G".
             7. 36th Battalion Machine Gun Corps.
             8. 8th   do.
          ✓ 9. War Diary.
            10. File.

SECRET. Copy No. 10

Operation Order No. 18.
by
Lieut.-Col. A. W. TATE.
Commanding 41st Battalion Machine Gun Corps.
15th April, 1918.

To O.C. "A" Echelon.

1. "A" Echelon will move from its present lines at DEAD END to-morrow morning the 16th instant to lines selected by O.C. "A" Echelon at H.4.central (approx.).

2. The maltese cart will move with "A" Echelon and remain with it.

3. Column will move off at 9 a.m. under Lieut. STOCKER who will report to Battalion Headquarters when ready to move.

4. On arrival a Runner will be sent back to Battalion Headquarters to report exact map location and to arrange with Signals for telephonic communication.

5. Animals and limbers must not be bunched together but scattered into small groups on being parked.

6. Acknowledge.

Issued at 8-45 p.m.
15-4-18.

A.W. Tate
Lt.-Colonel.
Commanding 41st Battn. M.G.Corps.

Copies to:

Copy No. 1. O.C. "A" Company.
2.   "   "B"   "
3.   "   "C"   "
4.   "   "D"   "
5. Transport Officer.
6. Quartermaster.
7. War Diary.
8. File.
9. spare

SECRET.   Copy No......5....

OPERATION ORDER NO. 19.
by
LIEUT.-COL. A. W. TATE.
Commanding 41st Battalion Machine Gun Corps.
16th April, 1918.

To: O.C. "A" Company, 41st Battn. Machine Gun Corps.
       " "B"   "   "   "   "   "   "

1.   In accordance with orders received from 41st Division, you will occupy 14 positions in the New Battle Zone, instead of 16 as previously ordered.
        Of the 4 forward guns in the Outpost Line, 2 of these will on withdrawal occupy positions in the 4th Line of the New Battle Zone.

2.   The remaining 2 guns will come into Brigade Reserve, and be at the disposal of G.O.C. Brigade.
        ("A" Company, 124th Infantry Brigade).
        ("B"   "   123rd Infantry Brigade).
        You will report to G.O.C. Infantry Brigade for further orders and arrange with him the position for these 2 Reserve Guns to be located.

                                                    A W Tate
Issued at 10 p.m.   Lt.-Colonel.
16-4-18.   Commanding 41st Battn. M.G.Corps.

Copies to:-
              Copy No. 1. G.O.C. 123rd Infantry Brigade.
                      2.   "   124th   "   "
                      3. 41st Division "G".
                      4. War Diary
                      5. File.

SECRET.   Copy No......4.

                    OPERATION ORDER NO. 20.
                              by
                    LIEUT.-COL. A. W. TATE.
                Commanding 41st Battalion Machine Gun Corps.
                         18th April, 1918.

To O.C. "A" Company.
   "   "B"   "

1.   Arrangements should be made immediately so that all guns
   in position in the forward zone that are not under direct
   hostile observation, can search dead ground forward of the new
   front line, so as to harrass the enemy in any area where he
   may be able to assemble not under our observation. From the map,
   it appears that the line JASPER FARM, C.29.b.5.8. RUPRECHT FARM,
   C.30.c.25.40. is suitable.
        The area forward of the front line should be examined if
   possible by personal reconnaissance to enable suitable targets
   as above to be selected.
        In addition to this long range area searching fire which
   must not be employed until it has been ascertained for certain
   that our outposts have been withdrawn in rear of this area.
   Arrangements should be made for laying down an S.O.S. Line on
   the most probable lines of approach, as close to our front line
   as possible, within safety limits.
        The location of the targets selected and guns employed
   should be forwarded to Battalion Headquarters as soon as possible.

                                         Wilfred Potter
                                              for
                                         Lieut.-Colonel.
Issued at 11-15 a.m.   Commanding 41st Bn. M.G.Corps.
18-4-18.

     Copies to:

              Copy No. 1. O.C. "C" Company.
                      2.   "   "D"   "
                      3.   41st Division "G".
                      4.   War Diary.
                      5.   File.

SECRET.

O.C. "A" Company.
"   "B"   "
"   "C"   "
"   "D"   "

Copy No. 7

1. "A" Company, 41st Battalion Machine Gun Corps will arrange to relieve the 1 Section at present in position in the Outpost Line, Right Brigade Sector, on the night of the 20th/21st inst.
   Completion of relief will be reported to O.C. Outposts and Machine Gun Battalion Headquarters by code word "Iron Rations".

2. "B" Company, 41st Battalion Machine Gun Corps will be relieved in the Left Brigade Sector by "C" Company, 41st Battalion Machine Gun Corps on the night of the 21st/22nd instant, and will relieve "D" Company, 41st Battalion Machine Gun Corps in the Intermediate Zone. Completion of relief to be reported as in para. 1.
   "C" Company will arrange with "B" Company for an Officer to reconnoitre the Outpost Line on the night of the 20th/21st instant.

3. "D" Company will relieve "C" Company in the Reserve Zone on the night of the 21st/22nd instant. Completion of relief to be reported to Battalion Headquarters as above.

4. Arrangements for reliefs to be made direct between Companies.

5. Acknowledge.

A. M. Tate
Lt.-Colonel,
Commanding 41st Battn. M.G.Corps.

20-4-18.

Copies to:

Copy No. 1. 122 Infantry Brigade.
         2. 123   "   "
         3. 124   "   "
         4. 41st Division "G".
         5. Quartermaster.
         6. Transport Officer.
         7. War Diary.
         8. File.
         9. O.C. Outposts.

SECRET.   Copy No......9......

O.C. "A" Company.-
    "B"   "
    "C"   "
    "D"   "

                                                        A/183

1.   "D" Company, 41st Battalion Machine Gun Corps will relieve
    "A" Company, in the Right Brigade Sector of the Forward Zone
    on the night of 24th/25th instant, and will send an Officer
    to reconnoitre the Outpost Line on the night of the 23rd/24th
    instant.

2.   "A" Company will relieve "B" Company in the Intermediate
    Zone on the night of the 24th/25th instant.

3.   "B" Company will relieve "D" Company in the Reserve Zone
    on the night of the 24th/25th instant.

4.   Arrangements for reliefs and necessary guides to be made
    direct between Companies concerned.

5.   Completion of reliefs will be reported to Battalion
    Headquarters by wiring "MORE OIL REQUIRED".
        "D" Company will also report completion of relief of
    Outpost Line to O.C. Outposts.

6.   Acknowledge.

                                    A. W. Tate
                                    Lieut.-Colonel.
23rd April, 1918.   Commanding 41st Battn. M.G. Corps.

    Copies to:
            Copy No. 1. 122nd Infantry Brigade.
                     2. 123rd Infantry Brigade.
                     3. 124th Infantry Brigade.
                     4. 41st Division "G".
                     5. Quartermaster.
                     6. Transport Officer.
                     7. O.C. Outposts.
                     8. Signalling Sergeant.
                     9. War Diary.
                    10. File.

SECRET.   Copy No... 11 ...

OPERATION ORDER NO. 21.
by
LIEUT.-COL. A. W. TATE.
Commanding 41st Battalion Machine Gun Corps.
Friday, 26th April, 1918.

To: O.C. "C" Company.
    "   "D"   "

1.   The following Operation Order received from Division:-

     G.568. 26th.
     "   41st Divn Order No. 245 AAA Outposts to be withdrawn
     "forthwith in conjunction with Outposts of 6th Divn and to
     "join their Battalions in the Battle Zone AAA The withdrawal
     "is to be affected by a general reduction of strength all
     "along the line with as much secrecy as possible AAA Touch
     "to be maintained throughout with Divisions on either flank
     "AAA Front line of Battle Zone will be held as main line of
     "resistance after withdrawal of Outposts AAA Completion of
     "moves to be reported to Battn. Hd.Qrs. AAA ACKNOWLEDGE AAA"

2.   The withdrawal of outpost guns should be arranged for
with O.C. Outposts.

     These guns will withdraw as previously arranged to their
prepared positions in the rear of the Forward Zone and take over
their Barrage Lines.

     Arrangements for necessary Transport to be made direct
between Companies concerned and "A" Echelon which has been
withdrawn to "B" Echelon.

     Number of limbers (Code word "Rabbits") required and time
required to be sent direct by telephone.

3.   ACKNOWLEDGE.

                                              A W Tate
26-4-18.   Lieut.-Colonel.
Issued at 2-15 p.m.   Commanding 41st Bn. M.G.Corps.

     Copies to:

               Copy No. 1. O.C. "A" Company.
                    2. "   "B"   "
                    3. 41st Division "G".
                    4. II Corps "G".
                    5. 123rd Infantry Brigade.
                    6. 124th Infantry Brigade.
                    7. O.C. Outposts.
                    8. 6th Battn. M.G. Corps.
                    9. 36th   "   "   "
                   10. War Diary.
                √ 11. File.

ORIGINAL

[Stamp: 41st BATTALION, MACHINE GUN CORPS. No. A426 Date 2.6.18]

Machine Gun Corps

41st Battalion

War Diary for May 1918

with

Appendices Nos 1 to 7.

WAR DIARY **Army Form C. 2118.**
or
INTELLIGENCE SUMMARY

41st Battalion,
The Machine Gun Corps.

MAY 1918

Place	Date	Hour	Summary of Events and Information	Remarks and references to Appendices
Ref BELGIUM and FRANCE Sheet 28. 1/40,000	1st		The Battalion was in the line: D Company in the forward area, A Company in the YPRES defences, B Company – Reserve Support Company with 2 Sections standing by to move with the 122 L. Bde., C Company in Reserve, B Schelton & Froven Camps, Battalion Headquarters at Chateau Rosie. Strength 40 Officers and 800 Other Ranks.	Ref.
	2nd.		The Corps Machine Gun Officer visited the rear sectors in the afternoon. The C.O. and Major GODSDON visited guns in the Peen Clear and warm day. All quiet in the line. During the night 'C' Company relieved and Yellow lines. 'A' Company in the YPRES defences, and 'A' Company on relief took over positions in the Peen and Yellow line vacated by 'C' Company.	Ref.
	3rd		C.O. visited Forward companies in the morning. 'D' Company was relieved by 'B' Company in the Support line.	Ref. A
	4th		A Conference of Company Commanders was held in the afternoon here the Instructions N.O. 5 and Corps M.G. chief points under discussion here the promotion of O.R.4.17	Ref A ①

Army Form C.2118

41st BATTALION, MACHINE GUN CORPS.

WAR DIARY
or
INTELLIGENCE SUMMARY
(Erase heading not required.)

Place	Date	Hour	Summary of Events and Information	Remarks and references to Appendices
	5th		N.C.O's and the Corporals with 2 the T.O. and O.C. 'C' Coy both reported to Tonquebert. Major E.H. INDEY, M.C. reported for 2 duty as 2nd in Command of the Battalion.	Aut. Cpt.
	6th		Thouroydan. C.O. visited lines in the morning. Major GADSDON rejoined 'D' Coy + took over command. The following Officers arrived from the base. Lieut. A.C. LINDLEY, Lieut. C.D. LOVERING, 2nd Lieut. K.G. FRAZER, 2nd Lieut. H.T. PARKER. Allotted to 'B' Coy. Excepting Lt. LINDLEY to 'D' Coy.	
	7th		C.O. visited 122nd Brigade in the morning. Rain nearly all day. C.O. + 2nd in Command visited forward companies. Heavy bombardment during the night. Several gas shells were sent over in the vicinity of VLAMY-FRINDAS Chateau. Mules were provided for 'A' Echelon.	Nil
	8th		Major Hupey went round lines of the positions in A Coy's area in the afternoon. Major Hupey visited Blongary, 2nd Lieut. H.K. WEST, Signalling Officer reported for duty. Casualties in 'D' Coy 1 killed, 2 wounded (shell). In the evening B. Coy relieved by 'A' Coy in the outpost line.	Cpt Vide OO 24 para 1
	9th		Clear weather. C.O. went round the Yellow line with the O.C. M.G. Coy. writeted O.C. 6, M.G. Batt. During the evening D Coy relieved 'C' Coy in the YPRES defences	Cpt Vide OO 24 Paras 2, 3

2449 Wt. W14957/Mgo 750,000 1/16 J.B.C. & A. Forms/C.2118/12.

WAR DIARY or INTELLIGENCE SUMMARY

Army Form C. 2118.

41ST BATTALION, MACHINE GUN CORPS.

Place	Date	Hour	Summary of Events and Information	Remarks and references to Appendices
	10th		C.O. 2nd in command visited forward guns in the morning. 11 O.R.s of 'B' Coy. arrived from the base, and posted "D" Coy. and inspected by the Commanding Officer. In the evening 2 Sections "C" Coy. relieved 2 sections of 6th Bath. M.G.C. in the YPRES defences. On the right 4 Guns A Coy. were relieved by 26th Batt. M.G.C. and relieved 6.9. guns 6th Bn. M.G.C. In the forward area.	vide O.O. No 25 paras 1 & 2.
	11th		— war diary taken over by 2nd in Command. C.O. visited forward guns lately taken over from 6th Battalion M.G. Corps in the YPRES DEFENCES. The battalion is now responsible for the sub of Menin YPRES defences. The 2 Sections of "C" Coy were relieved by the 2 sections of D Company, when the latter has been relieved by 36th Battalion M.G. Corps. Instructions were received to engage certain enemy field and heavy batteries with harassing fire. The enemy have pushed three batteries to within machine gun range of our emplacements.	(illegible)
	12th		C.O. and 2nd in command visited 124 & 10th Bde H.Q. with reference to rear area taken over during hostile sniping and visibility great/danger of having emplacements (crushed)(?)(?) spotted in day time. Enemy very quiet with hostile gun fire. Battn Signalling officer went up to forward area and arranged communications schemes between Coy. H.Q.s and forward sections Visual both by lamp and car was found possible from two sections H.Q. to the RAMPARTS YPRES. Companies are distributed as follows. A Company holding outpost line in front of YPRES " " " emplacement in Rampart. D " " " in Divisional Reserve in WARRINGTON CAMP C " " " in V3, V4 redoubts and 32 (green) Reserve line	(illegible)

Army Form C. 2118.

41ST BATTALION.
MACHINE GUN
CORPS.

No ....
Date ....

WAR DIARY
or
INTELLIGENCE SUMMARY
(Erase heading not required.)

Instructions regarding War Diaries and Intelligence Summaries are contained in F. S. Regs., Part II. and the Staff Manual respectively. Title Pages will be prepared in manuscript.

Place	Date	Hour	Summary of Events and Information	Remarks and references to Appendices
	13th	2am	"S.O.S." Enemy shell entered Dugout in the vicinity of SCHOOL HOUSE causing one casualty. Hostile Batteries (locations mentioned above) engaged by harassing fire during the night.	
		pm	Company in Divisional Reserve carried out training and general cleaning up. Enemy bombed back areas during the night.	
	14th		Enemy bombards cross roads 105 S of VLAMMERTINGHE causing delay in traffic. Enemy Headquarters and A & B Cos shell cut communications between Battalion Headquarters and A & B Companies. This took the S.A. all day to locate. Communication with A and D Companies at present being unsatisfactory owing to buried cable being broken between A and B Companies HQ. Visual station established on ramparts YPRES. Signalling to the Rear only possible. Enemy very active against our Observation Balloons – Two turned fired on. Enemy bombed back areas. Enemy aircraft – no result reported. During the night – approximately 7 Enemy though to be exploding an enemy Dump on our left.	
	15th		C.O. Lieut Colonel proceeded up to B Company. Draft of 1 Officer and 40 other ranks reported from CAMIERES	

WAR DIARY or INTELLIGENCE SUMMARY

41st Battalion, Machine Gun Corps.

Army Form C. 2118.

Place	Date	Hour	Summary of Events and Information	Remarks and references to Appendices
	15th (cont'd)		Enemy gas shelled parts of front line – no casualties – Schreen rather on the increase at WARRINGTON CAMP from an unknown cause – high temperature and signs of influenza reported by M.O. Enemy's GOTHAS very active during the night.	
	16th		"C" Coy relieved "A" in the front line. A Company going into Divisional Reserve. "B" Coy relieved "D" in the YPRES defences. "D" Company took over V³ V⁴ defences. Relief reports complete at 2am 17th. During the day enemy gas shelled YPRES and parts of the Reserve line. 500 rounds were expended on enemy aircraft. Enemy's GOTHAS bombed the back areas during the night.	Vide Appendix No. 5
	17th		Day very quiet – slight shelling of YPRES reported – 3 shells in MENIN GATE. Enemy aircraft active all day. C.O. & 2 i/c in Command went round new positions in rear of YELLOW LINE giving necessary instructions on construction of same. A water tank sunk into the ground is the only solution for our emplacements. What is urgently wanted in wet ground. Both aeroplanes bombed artillery & camps round Abeele, FLAMERTINGHE.	
	18th		2 i/c in Command visited YPRES defences in Company with Boyd's Machine Gun Officer with object of ascertaining whether concrete would improve the emplacements.	

WAR DIARY or INTELLIGENCE SUMMARY

Army Form C. 2118.

41st BATTALION MACHINE GUN CORPS

Place	Date	Hour	Summary of Events and Information	Remarks and references to Appendices
	18th		Conclusion arrived at was that slopes should the snipers through to the face of the Yanfark which would afford invisibility and cover for the team. Green line and above (pints). Enemy quiet most of the day. Having before day-break everyones very active. Harassing fire carried out by forward Company on I.12.b.57.89, I.11.b.65.60, I.11.b.20.50, I.29.d.57.80, I.24.d.50.90 (4000 rounds fired)	A/1)
	19th	10pm – 2am	Targets engaged by harassing fire as previous nights – i.e. Houzzier Batteries – have been moved out of range of our machine guns. R.E. started building fortified emplacement in a house 500x N. of VLAMMERTINGHE with loophole covering East of the village. R.E.'s who started work on emplacement – also in hut 800x west of VLAMMERTINGHE. This hut has brick walls over 2 feet thick and very strong. The reserve Coy (C) was shelled during the day. Shell bursting with instantaneous fuze 80x from a hut caused several of – a Sergeant died later his 2o rounds. During shortage of patrol time in the country every effort is being made to salvo them, as they are invaluable.	A/1)
	20th		C.O. visits green line and forward gun during the night. These two are being provided by Corp'l H.Q. for work in YPRES DEFENCES. "C" Coy moved Camp to A.27.B. Tents provided by Division. Gothas active during the night in Back Areas	A/1)

Army Form C. 2118.

41st BATTALION
MACHINE GUN
CORPS

WAR DIARY
or
INTELLIGENCE SUMMARY
(Erase heading not required.)

Instructions regarding War Diaries and Intelligence Summaries are contained in F. S. Regs., Part II. and the Staff Manual respectively. Title Pages will be prepared in manuscript.

July 1917

Place	Date	Hour	Summary of Events and Information	Remarks and references to Appendices
	20th (Cont'd)	10.30pm / 11pm	The following targets were engaged at times stated I.2.b.50.98	M.W
		11.30pm / 12pm	I.17.b.60.80 } 7000 rounds fired	
	21st	1.30 AM / 2 AM	I.17.c.35.40 I.22.d.90.00 I.23.d.74.54	M.W
		1.45pm	Enemy shelled vicinity of DEAD END 200x N of YPRES with a few gas shells (MUSTARD) sent 4½ batteries large columns of smoke were seen in the vicinity of VOORMEZEELE. Our heavy bombardment on right of	
		5.36pm	ZILLEBEKE LAKE caused enemy to send up no. of coloured lights chiefly Green.	
		12 pm	Heavy counter fire was carried out as above. An enemy aeroplane fires tracer bullets Ypres Railway during night. Also Trafflic bombarded the Town (about Iy f 2.2)	
		10pm / 10.30pm	I.22.b.80.90 }	
		11.15pm / 11.45pm	I.17.b.20.60 } 9000 rounds fired	
	22nd	12.30 AM / 1.0 AM	I.17.c.60.20 }	
		1.45am / 2.30am	I.23.b.60.80 I.17.c.40.60 I.15.b.30.55	
		10 AM	V3 V4 were shelled with gas shells during the night (early morning) causing 2 wounded (a.a. men) 3 evacuated with mustard gas poisoning. One of which was an officer. Enemy aeroplane dropped message evidently from British R.E. telling infantry to make two movement	M.W

2449 Wt. W14957/M90 750,000 1/16 J.B.C. & A. Forms/C.2118/12.

WAR DIARY
or
INTELLIGENCE SUMMARY
(Erase heading not required.)

Army Form C. 2118.

41st BATTALION
MACHINE GUN
CORPS.

Place	Date	Hour	Summary of Events and Information	Remarks and references to Appendices
	22 Cont^d	1.30 p.m.	Enemy aircraft active. YPRES Ramparts lightly shelled. Draft of 34 men reported from base. Harassing fires as below:-	
		10 – 10.30 am	I 17 a 80 50 I 22 b 88	
		11 – 11.40	I 12 a central I 17 a 2.5	
		12.45 – 1.15 am	I 17 b Central	
		2 am 2.45	I 18 a 75 60, I 18 b 6.15 I 16 b 90 40 I 17 a 80 55, I 11 c 01	22,600 rounds fired.
	23rd 28		Draft of 40 men reported from base. Company relief took place during night and early hours the morning as under. D Company relieved A Company in the forward zone. C Company relieved B Company in the YPRES Defences. E Company relieved D Company in Canal Bank (a bullet)	
		4 am.	No casualties – relief completed at 4 am. Enemy lights ½ to 0 bullet during afternoon. POTIJSE Road was under Enemy Machine Gun fire at intervals during the night. 2 Carrier pigeons were now kept in YPRES Defences – with H.Q. Company H.Q. Communication between the two HQ's is perfected by 2 power buzzer.	6
	24	Nearly 4 am Noon	Enemy put up no <u>of Green Lights</u>. Enemy high the rear of <u>CM Gunning and right of</u> the Ramparts in YPRES HA fences and with 4.2 guns. A few shells over VLAMERTINGHE Platoon. Enemy put in the YPRES PAPERINGHE road under a small bombardment through ?? the night Targets engaged as under.	

WAR DIARY
or
INTELLIGENCE SUMMARY

(Erase heading not required.)

Army Form C. 2118.

41st BATTALION MACHINE GUN CORPS.

Place	Date	Hour	Summary of Events and Information	Remarks and references to Appendices
	24th Aug 17		BIRR X Road – through of the night – 5000 rounds fired }	(initials)
			Outpost Buildings " " " " "	
			Outpost X roads " " " " "	
	25th	4 a.m.	Heavy shelled Ramparts.	(initials)
		10-10.30 a.m.	Enemy shells round of LILLE GATE close to one of our gun positions. Heavy calibred Shells fell on the Lille Road	
			Enemy machine gun active from direction of ZILLEBEKE	
		12 p.m.	Our Divisional Artillery carried out heavy gas Shell bombardment. Very little retaliation	
			Targets engaged as under :- I.66.20.55 }	
			I.12.6.80.70 } 8000 rounds fired	
			I.60.50.28 }	
			I.66.20.80 }	
	26th	2 a.m.	(C. O ride) forward guns during the night.	
		4.30 a.m.	Enemy machine gun active on MENIN ROAD turning roundabouts of MILL COT.	
			YPRES shelled during the day, and gas shells at night.	
			LILLE ROAD shelled heavily	
			MANOR FARM suspected as enemy "strong point".	
		11 a.m.	Draft of 7 Rank & Files and 1 N.C.O. reported from Base. Type of reinforcements coming up now from Base Weak	
			Too fatigued and worn out after have been exposed to lot of fighting.	
		7/8/17	Neighbourhood of GOLDFISH CHATEAU shelled with 5.9"s, also VLAMERTINGHE CHATEAU	(initials)
			The YPRES – POPERINGHE road shelled in the night – Enemy fires – rapid fire 100 per hour.	
			C.D. 42nd in command sent reconnaissance for Gun & tactical mile in the Green Line.	
			Enemy Aircraft active all day. New positions hits during YELLOW line proceeding	
			satisfactorily & are being successfully hidden by natural growing barricade of	
			8000 rounds here expended in harrassing fire	

WAR DIARY or INTELLIGENCE SUMMARY

Army Form C. 2118

41st Bn. MACHINE GUN CORPS.

Place	Date	Hour	Summary of Events and Information	Remarks and references to Appendices
	27th		Machine Gun Tactical meeting held on 24th July (O.C. & 2nd in Command & four Section Commanders)	
			VLAMERTINGHE CHATEAU Conveniences. Heavily shelled in early morning.	
			8 PROVEN S.P. shells fired in H32, 30.2.0. (main line)	
			Reinforced guard from the 12th into the YPRES Cloth Hall. This g was also taken over, preparations being made for the new	
			Harassing targets arranged in conjunction with artillery. Targets to be engaged on receipt of code word denoting the target — rate of fire laid down for each set of targets.	6/IB
		1.20	Enemy shelled YPRES and round AREA 9472 — Enemy planes very active over YPRES — Barrel was brought into action by night	
			2nd in command visits YPRES Defences this evening. 3 m.g. H.Q. moving forward of narrowing the night.	6/IB
	28th	12.30 a	Enemy shelled YPRES with gas shells. Machine guns kept firing. Four Saveys and round 9472. 2 guns got as a very heavy gas bombardment in the early hours of the morning. 825 rounds fired in harassing fire.	
			Transport and personnel of "B" Echelon forced to change camps owing to enemy shelling from front of Austrian Farm.	
		1.pm	VLAMERTINGHE Shelled all day and at intervals during the night. 6 fires per (possibly) of between D & E and YPRES (15) or crushed.	
			One enemy being chased all day — one enemy Machine reported as crashed.	
			Targets engaged with harassing fire as under:	
			C 30.C. 65·35· 2,000 rounds	
			C 30.C. " 2,000 "	
			I 12.b 35.58 2,000	
			I 12.a 85.70 2,000	
			H 17.k 20.50 2,000	
			B.I.R R Xroads 2,000	
				(at intervals during the night)
			One man wounded from shell fire	
			B Company relieved D Company in the forward zone	6/IB
			C Company relieved A Company in the YPRES Defences	

WAR DIARY or INTELLIGENCE SUMMARY

Army Form C. 2118.

41st Battalion MACHINE GUN CORPS

Place	Date	Hour	Summary of Events and Information	Remarks and references to Appendices
	29th		YPRES, VLAMMERTINGHE CHURCH shelled with descending fire all day.	
		2.30am & 1.30pm	MENIN ROAD and junction of SAVAGE POTIJZE ROAD shelled.	
			Large formation of enemy aircraft (30 planes) over forward zone.	
			1 officer and 35 O.R. supplied from A Company with Green Line as covering party for R.E. Tunnellers making Tunnel Emplacements in the Rampart YPRES - Two of these Emplacements are finished except for Quadrant Mountings (through preventing) which is slated. Targets Engaged with harassing fire as under. C. D.219 in command over (2) YPRES Drones Ava enemy aeroplane destroyed) & O Balloons.	
		10-11pm	Battery H.Q. & Rd Junction C 30 C 65-35 2500 rounds	
		10-11pm	Outpost Buildings & Rd Junction C 30 C 10.10 5th rounds 2000	
		10-11pm	BIRR X ROADS 2500 rounds	
		10-11pm	Junction of Roads and Tracks I 19 A 20-570 2500 rounds	
	30th		CLOTH HALL YPRES shelled with 5.9 guns.	
			No 14.-31. 32 guns layed on line I 11 a 9.5 - I 5 d 2.5 by one particular lining- to end Infantry raid. No case of gas reported - no Casualties made. One day barge Skull toll in YPRES Asylum. C.O. x 2nd in command inspected YELLOW LINE and Company in Divisional Reserve - Company training work on Emplacement, magazine & Bay Infantry.	
	6pm and 8pm		ATHERLEY furtherer H.4 & Cont.M. No.15 gun heavily shelled	

Army Form C. 2118.

WAR DIARY
or
INTELLIGENCE SUMMARY
(Erase heading not required.)

Instructions regarding War Diaries and Intelligence Summaries are contained in F. S. Regs., Part II. and the Staff Manual respectively. Title Pages will be prepared in manuscript.

[Stamp: 41st BATTALION MACHINE GUN CORPS.]

May 1918

Place	Date	Hour	Summary of Events and Information	Remarks and references to Appendices
	31st	3.30am	Part of Green Line shelled with gas	
	May		Heavy shelling on right of YPRES	
			Enemy aircraft very low over forward zone.	
		9am	One enemy plane brought down by gun fire, also claimed by our A.A. guns.	
		9.30	CLOTH HALL shelled	
		10.30	Enemy's Drying batteries very active	
		pm	Front line and ramparts systematically shelled with heavy artillery. Green line shelled intermittently all day - Positions R7 - R9 - R12 - R13 received much attention. C.O. & 2 i/c reconnoitred various YPRES Ramparts with reference to gun positions into near Barracks (using R8 two guns on platoon) in the event of being ordered to adopt new positions - it was decided to move one gun with 9 Company near the Prison. The other (Reserve) gun to move with another reserve gun from the Prison. Guns 19 & 20 to be moved into tunnelled positions in the ramparts from the railway embankment.	
			5000 rounds fired at aircraft	
			5000 rounds fired on harassing fire during the night.	

Lieut Colonel
41st Battalion Machine Gun Corps.

SECRET.   Copy No..............

OPERATION ORDER NO. 23.
by
LIEUT.-COL. A. W. TATE.
Commanding 41st Battalion Machine Gun Corps.
Wednesday, 1st May, 1918.

To O.C. "A" Company.
   " "B"   "
   " "C"   "
   " "D"   "

1. If the situation permits, "D" Company, 41st Battalion Machine Gun Corps, will be relieved by "B" Company in the Outpost Line on the night of the 3rd/4th May and will take up the 8 positions in the Reserve Zone of Defended Localities V3 and V4 vacated by "B" Company and place 8 guns in Reserve under G.O.C., 124th Infantry Brigade.

2. "A" Company will be relieved by "C" Company in the YPRES Defences on the night of the 2nd/3rd May, and will take over the positions in the YELLOW and GREEN Line vacated by "C" Company.

3. During the time that "D" Company is being relieved by "B" Company, "A" Company will hold the 8 guns in the YELLOW Line in readiness to move at 2 hours notice with the 124th Infantry Brigade.
   On completion of relief between "B" and "D" Companies "D" Company will hold 8 guns in readiness to move at 2 hours notice with 124th Infantry Brigade, and O.C. these 2 Sections will report to G.O.C. 124th Infantry Brigade at VLAMERTINGHE CHATEAU and will notify completion of relief to O.C. "A" Company.

4. Details of reliefs to be arranged direct between Companies and "A" Echelon.
   Completion of reliefs to be notified to Battalion Headquarters by wiring "ARE WE DOWNHEARTED".

5. Acknowledge.

Issued at 7-30 a.m.   Lieut.-Colonel.
2nd May, 1918.   Commanding 41st Battn. M.G.Corps.

Copies to:
        Copy No. 1. 41st Division "G".
                2. 122nd Infantry Brigade.
                3. 123rd Infantry Brigade.
                4. 124th Infantry Brigade.
                5. C.M.G.O.
                6. "A" Echelon.
                7. Quartermaster.
                8. Signal Sergeant.
                9. War Diary.
              10. File.

SECRET. Copy No. 10

OPERATION ORDER NO. 24.
by
LIEUT.-COL. A. W. TATE.
Commanding 41st Battalion Machine Gun Corps.
Monday, 6th May, 1918.

To: O.C. "A" Company.
"   "B"   "
"   "C"   "
"   "D"   "

If the situation permits:-

1. "B" Company will be relieved by "A" Company in the Outpost Line on the night of 8th/9th May, and will occupy the positions in the GREEN and YELLOW Lines respectively vacated by "A" Company.

2. "C" Company will be relieved by "D" Company in the YPRES Defences on the night of 9th/10th May, and will occupy the 8 positions in the Reserve Zone of Defended Localities V3 and V4 vacated by "D" Company, and will place 8 guns in Reserve under G.O.C. 124th Infantry Brigade.

3. During the time that "C" Company is being relieved by "D" Company, "B" Company will hold the 8 guns in the YELLOW Line in readiness to move at 2 hours notice with the 124th Infantry Brigade.
    On completion of relief between "C" and "D" Companies, "C" Company will hold 8 guns in readiness to move at 2 hours notice with 124th Infantry Brigade, and O.C. these 2 Sections will report to G.O.C. 124th Infantry Brigade at H.1.c.70.80. and will notify completion of relief to O.C. "B" Company.

4. Details of reliefs to be arranged direct between Companies and "A" Echelon.
    Completion of reliefs to be notified to Battalion Headquarters by wiring "FIVE MORE".

5. Acknowledge.

Issued at 7-30 a.m. Lieut.-Colonel.
7th May, 1918. Commanding 41st Battn. M.G.Corps.

Copies to:
Copy No. 1. 41st Division "G".
        2. 122nd Infantry Brigade.
        3. 123rd   "   "
        4. 124th   "   "
        5. C.M.G.O.
        6. "A" Echelon.
        7. Quartermaster.
        8. Signal Sergeant.
        9. War Diary.
       10. File.

SECRET.   Copy No......9......

                        OPERATION ORDER NO. 24.
                                   by
                         LIEUT.-COL. A. W. TATE.
                    Commanding 41st Battalion Machine Gun Corps.
                          Monday, 6th May, 1918.

To: O.C. "A" Company.
        "   "B"   "
        "   "C"   "
        "   "D"   "

            If the situation permits:-
1.   "B" Company will be relieved by "A" Company in the Outpost
        Line on the night of 8th/9th May, and will occupy the positions in
        the GREEN and YELLOW Lines respectively vacated by "A" Company.

2.   "C" Company will be relieved by "D" Company in the YPRES
        Defences on the night of 9th/10th May, and will occupy the 8
        positions in the Reserve Zone of Defended Localities V3 and V4
        vacated by "D" Company, and will place 8 guns in Reserve under
        G.O.C. 124th Infantry Brigade.

3.   During the time that "C" Company is being relieved by "D"
        Company, "B" Company will hold the 8 guns in the YELLOW
        Line in readiness to move at 2 hours notice with the 124th
        Infantry Brigade.
            On completion of relief between "C" and "D" Companies, "C"
        Company will hold 8 guns in readiness to move at 2 hours notice
        with 124th Infantry Brigade, and O.C. these 2 Sections will
        report to G.O.C. 124th Infantry Brigade at H.1.c.70.80. and
        will notify completion of relief to O.C. "B" Company.

4.   Details of reliefs to be arranged direct between Companies
        and "A" Echelon.
            Completion of reliefs to be notified to Battalion Headquarters
        by wiring "FIVE MORE".

5.   Acknowledge.

                                                    A. W. Tate
Issued at 7-30 a.m.   Lieut.-Colonel.
7th May, 1918.   Commanding 41st Battn. M.G.Corps.

Copies to:
            Copy No. 1.   41st Division "G".
                     2.   122nd Infantry Brigade.
                     3.   123rd   "   "
                     4.   124th   "   "
                     5.   C.M.G.O.
                     6.   "A" Echelon.
                     7.   Quartermaster.
                     8.   Signal Sergeant.
                     9.   War Diary.
                    10.   File.

SECRET.   Copy No...12...

OPERATION ORDER NO. 25.
by
LIEUT.-COL. A. W. TATE.
Commanding 41st Battalion Machine Gun Corps.
Friday, 10th May, 1918.

To: O.C. "A" Company.
    "   "B"   "
    "   "C"   "
    "   "D"   "

1. On the night 10th/11th May, the 6 guns of "A" Company occupying positions F.6., 7, 11, 13, 28. (two guns) will be relieved by 36th Battalion Machine Gun Corps and will relieve 6 guns of the 6th Battalion Machine Gun Corps in the Forward Area.

2. During the afternoon 10th May, the two sections of "C" Company standing by as Reserve to 124th Infantry Brigade, will relieve the two sections of the 6th Battalion Machine Gun Corps in the YPRES DEFENCES.

3. During the afternoon 11th May, 6 guns of "D" Company occupying positions I.9, 10, 11, 12, 13, 15. will be relieved by 36th Battalion Machine Gun Corps; also guns occupying positions I.3, and 14. will vacate their position. These 8 guns on relief by 36th Battalion Machine Gun Corps will relieve the guns of "C" Company mentioned in para. 2., in the YPRES DEFENCES.

4. The 8 guns of "C" Company, relieved, as stated in para. 3. will rejoin their Company in the V.3. V.4. Area, and the whole Company will then move into Divisional Reserve under G.O.C. 123rd Infantry Brigade, and take over the Camps now occupied by the 124th Infantry Brigade, with Headquarters at VLAMERTINGHE CHATEAU.

5. The two sections of "B" Company, at present occupying the YELLOW LINE will, during the 11th May move forward and occupy the positions in the V.3. V.4. Area vacated by "C" Company.

6. Further details as to guides, time of reliefs, etc., will be issued separately to Company Commanders as soon as possible.

7. Completion of reliefs to be reported to Battalion Headquarters by Code "TUESDAY".

8. Acknowledge.

Issued at 6 a.m.
10-5-18.

Lieut.-Colonel.
Commanding 41st Battn. M.G.Corps.

Copies to:
    Copy No. 1.   41st Division "G".
               2.   C.M.G.O.
               3.   122nd Infantry Brigade.
               4.   123rd Infantry Brigade.
               5.   124th Infantry Brigade.
               6.   36th Battalion Machine Gun Corps.
               7.   6th Battalion Machine Gun Corps.
               8.   O.C. "A" Echelon.
               9.   Quartermaster.
              10.   Transport Officer.
              11.   Signal Officer.
              12.   War Diary.
              13.   File.
              14.   Spare.

SECRET.   Copy No..........

                    OPERATION ORDER NO. 26.
                              by
                      LIEUT.-COL. A. W. TATE.
                Commanding 41st Battalion Machine Gun Corps.
                      Wednesday, 15th May, 1918.

To: O.C. "A" Company.
       "   "B"   "
       "   "C"   "
       "   "D"   "

1.   On the night of the 16th/17th May, "A" Company in the
Forward Area will be relieved by "C" Company in Divisional
Reserve. On relief "A" Company will go into Divisional
Reserve at (this position to be notified later) under G.O.C.
123rd Infantry Brigade (Brigade Headquarters at VLAMERTINGHE
CHATEAU).

2.   During the afternoon of the 16th May, "B" Company will
relieve "D" Company in YPRES DEFENCES, coming under the orders
of G.O.C. 122nd Infantry Brigade (Brigade Headquarters at
Machine Gun Farm). On relief "D" Company will take over
positions in V.3. and V.4. Area vacated by "B" Company.

3.   Details as to guides etc., will be arranged mutually
between Company Commanders.

4.   Completion of reliefs to be reported to Battalion
Headquarters by code "MAPCASE".

5.   Acknowledge.

Issued at 4 p.m.   Lieut.-Colonel.
15-5-18.   Commanding 41st Battn. M.G.Corps.

      Copies to:

              Copy No. 1. 41st Division "G".
                       2. C.M. G.O.
                       3. 122nd Infantry Brigade.
                       4. 123rd Infantry Brigade.
                       5. 124th Infantry Brigade.
                       6. 36th Battalion Machine Gun Corps.
                       7. 6th Battalion Machine Gun Corps.
                       8. O.C. "A" Echelon.
                       9. Quartermaster.
                      10. Transport Officer.
                      11. Signal Officer.
                      12. War Diary.
                      13. File.
                      14. Spare.

SECRET.   Copy No...............

OPERATION ORDER NO. 27.
by
LIEUT.-COL. A. W. TATE.
Commanding 41st Battalion Machine Gun Corps.
Tuesday, 21st May, 1918.

To: O.C. "A" Company.
 "   "B"   "
 "   "C"   "
 "   "D"   "

On the night of the 22nd/23rd May.

1. (a). "C" Company 41st Battalion Machine Gun Corps will be relieved by "D" Company in the Forward Area (under G.O.C.s 123rd and 124th Infantry Brigades, Headquarters at H.5.b.4.3. and Machine Gun Farm, H.5.c.9.9. respectively) and on relief will occupy the positions in the BRIELEN LINE (V.3. and V.4.) and VLAMERTINGHE (GREEN) LINE, vacated by "D" Company.

    (b). "B" Company will be relieved by "A" Company, in the YPRES DEFENCES and on relief will go into Divisional Reserve (under G.O.C. 122nd Infantry Brigade, Headquarters at VLAMERTINGHE CHATEAU) and will occupy the camp vacated by "A" Company.

2.   On the night of the 21st/22nd May, "C" and "D" Companies will inter-change one man per gun team to live at the position to be taken over from each other.
         "A" Company will send one man per gun team to live at the positions to be taken over from "B" Company.

3.   Details for relief to be arranged direct between Companies concerned.

4.   No movement to take place until dusk.

5.   Completion of relief to be reported to Battalion Headquarters, by wiring "3 SURPLUS".

6.   Acknowledge.

Issued at 11-45 a.m.
21-5-18.   Lieut.-Colonel.
                                          Commanding 41st Battn. M.G.Corps.

         Copies to:

                     Copy No.1. 41st Division "G".
                           2. C.R.G.O.
                           3. 122nd Infantry Brigade.
                           4. 123rd Infantry Brigade.
                           5. 124th Infantry Brigade.
                           6. 36th Battn. Machine Gun Corps.
                           7. 8th Battalion Machine Gun Corps.
                           8. O.C. "A" Echelon.
                           9. Quartermaster.
                          10. Transport Officer.
                          11. Signal Officer.
                          12. War Diary.
                          13. File.
                          14. Spares.

SECRET.

SECRET. Copy No. 13

OPERATION ORDER NO. 28.
by
LIEUT.-COL. A. W. TATE.
Commanding 41st Battalion Machine Gun Corps.
Monday, 27th May, 1918.

To: O.C. "A" Company.
        "B" "
        "C" "
        "D" "

On the night of the 28th/29th May.

1. (a). "D" Company, 41st Battalion Machine Gun Corps will be relieved by "B" Company in the Forward Area (under G.O.sC. 123rd and 122nd Infantry Brigades, Headquarters at H.5.b.4.3. and MACHINE GUN FARM, H.5.c.9.9. respectively) and on relief will go into Divisional Reserve (under G.O.C. 124th Infantry Brigade, Headquarters at VLAMERTINGHE CHATEAU) and will occupy the camp vacated by "B" Company.

   (b). "A" Company will be relieved by "C" Company in the YPRES DEFENCES, and on relief, will occupy the positions in the BRIELEN LINE (V.3. and V.4.) and VLAMERTINGHE (GREEN) LINE vacated by "C" Company.

2. On the night of the 27/28th O.C. "B" Company will send the Section Officers who will be responsible for Guns Nos. F.29, 30, 31, 32, 33, 34 to reconnoitre these positions.

3. Details of relief to be arranged direct between Companies concerned.

4. No movement to take place until dusk.

5. Completion of relief to be reported to Battalion Headquarters by wiring "YOUR A.Z. 53 RECEIVED".

6. Acknowledge.

Issued at 12-30 p.m.
27-5-18.

Lieut.-Colonel.
Commanding 41st Battn. M.G.Corps.

Copies to:

    Copy No. 1. 41st Division "G".
             2. C.M.G.O.
             3. 122nd Infantry Brigade.
             4. 123rd Infantry Brigade.
             5. 124th Infantry Brigade.
             6. 33th Battn. M.G.Corps.
             7. 6th Battn. M.G.Corps.
             8. Quartermaster.
             9. Transport Officer.
           10. Signal Officer.
           11. War Diary.
           12. File.
           13. Spare.

9044

41st Battalion
Machine Gun Corps

Diary for the Month of
June 1918

WAR DIARY or INTELLIGENCE SUMMARY

Army Form C. 2118.

41 B/n M.G. Corps

JUNE. 1918.

Place	Date	Hour	Summary of Events and Information	Remarks and references to Appendices
Ref BELGIUM 27 HAZEBROUCK S.A.	1st	6-8am	Right of front line shelled. Enemy planes very active & engaged by our guns - hostile A.A. guns. HAMMERTINGHE Chateau environment, heavily shelled during day by enemy especially active at 9pm.	17
		P.M.	Hostile artillery increased in activity towards evening. Few gas shells fired. Harassing fire [17.42258] [123.A.58.40] also LG fired during the night - warning given when sent to Coys. [21] [pass] [111.6.30.35]	
	2nd		Enemy very lively with salvos on roads in rear zone. Aeroplane very active until follow through close up to line.	
			49th Battln. M.G. Coys. relieved 16 1/2 Battn. Forward zone 9/t. YPRES defences. Relief successfully carried out without casualties. In spite of the 49th getting incapacitating certain orders we see to them by their C.O. Enemy shelled roads back area. Casualties nil.	
	3rd	—	Enemy very active with sniping artillery and considerable trenchmortars YPRES with very high explosive all day till 8 pm. Remainder of Battalion relieves continues in Divisional Reserve and Green & Blue line (DTA) relieves in daylight.	17
		10 P.M.	1/C.2.B. relieves afterwards. Enemy put a heavy gas H.E. barrage of run on the rampart of YPRES. Casualties 10 officers 17 men wounded from gas poisoning. 1/c.C.2.B. Company proceeded by line from MENDINGHAM to MATTEN Home to hills at BUYSSCHEURE.	

Army Form C. 2118.

WAR DIARY
or
INTELLIGENCE SUMMARY.
(Erase heading not required.)

415th M.G. Corps

JUNE 1918.

Place	Date	Hour	Summary of Events and Information	Remarks and references to Appendices
	4th	6 AM.	Forward 3 Coy YPRES Defences relieved. Proceeded by tram route to be billeted in BUYSSCHEURE. Owing to unavoidable in the number of sick amongst the limbers - all M.G. transport & stores by road - stopping en route for the night at ZIPPERS CAPPEL. Headquarters closed at LOVIE CHATEAU opened at BUYSSCHEURE.	Kt
	5	7 PM	Company training general clean up - remainder of transport arrived at BUYSSCHEURE. Owing by M.O. before accepting for infantry, we allowed two weeks forming regime by our training - men are unfit to tackle for gas clusters in thigh.	
	6th	PM.	C.O's conference of all officers - Subject general principals of training. Discipline. Department of own officers - running programme. Regular schools for both, nuts, workings and installations. Chocking of own. Stove relaying up of filler. Elementary M.G. Drill.	
	7th	11 AM	Companies carrying out training as per programme. 24th Cornwalls received I week's special leave.	
	8th		General training carried out around HGT M Volkers Labs "D" Coy.	
	9th		News received at 11.15 AM. to proceed to billets in EPERLECQUES. A dance for left BUYSSCHEURE at 8 AM. to Planes excellent billet. The transport was off the two to lorries from 2.30 PM to 3 PM. It rained during the march the Battalion arrived.	

WAR DIARY
INTELLIGENCE SUMMARY

41st M.G. Bn.

JUNE 1918.

Place	Date	Hour	Summary of Events and Information	Remarks and references to Appendices
	9th		O.R.'s in and villas for the night.	Cut.
	10th		Training carried on under Company arrangements. Coy drill and elementary work with Tactical Schemes for Officers. Baths were detailed for A+B Coys at Divisional Baths EPERLECQUES. Military Cross ces awarded to Capt. A.H. Asney late Besides Commander of C Coy. Quartermaster Lt. A.E. Reicanan + R.S.H. Gibson H.K.	Cut.
	11th		Training recently to previous performance. Coys rifles stoppages or miniature ranges in the vicinity of the village. Battalion transport inspected by Lt Col DOWLING	Cut.
	12th		A.C.I. 52. Divisional Train. Brig. Gen. LUCAS, D.S.O. G.H.P. visited the Battalion during the morning. Companies on the large range. This is the improve them in the afternoon Prevalence of although noted for the first time, 39 men being sick of I company absent of	Cut.
	13th		Visit by the Divisional Commander accompanied by G.S.O.2. The Companies were mostly training in their billets. B Company carried out a Tactical Exercise L. FORÊT d' EPERLECQUES.	Cut.
	14th		2 Sections of A Company went to GUEMY to cooperate with the 124th Brigade in Tactical Scheme. The remainder the Companies made The range A Performance was given for the battalion by the "CRUMPS" the football grand at EPERLECQUES.	Cut.

WAR DIARY or INTELLIGENCE SUMMARY

Army Form C. 2118.

41st M.G. Btn

JUNE 1918

Place	Date	Hour	Summary of Events and Information	Remarks and references to Appendices
	14th		Arrival of 2/Lts M'NAIR and HOWSIN.	Capt
	15th		All Companies carried out out-door Training. Departure of Capt HAMMATT and 5 OR's to Infantry substitutes scheme.	Lut
	16th		The "C.R.M.A.S." performed for the Bttn. at 6.30 p.m. Battalion parade 7-7.30 a.m. Church parade for British denominations were held at Div. Headquarters during the day. Another of service a Battalion football team played the 16th Hampshires Treat Team (1-2)	Ctd V. Training Programme
	17th		Companies training in Area. A photo committee was formed under Capt Day Lapsley V.C. and Lut G Action has been arranged. Vide Training Programme. D Company worked with 123rd Inf Bde. and C Coy with 124th Inf Bd.	Ctd Ctd
	18th		" " " "	
	19th 20th		Along Company laying & maintaining telephone and visual communication to. No. 6 section divisional signal Company and the Battalion & another Battalion & position A Company worked with 132nd Infantry Bde. 3 Officers, Lts. GREEN, R.C., MUIR-SMITH, LINDSAY, G. + 2/Lt Le reported for duty corporated for Baths during the day. (A+B Coys + HQ) C.O.'s Conference.	Ctd Ctd
	21st		All 4th Battalion to attend for retraining of the Bn. called out Company Training.	Ctd
	22nd		Baths for remainder of Bn. Training during the morning and inter-section matches in the afternoon.	Ctd

WAR DIARY *or* **INTELLIGENCE SUMMARY.**
(Erase heading not required.)

Army Form C. 2118.

V.
41st M.G. B/n.
JUNE 1918

Place	Date	Hour	Summary of Events and Information	Remarks and references to Appendices
	23rd		Voluntary Church services during the day.	
	24th		Training continued. In the afternoon a warning order was received. Detailed orders received in the evening. The Div. to move into the line.	Vide Administrative Ins.
	25th	At 7.30 a.m. the B/n moved to BUYSSCHEURE in the following order B,A,C,D, Coy Transport. The billets vacated by the 9th were re-occupied. The Battalion arrived and were settled in by 2.45 p.m.	
	26th		9th B/n. moved to the OUDEZEELE area. A Company moved with 122 I. Bde. to ABeele and near Bn. Headquarters and established at X roads. "D" in ATWELD. (Map 5.x.) Preparing for the Show.	
	27th		C.O. and 2 i.c. Coy. visited the line, with a views to relieving m.g. hands of 34th Division.	V. O.O. no
	28th			
	29th			
	30th		B+C Coys were furnished with "A" Echelon to Lies at ABEELE station D Coy to 4.23. D.S.T. settled in by 7.30 p.m. Preparing for the line during day. B,C,D Coys moved in by h Coys — quiet morning.	

SECRET.

To: O.C. "A" Company.
 " "B"   "
 " "C"   "
 " "D"   "
    Transport Officer.
    Quartermaster.
    Signal Officer.

WARNING ORDER.

1.   41st Division will be relieved by 49th Division on nights 2nd/3rd and 3rd/4th June.

        Machine Guns as in the Right Brigade Sector of the Forward Area and YPRES Defences will be relieved on the night of the 2nd/3rd and those as in the Left Brigade Sector on the night of the 3rd/4th.

        Remaining Companies will be relieved on the 3rd.

        Details for the relief will be issued later.

2.   Acknowledge.

                                            Lieut.-Colonel.
                                Commanding 41st Battn. M.G.Corps.

1st June, 1918.

SECRET.   Copy No........ 5 .... R.100.

ADMINISTRATIVE ORDERS:
by
LIEUT.-COL. A. W. TATE.
Commanding 41st Battalion Machine Gun Corps.
Sunday, 2nd June, 1918.

To: O.C. "A" Company.
     "   "B"   "
     "   "C"   "
     "   "D"   "
     Transport Officer.
     Quartermaster.
     Signal Officer.
     Medical Officer.

1.   Two Sections of "B" Company (less one gun team) and two Sections of "C" Company (plus 1 gun team) will on relief by 49th Battalion Machine Gun Corps on the night of the 2nd/3rd June, entrain at FORWARD DUMP, H.6.c.2.5. in the train that has brought up the 49th Battalion Company, and will detrain at REMY SIDING, and from there march to the new camp at F.27.a.2.6.
        An Officer from "C" Company should be sent to REMY SIDING at the commencement of the relief, to prevent the train from moving off until all the men are entrained.
        The necessary limbers of "A" Echelon of these two Companies to get these two Sections out of the line, will proceed direct by road to the new camp.

2.   (a). On relief by the 49th Battalion Company on the 3rd June, "D" Company will entrain at HAGLE, G.6.b.2.2. (train will probably be ready to start loading at 10-15 a.m.) and detrain at PUGWASH and proceed to the new camp, F.27.a.2.6.
        "A" Echelon will proceed by road.
        (b). "A" Company will entrain at HAGLE on relief detraining at REMY SIDING and proceed as in para. 2(a).

3.   The remainder of "B" and "C" Companies will, on relief on the night of 3rd/4th entrain at MACHINE GUN SIDING, H.12.a.8.5. detrain at REMY SIDING and proceed to the new camp.
        The remainder of "A" Echelon will proceed by road.

4.   Transport will move to the new camp on the morning of 3rd June, under arrangements to be made by the Transport Officer.

5.   Battalion Headquarters will move from LOVIE CHATEAU on 4th June and open at the new camp at an hour to be notified later.

6.   All ammunition, reserve rations, petrol tins, solidified alcohol, gum boots, gas clothing, and other trench stores, will be handed over to 49th Battalion Machine Gun Corps on relief, and a copy of receipt forwarded to Battalion Headquarters.

7.   "A" Company will hand over 224 belt boxes to 49th Battn. M.G.C.
        "B"   "   "   "   " 223   "   "   "   "   "
        "C"   "   "   "   " 224   "   "   "   "   "
        "D" Company will not hand over any belt boxes.

        On arrival at new camp, Companies will receive a similar number of belt boxes and tripods from 49th Battalion Machine Gun Corps on producing receipt for belt boxes and tripods handed over in the line.

8.   Guides will be provided by Battalion Headquarters to meet trains at detraining points, and to conduct parties to the camp.
        "A" and "D" Company will send a groom or cyclist to report immediately Battalion Headquarters and will act as guides for "A" Echelon.
        "B" and "C" Companies will send a groom or cyclist (one for each half of "A" Echelon).

9.   Companies will report arrival at the new camp to Battalion Headquarters.

10. RATIONS.

(i). For consumption on 3rd June.
Rations for two Sections of "B" Company and two Sections of "C" Company plus 7 men of "B" and 9 men of "C" remaining in the line will be issued as usual to-night.

(ii). The rations for the remainder of these two Companies will be issued to cooks, who will proceed early on the morning of the 3rd to the new camp with cookers, and prepare breakfast for the half Companies on arrival.

(iii). Breakfast rations for "A" and "D" Companies will be sent up to-night, the remainder of rations will be issued to cooks, who will proceed to new camp in sufficient time to prepare for the mid-day meal.

For consumption on 4th,
will be issued to cooks at the new camp.
An early breakfast will be prepared for the two Sections of "B" and two Sections of "C" Company coming out of the line.
Rations for gun numbers left in the line on the night of the 3rd/4th will be provided by the 49th Battalion Machine Gun Corps.

(iv). Rations for "A" Echelon will conform to these arrangements

11. Acknowledge.

Issued at 12-30 p.m.
2-6-18.

Lieut.-Colonel.
Commanding 41st Battn. M.G.Corps.

Copies to:

Copy No. 1. 41st Division "G".
2. " "Q".
3. 49th Battalion Machine Gun Corps.
4. War Diary.
5. File.
6. Spare.

SECRET.   Copy No........ 8.   R.103.

ADMINISTRATIVE INSTRUCTIONS PART II.
by
LIEUT.-COL. A. W. TATE.
Commanding 41st Battalion Machine Gun Corps.
Sunday, 2nd June, 1918.

To: O.C. "A" Company.
     "B"   "
     "C"   "
     "D"   "
     Transport Officer.
     Quartermaster.
     Signal Officer.
     Medical Officer.

1.   The two Sections of "B" Company (less one gun team) and
two Sections of "C" Company (plus one gun team) that are being
relieved in the Forward Area on the night of the 2nd/3rd June,
will depart from PROVEN Station, on 3rd June at 15 hours.
        No baggage is to be taken on this train with the exception
of a limited number of cooking utensils.
        Detraining station WATTEN arrive 18-30 hours.
        Personnel will entrain one hour before time of departure
reporting to D.A.Q.M.G. at the station.

2.   On 4th June, M.G.Battalion Headquarters and "A" and "D"
Companies will depart from PROVEN Station at mid-day, detraining
at WATTEN, arriving at 15-30 hours.
        Personnel will entrain one hour before time of departure
reporting to D.A.Q.M.G.
        No baggage as in para. 1.

3.   The remainder of "B" and "C" Companies will on 4th June,
depart from PROVEN Station at 22 hours, detraining at ST. OMER
at 2 hours, 5th June; entraining arrangements as in paras 1
and 2.

4.   Arrangements are being made by Division for the transport
of the personnel left in the line on the night of the 3rd/4th
June.

5.   Three G.S. limbered wagons and 10 draught horses of "B"
Company, with 5 attendant personnel and a similar number from
"C" Company, will depart from PROVEN Station at 16.00 hours
on 3rd June, detraining at WATTEN at 19-30 hours.
        This party will report to D.A.Q.M.G. at PROVEN, three
hours before time of departure.

6.   On 4th June, Headquarters Limber and two draught horses and
5 limbers and 16 draught horses from "A" Company, two Riding
Horses from Headquarters with attendant personnel will depart
from PROVEN at 8 hours, reporting 3 hours before time of
departure, detraining at ST. OMER, 11-30 hours.

7.   On the 3rd June, "B" Echelon Transport will march off not
later than 10-15 a.m. and proceed by road to BUYSSCHEURE under
orders issued separately to Transport Officer.
        The cookers of "A", "D" and "C" Companies will assemble
at Transport Lines, F.18.a.8.2. in time to move off with the
Transport.
        The Transport of Battalion Headquarters less Headquarters
limbered G.S. wagon detailed in para. 6 will join the Transport
opposite D.A.D.O.S. Stores F.17.c.10.80. at 10-30 a.m.

8.   The remainder of "A" Echelon of Companies and the cooker of
"B" Company will move off on the morning of the 4th June from
the new camp under Capt. RILEY.

9. Acknowledge.

Issued at 1 2-30 a.m.
3-6-18.

                                                  Lieut.-Colonel.
                            Commanding 41st Battn. M.G.Corps.

Copies to:

        Copy No. 1. 41st Division "G".
                 2.   "   "Q".
                 3. Capt. R. G. RILEY.
                 4. Lieut. STRINGER.
                 5. War Diary.
                 6. File.
                 7. Spare.

        Distribution of Maps.

                1. Capt. R. G. RILEY.
                2. Lieut. STRINGER.
                1. Transport Officer.

To O.C. "A" Company.
      "B"   "
      "C"   "
      "D"   "
Transport Officer.
Quartermaster.
Signal Officer.
Medical Officer.
R.S.M.

Ref. Map HAZEBROUCK 5a.

1.   The Battalion will move to-day to EPERLECQUES. Advanced parties and guides from each Company have already proceeded to the new area under the Adjutant.

2.   The whole of the Transport will move together under the Transport Officer, starting not later than 2 p.m.
"A" Echelons will report loaded to Battalion Transport Officer not later than 1-30 p.m.

3.   "B" Company will move off at 2-30 p.m.
       "C"   "   "   "   "   " 2-45 p.m.
       "D"   "   "   "   "   " 3-0 p.m.
       "A"   "   "   "   "   " 3-10 p.m.
       H.Q. "   "   "   "   " 2-15

Companies will march independently and observe strict march discipline.

Route to be followed:-
Road along South side of Battalion Transport Lines, ST. MOMELIN, across CANAL Northwards to LE BAS - SERQUES, MOULLE, EPERLECQUES.

4.   All tents will be struck immediately, handed over to Area Commandant, Main Street, BUYSSCHEURE, and a receipt obtained, which is to be forwarded to Battalion Headquarters.

5.   Billeting Certificates have been completed at Battalion Headquarters.

6.   All Billets and Camps must be left perfectly clean.

                                          Lieut.-Colonel.
9th June, 1918.   Commanding 41st Battn. M.G. Corps.

Army Form W. 3724.

TRAINING PROGRAMME FOR WEEK ENDING 22nd June, 1918.

Date.	Division and Location of H.Q. Corps.	Brigade and Location of H.Q.	Unit.	Description of Training.	Approximate Date of Commencement and Completion of Training. Time.	REMARKS. (Time and place of Divisional, Brigade and Battalion Exercises).
22-6-18.		41st Battn. M. G. Corps.				
			"A" Company.	Company Drill.	6-45 a.m. to 7-30 a.m. 9 a.m. to 3-30 p.m.	do.
			"B" Company.	Fire Control. Use of cover. Squad Drill. Barrage Drill.	do.	
			"C" Company.	Company Drill. Gas Drill. Kit Inspection. Immediate Action.	do.	
			"D" Company.	Company Inspection. Iron Rations, Box Respirators etc. - at disposal of Section Commanders.	do.	
			Signallers.	Day Scheme - moving stations.	do.	

Army Form W. 3724.

TRAINING PROGRAMME FOR WEEK ENDING 22nd June 1918.

Corps.	Division and Location of H.Q.	Brigade and Location of H.Q.	Unit.	Date.	Description of Training.	Approximate Date of Commencement and Completion of Training.	REMARKS. (Time and place of Divisional, Brigade and Battalion Exercises).
		41st Battalion M.G. Corps.	Transport Section.			Time.	
				17-6-18.	N.C.O.s Class Continued. Saddlery - Parts and fitting - Methods of folding blankets - Fitting of Stirrups - Position in saddle - Saluting mounted - Elementary instruction in horsemanship.		do.
				18-6-18.	Men instructed by their N.C.O.s in subjects as above.		
				19-6-18.	As for 18th. Lecture. "The foot and shoeing".		
				20-6-18.	Pack Saddlery - Fitting and packing.		
				21-6-18.	Limber Drill.		
				22-6-18.	Watering Order Parade. Saluting dismounted, rifle drill and Box Respirator Drill will be carried out each afternoon.		

Army Form W. 3724.

TRAINING PROGRAMME FOR WEEK ENDING 22nd June, 1918.

Corps.	Division and Location of H.Q.	Brigade and Location of H.Q.	Unit.	Description of Training.	Approximate Date of Commencement and Completion of Training.	REMARKS. (Time and place of Divisional, Brigade and Battalion Exercises).
Date.					Time.	
21-6-18.		41st Battn. M.G. Corps.				
			"A" Company.	Company Drill.	6-45 a.m. to 7-30 a.m.	
				Section Scheme. Barrage Drill. Immediate Action.	9 a.m. to 3-30 p.m.	do.
			"B" Company.	Arms Drill and Saluting Drill. Company Scheme. Attack on a village. Some guns employed in defence.	do.	
			"C" Company.	Company Drill. Barrage Drill.	do.	
			"D" Company.	Section Schemes. Sections working on their own. Box Respirator Drill.	do.	
			Signallers.	Buzzer. Fullerphone. Cable laying and jointing practice. Lecture on trench pole and cable laying.	do.	

TRAINING PROGRAMME FOR WEEK ENDING 22nd June, 1918.

Army Form W. 3724.

Corps.	Division and Location of H.Q.	Brigade and Location of H.Q.	Unit.	Description of Training.	Approximate Date of Commencement and Completion of Training.	REMARKS. (Time and place of Divisional, Brigade and Battalion Exercises).
Date.					Time.	
20-6-18.	41st Battn. M.G. Corps.					
		"A" Company.		Squad Drill and Saluting Drill.	6-45 a.m. to 7-30 a.m. 9. a.m. to 3-30. p.m.	do.
				Immediate Action. Judging Distance. Indication and Recognition. Direct overhead fire.	do.	
		"B" Company.		Company Drill. Sight setting and laying with fire direction with use of S.B.R. Stoppages. N.C.O.s Map Reading and use of Compass. Gas Drill. Physical Training Barrage Drill.		
		"C" Company.		Company Drill. Outpost Scheme.	do.	
		"D" Company.		Simple Scheme employing Pack Saddles - Time at disposal of Section Officers.	do.	
		Signallers.		Semaphore. Fullerphone. Buzzer - Flag - Lamp and Disc sending.	do.	

Army Form W.

TRAINING PROGRAMME FOR WEEK ENDING 22nd June, 1918.

Date.	Corps.	Division and Location of H.Q.	Brigade and Location of H.Q.	Unit.	Description of Training.	Approximate Date of Commencement and Completion of Training. Time.	REMARKS. (Time and place of Divisional, Brigade and Battalion Exercises).
19-6-18.			41st Battalion M.G. Corps.				
				"A" Company.	Company Drill and Arms Drill. Tactical Scheme Part II.	6-45 a.m. to 7-30 a.m. 9 a.m. to 3-30 p.m.	do.
				"B" Company.	Squad Drill. Company Scheme. Machine Guns in support of attack and consolidation of position.	do.	
				"C" Company.	Company Drill. Concealment of guns and use of back ground. Immediate Action with Gas masks. from direct overhead fire.	do.	
				"D" Company.	Fire Orders and Control in open country - Kit inspection.	do.	
				Signallers.	Buzzer. Buzzer Reading Test. Fullerphone Reading Test. Long distance visual.	do.	

Army Form W. 3724.

TRAINING PROGRAMME FOR WEEK ENDING 22nd June, 1918.

Corps.	Division and Location of H.Q.	Brigade and Location of H.Q.	Unit.	Description of Training.	Approximate Date of Commencement and Completion of Training.	REMARKS. (Time and place of Divisional, Brigade and Battalion Exercises).
Date.					Time.	
18-6-18.		41st Battn. M.G. Corps.				do.
			"A" Company.	Company Drill. Use of Cover. Barrage work. Use of clinometer & dial.	6-45 a.m. to 7-30 a.m. 9 a.m. to 11 a.m. 11-30 a.m. to 1 p.m.	
			"B" Company.	Arms Drill. Saluting Drill. Range and Stoppages.	6-45 a.m. to 7-30 a.m. 9 a.m. to 1 p.m.	
			"C" Company.	Company Drill. Aiming off for wind and movement. Stoppages.	do.	
			"D" Company.	Company with 123rd Infantry Brigade.		
			Signallers.	Flag Drill. Buzzer. Lamp - Flag - Disc Reading Test.	do.	

Army Form W. 3724.

TRAINING PROGRAMME FOR WEEK ENDING 22nd June, 1918.

Date.	Division and Location of H.Q.	Brigade and Location of H.Q.	Unit.	Description of Training.	Approximate Date of Commencement and Completion of Training. Time.	REMARKS. (Time and place of Divisional, Brigade and Battalion Exercises).
			41st.Batt̄n. M.G.Corps.			
17-6-18.			"A" Company.	Squad and Saluting Drill.	6-45 a.m. to 7-30 a.m. 9 a.m. to 3-30 p.m.	Reference 41st Div. G.604. 74/10. Map of training area not yet received. Will be notified to Divisional Headquarters later.
			"B" Company.	Squad Drill. Use of covered approaches. Judging Distance Fire Direction. Direct overhead fire.	do.	
			"C" Company.	Company Drill. Tactical Scheme.	do.	
			"D" Company.	Tactical Scheme. Defence of locality. Discussion of Scheme.	do.	
			Signallers.	Flag Drill, Buzzer, Lamp - Flag - Disc Reading Practice. Fullerphone Stations.	do.	

SECRET.   Copy No.............

AMINISTRATIVE ORDER.
by
LIEUT.-COL. A. W. TATE,
Commanding 41st Battalion Machine Gun Corps.
Tuesday, 25th June, 1918.

To: O.C. "A" Company.
    "   "B"   "
    "   "G"   "
    "   "D"   "
    Transport Officer.
    Quartermaster.
    Signal Officer.
    Medical Officer.
    R.S.M.

Ref. Map HAZEBROUCK 5a.

1. "A" Company will be attached to the 122nd Infantry Brigade
    and will march off at 9-30 a.m. June 26th, with their "A"
    Echelon, cooker and watercart proceeding via IE TOM - CASSEL -
    STEENVOORDE to ABEELE WEST AREA.
    Head of column to reach IE TOM by 10-54 a.m. and to fall in
    at rear of 122nd Infantry Brigade Column.
    O.C. "A" Company will report personally to G.O.C. 122nd
    Infantry Brigade at IE TOM at 11 a.m. to proceed with him and
    reconnoitre the line.

2. "B", "G", "D" Companies, Headquarters and Transport will
    parade in the Transport Field at 11-25 a.m. and proceed via
    BAVINGHEM - WALMERS CAPPEL to RIETVELD - ZERMEZEELE AREA. Head
    of the column to pass BAVINGHEM by 12 noon.
    Headquarters will march at the head of the column.
    50 yards distance to be maintained between Companies.
    Transport will march under the Transport Officer in rear of
    the column.

3. Advance Parties, consisting of 1 N.C.O. per Company, and
    1 Officer and 1 Runner both on bicycles from "A" Company, will
    report to the Adjutant at the Transport Lines at 7 a.m. and
    proceed by motor lorry.
    "A" Company Runner will meet supply wagons at Cross Roads
    IE TEMPIER N.W. of STEENVOORDE at 12 noon.

4. "A" Company will synchronise watches at Battalion Headquarters
    before marching off.

5. Supplies for consumption 27th will be drawn from railhead
    by 41st Divisional M.T. Company and delivered to Divisional Train
    Companies on arrival in new area at Refilling Points to be
    arranged between O.C. Train and O.C. Divisional M.T.Company.
    O.C. Train will notify time and place of Refilling Points to units who
    will send Guides to Refilling Points.

6. All tents will be struck, handed over to Area Commandant
    and a receipt obtained for same before marching off.
    Receipts to be forwarded to this Office.

7. Usual "Falling Out" Reports to be rendered to Battalion
    Headquarters on arrival at destination.

8. Acknowledge.

                                        A.W. Tate
                                        Lieut.-Colonel.
Issued at 10-40 p.m.   Commanding 41st Battn. M.G.Corps.
25-6-18.

Copy No. 1. 41st Division "G".
       2.   do.   "G".

SECRET.

ADMINISTRATIVE ORDER.
by
LIEUT.-COL. A. W. TATE,
Commanding 41st Battalion Machine Gun Corps,
Monday, 24th June, 1918.

To: O.C. "A" Company.
 " "B" "
 " "C" "
 " "D" "
 Transport Officer.
 Quartermaster.
 Signal Officer.
 Medical Officer.
 R.S.M.

1. The Battalion will move to-morrow 25th June and occupy the same billets that were vacated at BUYSSCHEURE.

2. "B" Company will start off at 9-30 a.m.
 "A" "   "   "   " " 9-35 a.m.
 "C" "   "   "   " " 9-40 a.m.
 "D" "   "   "   " " 9-45 a.m.
 Headquarters will march with "B" Company under Sergt. OSBORN, and will join the Company in the Square.
 The above order will be maintained and strict march discipline adhered to.
 Head of column to reach WATTEN by 11-15 a.m.
 Route to be followed is OUEST MONT, WATTEN, ST. MOMELIN.

3. The Transport will march under the Battalion Transport Officer, with the exception of the cookers, which will accompany their Companies.
 Hour of start 9-55 a.m.

4. All billets will be left in a clean and sanitary condition, and a certificate to this effect rendered to this Office before marching off.
 Rear parties will be left from each Company and Transport to ensure that these orders are carried out.
 This party will march under the Provost Sergeant from the Square EPERLECQUES at 11 a.m.

5. Advance parties have already been sent on to arrange about billets.

6. Sick who are being treated regimentally and who are unfit to march will be evacuated to the affiliated Field Ambulance forthwith.

7. Supplies for consumption 26th will be drawn from Railhead on the 25th as on 24th, and delivered to Units on arrival.
 On 26th instant, Divisional A. T. Company will draw for all Units at Railhead and deliver to Refilling Points as arranged between them and O.C. Divisional Train.

8. One lorry will report to Battalion Headquarters at 8 a.m. This lorry will remain with the Battalion until the night of the 26th, when it will be returned to Divisional M. T. Company.

9. Standing Orders of Second Army Training Areas will be complied with. Amount of practice ammunition handed over to Sub-Area Commandant will be notified to this Office.

10. Companies will notify their arrival to Battalion Headquarters and render the usual "Falling out" Reports.

11. Battalion Headquarters will close at EPERLECQUES at 10 a.m. and reopen at BUYSSCHEURE at 12-30 p.m.

12. Acknowledge.

A. Tate
Lieut.-Colonel,
Commanding 41st Battn. M.G.Corps.

Issued at 9-30 p.m.
24-6-18.

Copy No. 1. 41st Division "G".
     2.   do.   "Q".

Copy No............

SECRET.

OPERATION ORDER NO. 31.
by
LIEUT.-COL. A. W. TATE.
Commanding 41st Battalion Machine Gun Corps.
Friday, 28th June, 1918.

Ref. Map Sheet. HAZEBROUCK 5a and Sheet 27.

To: O.C. "A" Company.
　　　　 "B" 　"
　　　　 "C" 　"
　　　　 "D" 　"
Transport Officer.
Quartermaster.
Signal Officer.
Medical Officer.
R.S.M.

1.   "D" Company will be attached to the 122nd Infantry Brigade in the Left Sub-Sector and will relieve the Machine Guns of the 103 French Infantry Regiment.
     "B" Company will be attached to the 123rd Infantry Brigade in the Centre Sub-Sector and will relieve the Machine Guns of the 104 French Infantry Regiment.
     "C" Company will be attached to the 124th Infantry Brigade in the Right Sub-Sector, and will relieve the Machine Guns of the 102 French Infantry Regiment.
     "A" Company will be in Divisional Reserve.

2.   217th Regiment of the 71st French Division will be on the Right, and the 6th British Division on the left of the 41st Division.
     After relief, the 7th (French) Division will move into the Reserve Area now occupied by the 41st Division.

3.   Detailed arrangements for relief, provision of guides etc., have already been made by Company Commanders concerned when reconnoitring their Sub-Sectors on the morning of 28th June.

4.   <u>Night 30th June/1st July.</u>
     "D" Company will relieve 6 guns in the Forward Area and 2 guns in the Support Area of the 123rd Infantry Brigade.
     "B" Company will relieve 2 guns in the Support Area and 4 guns in the Reserve Area.
     "C" Company will relieve 2 guns in the Forward Area, 4 guns in the Support Area on the Right Flank, and 4 guns in the Reserve Area.
     <u>Night 1st/2nd July.</u>
     "D" Company will relieve 6 guns in the Support Area.
     "B" Company will relieve 6 guns in the Forward Area and 2 guns in the Support Area of the 124th Infantry Brigade.
     "C" Company will relieve 6 guns in the Support Area.
     The exact positions of these guns have already been pointed out to Company Commanders in co-operation with the French Machine Gunners.

5.   (a) "B", "C" and "D" Companies will move forward their teams complete with "A" Echelon, 1 water cart and cookers to bivouacs in field in North half of square L.33.d.
     "A" Echelons will remain in this field after relief is complete. "B" Echelon will remain with Battalion Headquarters.

(b) Officers Commanding Companies, Section Officers and 1 man per gun team of guns relieving on night of 30th June/1st July, will reconnoitre positions to be taken over, and Nos. 1 will remain in.

(French Machine Gunners are leaving in 1 man per gun and 1 N.C.O. per ½ Section for 24 hours after relief)

They will report to Commandant I.D. at Point L.29.c.9.2. as follows:-

Representatives 122nd Infantry Brigade. 9 p.m.
    do.   123rd Infantry Brigade. 9-30 p.m.
    do.   124th Infantry Brigade. 10 p.m.

1 Lorry will be at Machine Gun Battalion Headquarters at 7-30 p.m. to take this party forward.

June 30th.

6. Advance parties for the remaining sections, as in para. 5(b) will report at the same point and at the same hours.

7. <u>July 2nd.</u>
"A" Company will move to L.23.c.1.2.

8. Company Commanders will arrange with Infantry Brigades to live at, or as near as possible to, Brigade Headquarters.

9. Completion of reliefs to be notified to Brigades concerned.

10. When in bivouacs, it is of the utmost importance that Battalions should take every precaution to avoid detection.

<u>At night</u>, Lights are to be reduced to a minimum and are to be carefully screened and no fires are to be lighted.

<u>By day.</u> There should be one Officer per Company always on duty to ensure that men do not expose themselves unnecessarily, and aeroplane sentries are to be posted to give notice of approaching aircraft.

Excessive smoke must be avoided.

The Divisional Commander directs that the reasons for such special secrecy, vizL to prevent the enemy from obtaining indications that a relief of the French by the British is in progress should be carefully explained to all ranks.

All ranks must be equally careful when in the forward area.

11. Acknowledge.

Issued at 7 a.m.
29-6-18.

Lieut.-Colonel.
Commanding 41st Battn. M.G.Corps.

Copies to: Copy No. 1. 122nd Infantry Brigade.
    2. 123rd Infantry Brigade.
    3. 124th Infantry Brigade.
    4. 41st Division "G".
    5.   "   "   "Q".
    6. C.R.A.
    7. C.R.E.
    8. 6th Division.
    9. 71st French Division.
    10. 7th French Division (4 Copies).
    11. War Diary.   2 "
    12. File.
    13. Spare.

Appendices for Orig.   Copy No......11...dy/s

SECRET.   OPERATION ORDER NO. 31.
by
LIEUT.-COL. A. W. TATE.
Commanding 41st Battalion Machine Gun Corps.
Friday, 28th June, 1918.

Ref. Map Sheet. HAZEBROUCK 5a and Sheet 27.

To: O.C. "A" Company.
    "B"   "
    "C"   "
    "D"   "
    Transport Officer.
    Quartermaster.
    Signal Officer.
    Medical Officer.
    R.S.M.

1. "D" Company will be attached to the 122nd Infantry Brigade in the Left Sub-Sector and will relieve the Machine Guns of the 103 French Infantry Regiment.
"B" Company will be attached to the 123rd Infantry Brigade in the Centre Sub-Sector and will relieve the Machine Guns of the 104 French Infantry Regiment.
"C" Company will be attached to the 124th Infantry Brigade in the Right Sub-Sector, and will relieve the Machine Guns of the 102 French Infantry Regiment.
"A" Company will be in Divisional Reserve.

2. 217th Regiment of the 71st French Division will be on the Right, and the 6th British Division on the left of the 41st Division.
After relief, the 7th (French) Division will move into the Reserve Area now occupied by the 41st Division.

3. Detailed arrangements for relief, provision of guides etc., have already been made by Company Commanders concerned when reconnoitring their Sub-Sectors on the morning of 28th June.

4. Night 30th June/1st July.
"D" Company will relieve 8 guns in the Forward Area and 2 guns in the Support Area of the 123rd Infantry Brigade.
"B" Company will relieve 2 guns in the Support Area and 4 guns in the Reserve Area.
"C" Company will relieve 2 guns in the Forward Area, 4 guns in the Support Area on the Right Flank, and 4 guns in the Reserve Area.
Night 1st/2nd July.
"D" Company will relieve 6 guns in the Support Area.
"B" Company will relieve 6 guns in the Forward Area and 2 guns in the Support Area of the 124th Infantry Brigade.
"C" Company will relieve 6 guns in the Support Area.
The exact positions of these guns have already been pointed out to Company Commanders in co-operation with the French Machine Gunners.

5. (a) *June 29th.* "B", "C" and "D" Companies will move forward their teams complete with "A" Echelon, 1 water cart and cookers to bivouacs in field in North half of square L.33.d.
"A" Echelons will remain in this field after relief is complete. "B" Echelon will remain with Battalion Headquarters.

(b) Officers Commanding Companies, Section Officers and man per gun team of guns relieving on night of 30th June/1st July, will reconnoitre positions to be taken over, and Nos. 1 will remain in.

(French Machine Gunners are leaving in 1 man per gun and M.C.O. per ½ Section for 24 hours after relief)

They will report to Commandant I.D. at Point L.29.c.9.2. as follows:-

    Representatives 122nd Infantry Brigade.   9 p.m.
         do.   123rd Infantry Brigade.   9-30 p.m.
         do.   124th Infantry Brigade.   10 p.m.

1 Lorry will be at Machine Gun Battalion Headquarters at 8.30 p.m. to take this party forward.

June 30th.

6. Advance parties for the remaining sections, as in para. 5(b) will report at the same point and at the same hours.

7. July 2nd.
"A" Company will move to L.23.c.1.2.

8. Company Commanders will arrange with Infantry Brigades to live at, or as near as possible to, Brigade Headquarters.

9. Completion of reliefs to be notified to Brigades concerned.

10. When in bivouacs, it is of the utmost importance that Battalions should take every precaution to avoid detection.
At night, Lights are to be reduced to a minimum and are to be carefully screened and no fires are to be lighted.
By day. There should be one Officer per Company always on duty to ensure that men do not expose themselves unnecessarily, and aeroplane sentries are to be posted to give notice of approaching aircraft.
Excessive smoke must be avoided.
The Divisional Commander directs that the reasons for such special secrecy, viz. to prevent the enemy from obtaining indications that a relief of the French by the British is in progress should be carefully explained to all ranks.
All ranks must be equally careful when in the forward area.

11. Acknowledge.

Issued at 7 a.m.
29-6-18.

                        Lieut.-Colonel.
                        Commanding 41st Battn. M.G. Corps.

Copies to: Copy No. 1. 122nd Infantry Brigade.
                        2. 123rd Infantry Brigade.
                        3. 124th Infantry Brigade.
                        4. 41st Division "G".
                        5.   "   "   "Q".
                        6. C.R.A.
                        7. C.R.E.
                        8. 6th Division.
                        9. 71st French Division.
                       10. 7th French Division (4 Copies).
                     11. War Diary.   2 "
                     12. File.
                     13. Spare.

ADMINISTRATIVE INSTRUCTION NO. 1.
ISSUED IN CONNECTION WITH OPERATION
ORDER NO. 31.

To O.C. "A" Company.
      "B" "
      "C" "
      "D" "
Transport Officer.
Quartermaster.
Signal Officer.
Medical Officer.
R.S.M.

1. AMMUNITION.
Divisional Dump will be situated at L.34.a.9.7., and can be drawn on from noon 30th June.
Brigade Dumps will be situated:-
    Right Brigade.   M.5.a.3.6.
    Centre Brigade. M.5.a.5.9.
    Left Brigade.   G.35.d.9.2.

The ammunition to form these dumps will be delivered by the S.A.A. Section on the evening of the 29th June.

Arrangements have been made with the 7th French Division for a sufficient number of French Pistols and S.O.S. Signals to be left in the Line until the British S.O.S. Signal is taken into use.

Brigades will arrange to take these over.

On the 2nd July 1918 they will be collected and returned to Divisional Headquarters for transmission to the French.

2. SUPPLIES.
Railhead - STEENVOORDE from 29th instant.

The Divisional Train will draw from Railhead by horse transport from 30th instant and will deliver to units transport lines.

Battalion Transport normally proceeds as far East as the following points:-
    Right Brigade.   M.11.d.6.6.
    Centre Brigade.   M.12.b.0.3.
    Left Brigade.   M.6.d.9.7.

Reserve rations are dumped in the area as follows:-

Right Brigade,	SCHERPENBERG TUNNELS.	Front Line Bn.	500 rations.
		Support Bn.	500 rations.
	G.27.d.4.3.	Reserve Bn.	2000 rations.
Centre Brigade,	M.18.b.5.1.	Front Line Bn.	500 rations.
	M.12.c.9.4.	Support Bn.	500 rations.
Left Brigade,	N.7.c.2.3.	Front Line Bn.	500 rations.
	M.6.d.4.6.	Support Bn.	500 rations.

These rations will be taken over by Brigades on relief, and they will be responsible for their safe custody.

3. WATER.
The water supply in the Forward Area is poor, and is reported as being badly contaminated, the greatest care must therefore be taken as regards chlorination.

There are water cart filling points at:-
    REMY SIDING.
    S.W. of HOOGRAAF CABT.
    ABEELE STATION.

Barrel reservoirs have been made by the French at :-
    Right Brigade,   M.11.b.6.2.
    Centre Brigade, M.5.a.6.6.
    Left Brigade,   M.6.a.0.9.

Petrol tins will be issued on the following scale:-
    M.Gun Companies,   40.

If in positions where water carts cannot be used.

Instructions as to drawing will be issued later.

- 2 -

4. R.E. MATERIAL.
    Divisional Dump STEENAKER L.32.d.4.0.

5. PROVOST INSTRUCTIONS.
    Lorries may not proceed further east than BOESCHEPE - WIPPENHOEK Road in daylight.

    Horse Transport may not proceed further East than N. & S. Grid Line between squares G.31 and 32 in daylight.

    Steel helmets and Box Respirators in the alert position will be worn by all ranks East of the N. Grid Line between Squares G.31 and 32.

6. Acknowledge.

20-6-18.
Issued at 11-30 a.m.

Lieut.-Colonel,
Commanding 41st Battn. M.G. Corps.

Secret

ADMINISTRATIVE INSTRUCTION NO. 1.
ISSUED IN CONNECTION WITH OPERATION
ORDER NO. 31.

To O.C. "A" Company.
      "B"   "
      "C"   "
      "D"   "
Transport Officer.
Quartermaster.
Signal Officer.
Medical Officer.
R.S.M.

1. **AMMUNITION.**
Divisional Dump will be situated at L.34.a.9.7., and can be drawn on from noon 30th June.
    Brigade Dumps will be situated:-
        Right Brigade.   M.5.a.3.5.
        Centre Brigade.   M.5.a.5.9.
        Left Brigade.   G.35.d.9.2.
The ammunition to form these dumps will be delivered by the S.A.A. Section on the evening of the 29th June.
Arrangements have been made with the 7th French Division for a sufficient number of French Pistols and S.O.S. Signals to be left in the Line until the British S.O.S. Signal is taken into use.
Brigades will arrange to take these over.
On the 2nd July 1918 they will be collected and returned to Divisional Headquarters for transmission to the French.

2. **SUPPLIES.**
Railhead - STEENVOORDE from 29th instant.

The Divisional Train will draw from Railhead by horse transport from 30th instant and will deliver to Units transport lines.
Battalion Transport normally proceeds as far East as the following points:-
        Right Brigade.   M.11.d.6.6.
        Centre Brigade.   M.12.b.0.3.
        Left Brigade.   M.6.d.9.7.
Reserve Rations are dumped in the area as follows:-
Right Brigade. SCHERPENBERG TUNNELS. Front Line Bn,   500 rations.
                                               Support Bn,   500 rations.
              G.27.d.4.3.   Reserve Bn,   2000 rations.
Centre Brigade. M.18.b.5.1.   Front Line Bn,   500 rations.
              M.12.c.9.4.   Support Bn,   500 rations.
Left Brigade.   N.7.c.2.3.   Front Line Bn,   500 rations.
              M.6.d.4.6.   Support Bn.   500 rations.
These rations will be taken over by Brigades on relief, and they will be responsible for their safe custody.

3. **WATER.**
The water supply in the Forward Area is poor, and is reported as being badly contaminated, the greatest care must therefore be taken as regards chlorination.
    There are water cart filling points at:-
        REMY SIDING.
        S.W. of HOOGRAAF CABT.
        ABEELE STATION.
Barrel reservoirs have been made by the French at :-
        Right Brigade,   M.11.b.6.2.
        Centre Brigade,   M.5.a.6.6.
        Left Brigade,   M.6.a.0.9.
Petrol tins will be issued on the following scale:-
        M.Gun Companies,   40.
If in positions where water carts cannot be used,
Instructions as to drawing will be issued later.

4. R.E. MATERIAL.
   Divisional Dump STEENAKER L.32.d.4.0.

5. PROVOST INSTRUCTIONS.
   Lorries may not proceed further east than BOESCHEPE - WIPPENHOEK Road in daylight.
   Horse Transport may not proceed further East than N. & S. Grid Line between squares G.31 and 32 in daylight.

   Steel helmets and Box Respirators in the alert position, will be worn by all ranks East of the N. Grid Line between Squares G.31 and 32.

6. Acknowledge.

29-6-18.
Issued at 11-30 a.m.

Lieut.-Colonel.
Commanding 41st Battn. M.G. Corps.

SECRET.

To O.C. "A" Company.
   "B" "
   "C" "
   "D" "
   Transport Officer.

[Stamp: 41st BATTALION MACHINE GUN CORPS.]

MACHINE GUN AMMUNITION DUMPS.

1.   4 S.A.A. Dumps will be established at the following points in the Forward Area :-
          M.11.a.2.1.   80,000 rounds.
          N.7.c.4.5.   120,000   "
          M.12.d.1.4.   120,000   "
          M.11.d.8.1.   120,000   "

       Companies will draw from these dumps to bring their gun positions up to the necessary establishment.

2.   Battalion Transport Officer will arrange to draw the ammunition from the Divisional Ammunition Dump L.34.a.9.7. to-day and to dump it at the positions mentioned in para. 1.

3.   "A" Company will provide an unloading party of 40 men under an Officer.
       2 Lorries from Division will pick up this party at "A" Company Headquarters at 8 p.m. to-night and will drop them at G.34.d.0.6. where they will meet the S.A.A. Limbers at 10 p.m. Lorries will return immediately. This party will return in the empty limbers.

4.   O.C. "A" Company will arrange for an N.C.O. for each unloading party to previously reconnoitre a suitable place for the dump, at, or as close as possible to the positions mentioned in para. 1.
       These N.C.O.s will act as guides.
       The exact positions of dumps will be reported by O.C. "A" Company to Battalion Headquarters as soon as possible.

5.   "A" Company will provide two limbers to report to the Battalion Transport Officer at 8 p.m. at the Divisional Ammunition Dump.

                                        Lieut.-Colonel.
29-6-18.   Commanding 41st Battn. M.G.Corps.

Copies to:

               Copy No. 1. 41st Division "Q".
                        2.   do.   "G".
                        3. 122nd Infantry Brigade.
                        4. 123rd Infantry Brigade.
                        5. 124th Infantry Brigade.
                        6. War Diary.
                        7. File.

"41st Battalion Machine Gun Corps" 151 5

WAR DIARY

So the Monthly

July 1918

"1st Division"
1-8-18

Army Form C. 2118.

WAR DIARY
or
INTELLIGENCE SUMMARY.
(Erase heading not required.)

Map Ref BELGIUM 27 — July 1918

Place	Date	Hour	Summary of Events and Information	Remarks and references to Appendices
	1st	9 a.m.	Remaining 1 Coy of B Coy prepare to go if line brought positions. Reconnoitred approaches. Night by Station Officers.	
	2	9.30 a.m.	Bn H.Q. moved L.31.d.40. at 9.30 a.m. arrive destination 2 p.m. – 28 reinforcements for 4th S.M. Q.C. join the Bn. Bn H.Q. were forwarded to STEENAKER DUMP.	
	3	10 a.m.	C.O. visited Forward Coy H.Q. in line also Pts T.22-39 & 3rd Brigade Bn H.Q. 'B' Echelon moved to K.2.S.C.P.8. settled in by 6 p.m. Two reinforcement officers reported - Lieut. WILKES and 2/Lt MEEK posted to 'D' Coy. 7/Lt MITCHELL - Capt. PARKS admitted to C.C.S. midnight 12 m. with influenza.	
	4		Day spent in erecting huts for Bn. H.Q. and pulling ready forms established.	
		7 p.m.	'B' Echelon arrived at Rd. B.6.5. The C.O. visited right sector of guns (C Coy) at 10 p.m. in the line.	
	5		C.O. visited Coy H.Q. 5 p.m. 3 huts erected at Bn. Coy (X.19) M.G. Officers called at H.Q. saw C.O.	
	6	7 a.m.	At Tinbrum arrival at H.Q. proceeds on line 9 a.m. H.Coy where D n m knight (with seeds) visit complete 2.15 a.m.	
	7	9 a.m.	Bn Stat. Parade. Capt. E. Sennies at 10 a.m. & 6.30 p.m. at X.30 a centrale. C.O. gave up the line to Coys 9 p.m. Lt Reinman returned from leave.	
	8		C.O. Inspect. new draft. who join Bn Coys today. Lieut. Eccleston in a.m. Lt KEGAN returned from leave. Heavy firm at night. The Corps Commander inspected 'D' Coy at their billets 11.45 a.m.	

Army Form C. 2118.

WAR DIARY
or
INTELLIGENCE SUMMARY.
(Erase heading not required.)

July 1918

Place	Date	Hour	Summary of Events and Information	Remarks and references to Appendices
	9	10 a.m.	Drafts for A-B-C Coys join respective Coys. C.O. and Adjutant visit Q.M. Stores and 'B' Coy belm in afternoon	KT
	10.		C.O. visits forward Coy H.Q. A-B + C Coys in afternoon. Heavy rain and thunder.	KT
	11		C.O. goes up line with C.R.E. and G.S.O.I siting strong points and rear line for defence. 'B' Coy relieved by D' Coy in centre sector. relief complete 2 a.m. Maj. GRIDSTON and LT. FLAXENMORVED on leave. LT ELLIS joins B/n posted to 'B'.	KT
	12	a.m.	Very wet. C.O. visits 35 Div M.G. H.Q. 4.30 p.m.	KT
	13.	9 a.m	H.Q. go to the above 'B' Coy. C.O. visits left and centre Brigades in the line during morning.	KT
	14	12.15 a.m	C.O. goes up line to left sector and goes round guns. visits Right and Centre Brigades and M.G. Coys in afternoon.	KT
	15	10.	O.C. visits 6th Div M.G. H.Q. and A. Echelon in p.m. LT HAZE returns from Red Camp and LT RUDDEL from leave.	KT
	16		C.O. goes up line with Div I.O. 10.123 Brigade and visits model of new Pill Box at ARQUES. 'B' Coy relieves 'C' in Right sector.	KT
	17		C.O. visits 122 Brigade in left sector	KT
	18		C.O. visits strong points in rear area	KT
	19		C.O. visits left Coy H.Q. LT NEBSTER joins B/n posted to C Coy. T. A.D.V.S.	KT

Army Form C. 2118.

WAR DIARY
or
INTELLIGENCE SUMMARY.
(Erase heading not required.)

July 1918

Place	Date	Hour	Summary of Events and Information	Remarks and references to Appendices
	19		Called Funks arrangement for inspection of horses on Monday by D.A.D.V.S.	KF
	21	10 AM	C.O. goes up line to Right Brigade. 'C' Coy relieves 'A' Coy in left sector tonight.	KF
	22.		D.A.D.V.S. inspects all animals in Transport. C.O. goes up line to A Bayonet 9.M.G. Coy H.Q. with G.O.C., visits Reserve line also, goes up again in P.M. to Brigades and Coys.	KF
	23.		C.O. goes up line with G.R.E. 10 am. 2Lt. TURPIN returns from leave.	KF
	24		C.O. goes up line with 9. C.O. who goes up line with American officers of 105th Regt (M.G.s) call to see C.O. up P.M. to Brigades H.Q. then attached to Right sector 9 up P.M. to Brigade H.Q.	KF
	25.		Working Parties for 105th A.M.G. Bn (2 Coys) who are attacks to 105th A.M.G. Bn. A.M.G.Bn detailed 80 4M.G.Bn from tonight. 2/Lt PARKER reports Bn. A.M.G.Bn detailed 80 To 'B' Echelon. C.O. & O.C. 103rd A.M.G.Bn visit Left and Right Brigades and rear line.	KF
	26.	6 am	C.O. & A.M.G. O.C. visit 'B' Echelon	
	27	10.30	C.O. holds conference with O.C. Coys at Left Coy H.Q. Lt TIPLADY & 2/Lt FIELDING join Bn posted to 'D'&'C' Coys.	KF
	28.		Wet.	

Army Form C. 2118.

WAR DIARY
or
INTELLIGENCE SUMMARY.
(Erase heading not required.)

July 1918

Instructions regarding War Diaries and Intelligence Summaries are contained in F. S. Regs., Part II. and the Staff Manual respectively. Title pages will be prepared in manuscript.

Place	Date	Hour	Summary of Events and Information	Remarks and references to Appendices
	29	2.30pm	C.O. held a conference at Bn H.Q. There were present the C.M.G.O., O.C. 63rd Div M.G. and O.C. 27 A.M.G. Bn.	KT
	30		Officers of 106 A.M.G. Bn called at H.Q. watching ours from 105 A.M.G.C. C.O. goes up line with them in p.m.	KT
	31	4pm	106th A.M.G. Bn takes over from 105th A.M.G. Bn. Col Jackson (A.M.G.O.) called. Saw C.O. 'D' Coy relieve 'B' Coy in Right sector tonight.	KT

R. M. Fah, LIEUT. COL.,
COMMANDING 41st BATTALION
MACHINE GUN CORPS

R.121

To: O.C. "A" Company.
         "B"   "
         "C"   "
         "D"   "
      Quartermaster.
      Transport Officer.
      Medical Officer.
      Signal Officer.
      R.S.M.

1.   Battalion Headquarters will move to-morrow temporarily to Huts at STEENAKER DUMP, L.32.d.4.0. and later to L.19.c.1.0.

        The party, under the R.S.M. will move off at 9-30 a.m. and march via STEENVOORDE and ABEELE.

        An Advance Party on cycles will proceed at 8 a.m. and will send a guide to meet the party at ABEELE Station. Haversack rations will be carried.

2.   "B" Echelon, under the Battalion Transport Officer will move off at 10 a.m. and porceed to K.25.c.8.8.

1st July, 1918.

                                    Lieut.-Colonel.
                         Commanding 41st Battn. M.G.Corps.

Secret

OPERATION ORDER NO. 32.
by
LIEUT.-COL. A. W. TATE.
Commanding 41st Battalion Machine Gun Corps.
Thursday, 4th July, 1918.

To: O.C. "A" Company.
       "B"   "
       "C"   "
       "D"   "
Transport Officer.
Quartermaster.
Battalion Signalling Officer.
Medical Officer.

1.   "A" Company will relieve "D" Company in the Left Sub-Sector on the night of the 6/7th July.

       "A" Company will arrange with "D" Company to send Nos. 1 of guns into the line on the previous night.

       "D" Company will take over the billets vacated by "A" Company, and will be in Divisional Reserve, ready to move forward immediately if required.

2.   O.C. "A" Company will go over the rear area with O.C. "D" Company the day of the relief, and will point out suitable positions to be taken up in case of an attack. All Officers of the Reserve Company will reconnoitre this area.

3.   Handing over Files, Trench Maps, Periscopes etc., will be handed over on relief.

4.   Completion of relief to be notified to Brigade concerned and to Battalion Headquarters by Battalion Code.

5.   Acknowledge.

Issued at ..7.p.m....
4-7-18.

                 K. Foster.
                 2nd Lieut.
                 A/Adjutant,
for O.C. 41st Battn. M. G. Corps.

Copies to:-
       Copy No. 1. 122nd Infantry Brigade.
              2. 123rd Infantry Brigade.
              3. 124th Infantry Brigade.
              4. 41st Division "G".
              5. 41st Division "Q".
              6. Divisional Signal Officer.
              7. 6th Division.
              8. War Diary.
              9. File.
            10. Spare.

SECRET.   Copy No. ....

OPERATION ORDER NO. 33.
by
LIEUT.-COL. A. W. TATE.
Commanding 41st Battalion Machine Gun Corps.
Tuesday, 9th July, 1918.

To: O.C. "A" Company.
     "   "B"   "
     "   "C"   "
     "   "D"   "
     Transport Officer.
     Quartermaster.
     Battalion Signalling Officer.
     Medical Officer.
     O.C. No. 5 Section, Divl. Sig. Coy.

1.   "D" Company will relieve "B" Company in the Centre Sub-Sector on the night of the 11th/12th July.

        "D" Company will arrange with "B" Company to send Nos. 1 of guns into the line on the previous night.

        "B" Company will take over the billets vacated by "D" Company, and will be in Divisional Reserve, ready to move forward immediately if required.

2.   O.C. "D" Company will go over the rear area with O.C. "B" Company the day of the relief, and will point out suitable positions to be taken up in case of an attack. All Officers of the Reserve Company will reconnoitre this area.

3.   Handing over Files, Trench Maps, Periscopes etc., will be handed over on relief.

4.   Completion of relief to be notified to Brigade concerned and to Battalion Headquarters by Battalion Code.

5.   Acknowledge.

                                                  A. W. Tate
                                               Lieut.-Colonel.
                                    Commanding 41st Battn. M.G.Corps.

Issued at 2 p.m.
9-7-18.

Copies to:-

                 Copy No. 1. 122nd Infantry Brigade.
                          2. 123rd Infantry Brigade.
                          3. 124th Infantry Brigade.
                          4. 41st Division "G".
                          5. 41st Division "Q".
                          6. Divisional Signal Officer.
                          7. 6th Division.
                          8. War Diary.
                          9. File.
                         10. Spare.

SECRET.   Copy No. ...7......

OPERATION ORDER NO. 34.
by
LIEUT.-COL. A. W. TATE.
Commanding 41st Battalion Machine Gun Corps.
Sunday, 14th July, 1918.

To: O.C. "A" Company.
       "B"   "
       "C"   "
       "D"   "
      Transport Officer.
      Quartermaster.
      Battalion Signalling Officer.
      Medical Officer.
      O.C. No. 5 Section, Divl. Signal Coy.

1.   "B" Company will relieve "C" Company in the Right Sub-Sector on the night of the 16th/17th July.

        "B" Company will arrange with "C" Company to send Nos. 1 of guns into the line on the previous night.

        "C" Company will take over the billets vacated by "B" Company, and will be in Divisional Reserve, ready to move forward immediately if required.

2.   O.C. "B" Company will go over the rear area with O.C. "C" Company the day of the relief, and will point out suitable positions to be taken up in case of an attack. All Officers of the Reserve Company will reconnoitre this area.

3.   Handing over Files, Trench Maps, Periscopes etc., will be handed over on relief.

4.   Completion of relief to be notified to Brigade concerned and to Battalion Headquarters by Battalion Code.

5.   Acknowledge.

                                                 2nd Lieut.
Issued at 2 p.m.   A/Adjutant.
        14-7-18.   41st Battn. M.G.Corps.

        Copies to:

                        Copy No. 1. 122nd Infantry Brigade.
                                 2. 123rd Infantry Brigade.
                                 3. 124th Infantry Brigade.
                                 4. 41st Division "G".
                                 5. Divisional Signal Officer.
                                 6. 41st Division "Q".
                                 7. 6th Division.
                                 8. War Diary.
                              ✓ 9. File.
                                10. Spare.

SECRET.

War Diary
R.146.

To: O.C. "C" Company.
    "   "D"   "

The 35th Division are carrying out a raid on enemy trenches in M.24.c. and d. on the night of July 14th/15th.

The 41st Divisional Artillery are co-operating by creating a diversion on the Left Flank of the raid.

Four 18 pounders are enfilading the Railway from M.24.d.35.35. to M.30.b.2.8.

Two 18 pounder batteries are searching and sweeping Square N.19.b.

The 41st Battalion Machine Gun Corps will assist with the following fire.

<u>Right Company.</u>   4 Guns - will cover track from N.19.b.30.65.
                        to N.19.b.95.20. and fire on located Machine
                        Gun at N.19.b.28.57.

<u>Centre Company.</u> 4 Guns - Road from N.19.d.40.98 to N.19.d.90.40.
                        Suspected Trench Mortar at N.19.d.90.95.
                        Railway Track from N.19.c.95.80. to N.19.d.95.60.

Rates of fire will be Zero to Zero plus 5, 150 rounds per gun per minute. Zero plus 5 to Zero plus 20, 80 rounds per gun per minute. Guns will then cease fire.

Watches will synchronised at Brigade Headquarters and the Signal for the guns to fire will be the opening of the Artillery Barrage.

Zero hour will be 11-45 p.m.

Acknowledge.

                                          Lieut.-Colonel.
Issued at 6 p.m.
14-7-18.   Commanding 41st Battn. M.G.C.

Copies to:

                    Copy No. 1. 41st Division "G".
                             2. C.R.A. 41st Division.
                             3. 35th Battn. M.G.Corps.
                             4. 123rd Infantry Brigade.
                             5. 124th Infantry Brigade.
                             6. War Diary.
                             7. File.

SECRET.   Copy No..... 10 .....

OPERATION ORDER NO. 35.
by
LIEUT.-COL. A. W. TATE.
Commanding 41st Battalion Machine Gun Corps.
Friday, 19th July, 1918.

To: O.C. "A" Company.
         "B"   "
         "C"   "
         "D"   "
      Transport Officer.
      Quartermaster.
      Battalion Signalling Officer.
      Medical Officer.
      O.C. No. 5 Section, Divl. Signal Coy.

1.   "C" Company will relieve "A" Company in the Left Sub-Sector on the night of the 21st/22nd July.

2.   "C" Company will arrange with "A" Company to send Nos. 1 of guns into the line on the previous night.

       "A" Company will take over the billets vacated by "C" Company, and will be in Divisional Reserve, ready to move forward immediately if required. All Officers of the Reserve Company will reconnoitre this area.

3.   Handing over Files, Trench Maps, Periscopes etc., will be handed over on relief.

4.   Completion of relief to be notified to Brigade concerned and to Battalion Headquarters by Battalion Code.

5.   Acknowledge.

                                            2nd Lieut,
                                            A/Adjutant.
Issued at 2-30 p.m.   for O.C. 41st Battn. M.G. Corps.
19-7-18.

   Copies to:

           Copy No. 1.   122nd Infantry Brigade.
                    2.   123rd Infantry Brigade.
                    3.   124th Infantry Brigade.
                    4.   41st Division "G".
                    5.   Divisional Signal Officer.
                    6.   41st Division "Q".
                    7.   6th Division.
                    8.   War Diary.
                    9.   File.
                   10.   Spare.

S E C R E T.   Copy No............

OPERATION ORDER NO. 36.
by
LIEUT.-COL. A. W. TATE.
Commanding 41st Battalion Machine Gun Corps.
Wednesday, 24th July, 1918.

To: O.C. "A" Company.
     "   "B"   "
     "   "C"   "
     "   "D"   "
     Transport Officer.
     Quartermaster.
     Battalion Signalling Officer.
     Medical Officers.
     O.C. No. 5 Section, Divl. Signal Coy.

1.   "A" Company will relieve "D" Company in the Centre Sub-Sector on the night of the 26th/27th July.

2.   "A" Company will arrange with "D" Company to send Nos. 1 of guns into the line on the previous night.

        "D" Company will take over the billets vacated by "A" Company, and will be in Divisional Reserve, ready to move forward immediately if required. All Officers of the Reserve Company will reconnoitre this area.

3.   Handing over Files, Trench Maps, Periscopes etc., will be handed over on relief.

4.   Completion of relief to be notified to Brigade concerned and to Battalion Headquarters by Battalion Code.

        ACKNOWLEDGE.

                                                    2nd Lieut.
Issued at 10-30 a.m.   a/Adjutant.
24-7-18.   for O.C. 41st Battn. M.G. Corps.

Copies to:

                    Copy No. 1.   122nd Infantry Brigade.
                             2.   123rd   do.
                             3.   124th   do.
                             4.   41st Division "G".
                             5.   Divisional Signal Officer.
                             6.   41st Division "Q".
                             7.   6th Division.
                             8.   War Diary.
                             9.   File.
                            10.   Spare.

****

SECRET.   OPERATION ORDER NO. 57.   Copy No......
                                by
                       LIEUT.-COL. A. W. TATE,
                  Commanding 41st Battalion Machine Gun Corps,
                       Thursday, 25th July, 1918.
                       ─────────────────

To O.C. "A" Company.
      "B"   "
      "C"   "
      "D"   "
Quartermaster.
Transport Officer.
Medical Officer.
O.C. No. 5 Section, Divl. Signal Coy.

1.   "B" and "D" Companies, 105th American Machine Gun Battalion, will be attached to 41st Battalion Machine Gun Corps for a period of 6 days commencing on July 25th.

2.   The attachment will be divided into three periods, each lasting two days.
        Period i.   The attachment of a proportion of personnel to gun teams.
              ii.   The relief of a portion of the guns in the line.
              iii. Relief of complete sections.

3.   On the night of July 25th/26th, 6 Officers and 154 Other Ranks of 105th A.M.G.B. will be attached to the three Companies in the line - "B" Company on the left, "D" Company on the right. Headquarters of O.C. "B" Company will be at Headquarters, Left Company, 41st Battn. M.G.C. and Headquarters of "D" Company at Headquarters of Right Company, 41st Battn. M.G.C.
        Three American Other Ranks and a proportion of N.C.O.s, will be attached to each of the guns in the line for Period i.
        O.s.C. Companies, 41st Battn. M.G.C. will therefore arrange to withdraw a proportion of their men to their "A" Echelons, not less than two men per team to be left in.

4.   Detailed arrangements for the attachment and for guides to meet the incoming detachments have already been made between British and American Companies concerned.
        Rations for the first 24 hours will be taken in on the man.

5.   On the night of July 26th/27th, the guns of the American teams mentioned in Period ii. para. 2, will be brought up to Company Headquarters in readiness for the following night.

6.   On the night of July 27th/28th, Period ii. will commence; detailed instructions will be issued later.

7.   On the night of July 29th/30th, Period iii. will commence.

8.   Arrangements for rations and transport will be made direct between American and British Transport Officers, Quartermaster and Supply Officers.

9.   Transport, Supply Officers Department and Details of 105th A.M.G.B. will move to "B" Echelon, 41st Battn. M.G.C. on the evening of July 25th, and O.C. 105th A.M.G.B. will make his Headquarters with 41st Battn. M.G.C.

10.   When not carrying out individual attachment, all American Units will invariably serve under the immediate command of their own Officers. American M.G. Platoons or Companies will be under the Command of the unit or formation to which they are attached.

11.   ACKNOWLEDGE.

                                        K Fraser
Issued at 4 p.m.   2nd Lieut. A/Adjutant.
25-7-18.   for O.C. 41st Battn. M.G.Corps.

Copies to :-
            Copy No. 1.   41st Division "G".
                     2.   "   "   "Q".
                     3.   122nd Infantry Brigade.
                     4.   123rd   do.
                     5.   124th   do.
                     6.   C.R.E. 41st Division.
                     7.   C.R.A.   do.
                     8.   O.C. 105th American Machine Gun Battn.
                     9.   O. M. G. C.
                     10. War Diary.
                     11. File.

SECRET.   Copy No. 10

To: O.C. "A" Company.
    "B"   "
    "C"   "
    "D"   "
    Quartermaster.
    Transport Officer.
    Medical Officer.
    O.C. No. 5 Section, Divl. Signal Coy.

Reference Operation Order No. 37 of this Office dated 25th July, para. 6.

1. "B" and "D" Companies, 105th American Machine Gun Battalion will relieve the following guns of the 41st Battalion Machine Gun Corps.

   "B" Company - Right Sector. 12 Guns.
   R.13., 14., 15., 8., 9., 10., 11., 12., C.15., C.16., C.10., and 11.

   "D" Company - Left Sector. 12 Guns.
   L.12 - 15., L.13 - 14., L.11 - 16., L.5 - 6., C.7 - 8., C.13 - 14.

2. American Teams will consist of 5 Other Ranks, inclusive of N.C.O.s; and 41st Battalion Machine Gun Corps will leave in 1 N.C.O. per team.
   These teams will be under the command of the American N.C.Os.

3. Surplus personnel will make up the teams of the guns depleted by the adjustment in para. 2 above, so that there will be a greater proportion of British personnel at each position not relieved, under the command of British N.C.Os.

4. All guns will be under the command of the British Right, Centre and Left Machine Gun Company Commanders in whose areas they are respectively situated.

5. Completion of relief to be reported to Brigades; and to Battalion Headquarters by Battalion Code.

6. ACKNOWLEDGE.

                                             2nd Lieut. A/Adjutant.
Issued at 2 p.m.   for O.C. 41st Battn. M.G.Corps.
27-7-18.

Copies to:
           Copy No. 1.   41st Division "G".
                2.   "   "   "Q".
                3.   122nd Infantry Brigade.
                4.   123rd   do.
                5.   124th   do.
                6.   C.R.E. 41st Division.
                7.   C.R.A.   do.
                8.   O.C. 105th American Machine Gun
                                              Battalion.
                9.   C. M. G. O.
               10.   War Diary.
               11.   File.

                    ****

SECRET.

Ref. R. 187.
Copy No.......... 10

To: O.C. "A" Company.
       "B" "
       "C" "
       "D" "
Quartermaster.
Transport Officer.
Medical Officer.
O.C. No. 5 Section, Divl. Signal Coy.
O.C. "B" Company, 105th A.M.G.Battn.
 " "D" " " " "

Reference Operation Order No. 37 of this Office dated July 25th, para. 7.

1.   On the night of July 29th/30th, Os.C. "B" and "D" Companies, 105th American Machine Gun Battalion will take over command of the positions detailed in para. (i) of Operation Order No. R. 184 of 27-7-18.

      They will be under the orders of the G.Os.C. Sectors in which their Sections are situated, and to whom they must report on taking over

      The usual daily returns will be rendered direct to O.C. 41st Battalion Machine Gun Corps.

2.   The British Officers and N.C.Os. at present at the positions to be taken over, will be withdrawn.

      The remaining American personnel will remain attached to the gun positions that are not being relieved.

3.   Receipts will be exchanged for all tripods, clinometers, ammunition and trench stores taken over on relief, and a duplicate forwarded to this office.

      American Company Commanders will see that any ammunition expended is replaced, and that the dumps at all positions are maintained.

4.   Completion of relief to be reported to Brigade and Battalion Headquarters.

Issued at 12-50 p.m.
28-7-18.

                            2nd Lieut. A/Adjutant.
                  for O.C. 41st Battn. M.G.Corps.

Copies to:

              Copy No. 1. 41st Division "G".
                     2. " " "Q".
                     3. 122nd Infantry Brigade.
                     4. 123rd Infantry Brigade.
                     5. 124th Infantry Brigade.
                     6. C.R.E. 41st Division.
                     7. C.R.A.   do.
                     8. O.C. 105th American Machine Gun
                                          Battalion.
                     9. C.M.G.O.
                    10. War Diary.
                    11. File.
                    12. Spare.

****

SECRET.   Copy No. 11

OPERATION ORDER NO. 38.
by
LIEUT.-COL. A. W. TATE.
Commanding 41st Battalion Machine Gun Corps.
Monday, 29th July, 1918.

To: O.C. "A" Company.
         "B"   "
         "C"   "
         "D"   "
     Transport Officer.
     Quartermaster.
     Medical Officer.
     O.C. No. 5 Section, Divl. Signal Company.

1.   "D" Company will relieve "B" Company in the Right Sub-Sector on the night of the 31st July/1st August.

2.   "D" Company will arrange with "B" Company to send Nos. 1 of guns into the line on the previous night.

        "B" Company will take over the billets vacated by "D" Company, and will be in Divisional Reserve, ready to move forward immediately if required. All Officers of the Reserve Company will reconnoitre this area.

3.   Handing over files, trench maps, periscopes etc. will be handed over on relief.

4.   Completion of relief to be notified to Brigade concerned and to Battalion Headquarters by Battalion Code.

5.   ACKNOWLEDGE.

Issued at 11-45 a.m.   2nd Lieut. A/Adjutant.
29-7-18.   for O.C. 41st Battn. M. G. Corps.

Copies to:
              Copy No. 1.   122nd Infantry Brigade.
                       2.   123rd Infantry Brigade.
                       3.   124th Infantry Brigade.
                       4.   41st Division "G".
                       5.   Divisional Signal Officer.
                       6.   41st Division "Q".
                       7.   6th Division.
                       8.   O.C. 105th American Machine Gun
                                                  Battalion.
                       9.   War Diary.
                      10.   File.
                      11.   Spare.

****

SECRET.   Copy No............ 11

OPERATION ORDER NO. 39.
by
LIEUT.-COL. A. W. TATE.
Commanding 41st Battalion Machine Gun Corps.
Tuesday, 30th July, 1918.

To: O.C. "A" Company, 41st Battn. M.G.C.
    "   "B"   "   "   "   "
    "   "C"   "   "   "   "
    "   "D"   "   "   "   "
    Quartermaster.
    Transport Officer.
    Medical Officer.
    O.C. No. 5 Section, Divl. Signal Coy.
    O.C. "B" Company, 105th American M.G. Battn.
    "   "D"   "   "   "   "   "
    "   "A"   "   106th   "   "   "
    "   "B"   "   "   "   "   "

1. On the night 31st July/1st August, "B" and "D" Companies, 105th American Machine Gun Battalion will be relieved by "A" and "B" Companies, 106th American Machine Gun Battalion.

2. Three American Other Ranks and a proportion of N.C.O.s (as in Operation Order No. 37, dated 25-7-18) will be attached to each of the guns in the line for Period i.
   O.C. Companies, 41st Battalion Machine Gun Corps will arrange to leave a sufficient number of men in the line to bring teams up to their necessary strength.

3. Arrangements for relief will be made direct between O.C. Company concerned.

4. ACKNOWLEDGE.

Issued at 4 p.m.   2nd Lieut. A/Adjutant.
30-7-18.   for O.C. 41st Battn. M.G. Corps.

Copies to:
        Copy No. 1.   41st Division "G".
             2.   "   "   "Q".
             3.   122nd Infantry Brigade.
             4.   123rd   do.
             5.   124th   do.
             6.   C.R.E. 41st Division.
             7.   C.R.A.   do.
             8.   O.C. 105th American Machine Gun Battn.
             9.   " 106th   do.
            10.   C.M.G.O.
            11.   War Diary.
            12.   File.
            13.   Spare.

                    ****

M 6

41st BATTALION,
MACHINE GUN
CORPS.

War Diary
for the Month of
August 1918

Army Form C. 2118

WAR DIARY
or
INTELLIGENCE SUMMARY
(Erase heading not required.)

AUGUST 1918

Place	Date	Hour	Summary of Events and Information	Remarks and references to Appendices
	1		Commanding officer goes up line with 106 A.M.G. O.C. to Right Centre and left sectors.	A
	2		Wet. 2nd Lieuts FERGUSON & ASHBROOKE join Batt. proceed to C & D Coys also 2/Lieut HILLS reported for duty as Assistant Transport Officer.	A
	3		C.O. goes up line in p.m. – Lt HANSON returns from leave – C.O. goes to left & centre Btys & Coys with 122 Brigadier to rear line	A
	4		C.O. goes up line to left & centre Coy & midnight visits Coys in line with 106 M.M.G.C. O.C.	
	5		Officers from 105–6 A.I.M.G.C. go up line with C.O. to Right Centre & left Coys also to Reserve Coy w/m LT BUTLER reports for duty as Assistant Transport Officer. B Coy relieve C in left sector tonight 106 M.M.G Battn	A
	6		C.O. goes up to left & centre Brigade with O.C. 105/96 A.I.M.G.C.	
	7		C.O. visits B section with O.C. 105/96 A.I.R.M.G.C.	

WAR DIARY of 41st Bn MACHINE GUN Bn.

INTELLIGENCE SUMMARY

Army Form C. 2118.

for Month of AUGUST 1918.

Place	Date	Hour	Summary of Events and Information	Remarks and references to Appendices
KEMMEL SECTOR	8/8/18		A Limb Day. Bombing Offr. Visited Reserve Coys during forenoon. Major J. Muhris assumed duties of 2/in Command during afternoon. 6 quiet 24 hours in Sector. No casualties	[initials]
KEMMEL SECTOR	9/8/18		A Limb Day. C.O. & 2/in Comm. Visit Coys in line during forenoon. Snvenshot Posts carried out by Minor operation by R.E. during night of 8/9 by M.G.s Co-operated. Hostile retaliation slight. 1 gun destroyed & 1 gun damaged by 15 Cmp. by shells. 2 casualties 1 O.R. Wounded. Parents long moved forward to assist in operation remaining this nights 10 & 11 O.R. Frainly quiet 24 hours. O.O.R. result.	[initials]
KEMMEL SECTOR	10/8/18		A Limb Day. C.O. Visited "A" Echelon during forenoon. 2/in Command Visited "B" Echelon Transport during afternoon. O.C. 10th M.G. Re visited Bn Hd Qrs in Connection with Period of attachment to Battn. 2/in Command visited all guns in Right Bn Sector during night. Harassing fire carried out throughout night. A quiet 24 hours up to 12 mn. 2 casualties Nil. Sick 2 Ors. 63 O.Rs. "C" Coy Relieved "A" Coy in Centre Bde Sector Relay completed without incident.	[initials]
KEMMEL SECTOR	11/8/18		A Fine day. After a heavy bombardment commencing at 3 a.m. enemy counter-attacked against ground gained by left Bde. Attack which was met with a Compenies was repulsed & their remnants mother. Several Prisoners taken. C.O. Visited left Coy Hd Qrs. re-organization of Barrage lines. 3/in Comm. Visited all Coy Hd Qrs with Offr. of 10th M.G Bn. A.E.F. to arrange details for attachment of personel Guns carried out harassing fire throughout the night. 2 casualties 1 O.R. wounded. Operation Orders Nr 46 & 47 issued. Copies herewith attached.	[initials]
KEMMEL SECTOR	12/8/18		A fine day. 2/in Comm to Reason Coy to hold Court of Inquiry. 10th Amer M/G Re Coy unit have here for instruction during night relieving 10th & 11th Amer M/G Coys & attachment to D.O. No 47 Issued. A Normal 24 hours in the area. Narod. fire no worse throughout night. Casualties 2 O.R. killed. Sick 3 O.R. to Hos. Strength Increase I.O.R. from Hos. Strength Decrease 1 O.R. Strength of Offrs B/62 O.Rs. 50 Offrs 862 O.Rs	[initials]

Army Form C. 2118.

WAR DIARY of 41ST BATTALION
INTELLIGENCE SUMMARY
(Erase heading not required.) MACHINE GUN CORPS. for AUGUST 1918

Instructions regarding War Diaries and Intelligence Summaries are contained in F. S. Regs., Part II. and the Staff Manual respectively. Title Pages will be prepared in manuscript.

Place	Date	Hour	Summary of Events and Information	Remarks and references to Appendices
KEMMEL SECTOR	13/8/18		A fine day, very hot & bright. C.O. visited Coy Hd Qrs in Line with O.C. 104 Amn M.G.Bte during afternoon. C. Coy burst out its Coy Hd Qrs in the line during afternoon of 12th inst. (accidental). Guns in Line carried out harassing fire as usual throughout the night. Except for heavy hostile artillery reply to Counter Preparation between 3 & 4 am a normal 24 hours in the Area. Casualties 1 O.R. Wounded. Sick to C.C.S. 1 Off. (Maj HINSHENWOOD) 2 O.Rs. (Sector Strength 2 O.Rs.(1 to C.C.S. 1 deserter)	
KEMMEL SECTOR	14/8/18		A fine day. 2/i- Comm to Area Commdt ABEELE Area to reconnoitre new area for B. Echelon Transport. C.O. & Capt. Oking Commdg 104 MG Bte Amn Con visited the line during the night. Hostile artillery very active during night, especially on Right & Centre Bdes areas. Casualties 1 O.R. Sick to C.C.S. 2 O.Rs. From 104 5 O.Rs. Strength increase Nil. Strength decrease 1 O.R. (1 to C.C.S. Evacuated for 24 hours above Normal) Hostile activity carried out harassing fire throughout the night. Hostile activity.	
KEMMEL SECTOR	15/8/18		A fine day, very hot. 2/i- Comm to 30 M.G.Bn Hd Qrs on liaison duty during afternoon. Bn Commandant visited all Coy's Sector during night. Normal 24 hours in the line. A Coy Relieved D Coy in Right B'de Sector during night 14/15th. Relief completed without incident. Harassing fire carried out throughout the night. B Coy to Reserve. Casualties. D/M Lts 1 O.R. W'd. 3 O.Rs. 2 moved 5 O.Rs. C Section of 104 Amn MG Bte were sample bombarded near SHERPENBERG during night 14/15th inst. 10 Casualties amongst D.Rs & Mule Pack 2.O.Rs E.C.C.S. Sgt Thompson to U.K. for Commission. 2 O.R. Reinforcements. Strength Decrease to M.G. Casualties Coy & Pac America. 5 personal attached to Army Apprentice	
KEMMEL SECTOR	16/8/18		A fine day. 2/i- Comm to 104 Bde B'felde as Pres. F.G.C.M. Periods 3 for 104 AMG Btc committed, C.O. to line during afternoon. O.C.104 AMG Btc visited the line during night. During the night several parties of the enemy attempted to approach left Posts under cover of a heavy bombardment but were repulsed in each case. Hostile artillery action throughout the night including some gas shelling. Hostile fire action during night. Our artillery responded to S.O.S. calls during the night. Harassing fire by M.Gs carried out throughout the night. Casualties amongst B.O.S. knives on response to signals. Casualties Nil. Sick to C.C.S. 1 Off. (2/Lt PARTRIDGE) Strength Increase Nil. Strength Decrease 1 Off (2/Lt PARTRIDGE)	

WAR DIARY of 41st BN. MACHINE GUN CORPS

INTELLIGENCE SUMMARY

(Erase heading not required.) for MONTH of AUGUST 1918.

Instructions regarding War Diaries and Intelligence Summaries are contained in F.S. Regs, Part II. and the Staff Manual respectively. Title Pages will be prepared in manuscript.

Army Form C. 2118

Place	Date	Hour	Summary of Events and Information	Remarks and references to Appendices
KEMMEL SECTOR	17/8/18		A fine forenoon. Windy. Rain during afternoon + during night. C.O visited R. Coy. H.d Qrs during afternoon in connection with forthcoming operation by 30th Bri. O.O No 149 received re operation of 30 Bri. O.O No 50 received re Relief of American Bri. personnel in line. Hostile artillery active throughout 24 hours. Our M.Gs carried out harassing fire throughout the night. Casualties Nil. Sick to Hos. 6. O.Rs. Sick from Hos. 4. O.Rs. Struck off. Strength decrease 2. O.Rs.	MWT
KEMMEL SECTOR	18/8/18		A fine day. 2/i-Cmm to Reserve Coy during afternoon. C.O + Adjt to Centre Coy during evening. O.O.P.51 issued re operation of 30 Bri. O. Normal 24 hours in the line. Harassing fire carried out as usual during night. 10 4" and M.G Rt. Personal withdrawn from line during night. Withdrawal completed without incident. Casualties Nil. Sick to Hos. 20. O.Rs. Sick from Hos. 8 O.Rs. Strength Increase 2. O.Rs	MWT
KEMMEL SECTOR	19/8/18		A fine day. 2/i- Command to 30 Bri during forenoon. C.O to Right Coy H.d Qrs during afternoon. A normal 24 hours in the line. 2/i- Cmmd to Right Coy H.Q during afternoon. Open Order No.52 received re Relief of 13 Coy by 13 Coy on Centre Sector. No casualties. Sick to Hos 12. O.Rs. Sick from Hos 6 O.Rs. Strength Increase 3. O.Rs. Brave decrease	MWT
KEMMEL SECTOR	20/8/18		A fine day. Coy Offrs to Bn Hd Qrs during forenoon. C.O to Left Coy Hd Qrs during afternoon. 2/i- Cmm to R Coy Hd Qrs during afternoon. Conference + Preparations for Co-operation with 30 Bri operations completed. Op No 30 an order card of a heavy bombardment, the enemy attempted to Rush our Right Posts on Centre Bde Area, they were repulsed with loss. Otherwise a normal 24 hours on the line. B Coy Relieved B Coy on Centre Sector during the night 20/21 Relief completed without incident. Right Section Regt Coy Hd Qrs blown in during the night by shells Casualties 1. O.R. Wounded. Sick to Hos 5. O.Rs. Sick from Hos 4. O.Rs. Strength Increase Nil. Strength decrease 5. O.Rs. Strength of Battn 119 Offrs 866 O.Rs.	MWT
KEMMEL SECTOR	21/8/18		A fine day/temp hot. 2/in Cmmd + 30 Bri Cmmd + Bn Adv Hd Qrs at LA MONTAGNE QUARRY re known re operation of morning of 21st instr + Right + Centre Coys carried out operations in Co-operation with 30 Bri M.G.C. 30 Bri attacked at 2.55am carried all objectives were gained + 134 prisoners + 2 M.Gs captured. Prisoners belong to 3 Regt & 11/15 Reserve Div. (Cameron Hld operations). A count of Enquiry was held in 19th inst (Maj Chalmers Presiding) + Engineer M.G Section 2 Recycles (118. 1 Day). Harassing fire throughout night. Round fired for 7 days ending 19/20 Aug 108,000 Rds. Casualties. 2.O.Rs Wounded. Sick to Hos 1.O.R. Sick from Hos 4 O.Rs. Strength Increase 1.O.R. from C.C.S. Strength decrease 4. O.Rs (2 C.C.S, 2 Wd).	MWT

WAR DIARY of 41st Bn MACHINE GUN CORPS

Army Form C. 2118.

INTELLIGENCE SUMMARY.

(Erase heading not required.) for Month of AUGUST 1918.

Place	Date	Hour	Summary of Events and Information	Remarks and references to Appendices
KEMMEL SECTOR	22/8/18		A fine day, very hot. Very close during the night. C.O. to Bde during afternoon. Centre Coy Hd Qrs vacated hearily & periodically shelled during evening. W.Qrs ordered to move place as High Coy Hd Qrs Hostile arty activity throughout the day. Otherwise as normal. 24 hours in area. Harassing fire carried out as usual throughout the night. Casualties Nil. Sick to Hos 12.O.Rs. Sick from Hos 5 O.R. 1 Off C.W Porter rejoining from Banks. Strength Increase 1 Off 5 O.Rs Decrease 5 C.C.S.	[initials]
KEMMEL SECTOR	23/8/18		A fine day, cooler. 24 communicated to B.B Echelons & QrMr Stores & Reserve Coy during afternoon. C.O. & 2i/c Coy to Divisional eng. Twenty. Artillery on both sides very active throughout the day & night. Rain during the night. Orders for relief of Coy in the line to Coy B. Hun No 10 Sept Sta B3 issued in connection with Relief of Coy — title. Warning orders re distribution of Platoons between Coy Hd Qrs & Battn Coy Hd Qrs compl'd. Harassing fire carried out throughout the night. Casualties 2 O.R. wounded. Sick 15 Nos 7 O.Rs from Bde & Strength Decrease 23 O.Rs from Bde depot Strength Increase 6 O.Rs 15 C.C.S.	[initials]
KEMMEL SECTOR	24/8/18 Saturday		A fine day. Rain during early hours of the morning. During early hours of the morning, after a heavy bombardment the enemy attacked on our Right Bde front with a Battn of 72 R.I. Regt., except for his occupation of 3 of our advanced post the attack was repulsed, leaving 3 prisoners in our hands. C.O & Adjt visited left & right Coy Hd Qrs. during the afternoon. 2i/c communicated Res Coy & B Echelon during afternoon. Relief of B & S Coy on the line was car North. Left Bde carried out a counter attack during evening with object of recovering posts lost during morning. Posts 2 & 3 re-occupied. Harassing fire carried out throughout the night. Except for early morning's activity quiet 24 hours on the line. Casualties Nil. Sick to Hos 4 O.Rs. Strength Increase Nil. Strength Decrease 27 O.Rs from Corps Area 2.O.Rs to C.C.S. from Corps Area.	[initials]
KEMMEL SECTOR	25/8/18 Sunday		A fine day. Rain during evening & night. C.O. visited left Coy Hd Qrs during afternoon. Divisn lectures at B.F Qrs during evening. B Coy Released C Coy — Banks State during night. Relief completed without incident. C Coy to Banks Village. Patrols carried out throughout the night. As normal 24 hours in the area. Casualties 2.O.Rs Wounded. Sick to Hospital 5.O.Rs. Sick from Hos 3.O.Rs. Strength Increase Nil. Strength Decrease To U.K. Sick 1 Off. (Maj Knuckleweed) To C.C.S. 2 O.Rs Transfers from Corps Area 11 O.Rs. Strength of Battalion — 50 Offrs 851 Other Ranks	[initials]

WAR DIARY of 41st BN. MACHINE GUN CORPS

Army Form C. 2118

INTELLIGENCE SUMMARY

(Erase heading not required.)

for MONTH of AUGUST 1918.

Place	Date	Hour	Summary of Events and Information	Remarks and references to Appendices
KEMMEL SECTOR	26/8/18	Mon.	A Changeable day. Rain at intervals throughout the day & night. C.O visited R. Bde H.Q. during afternoon. C.M.G.O & Corps visited Bn. Hd. Qrs. during afternoon. A.D.M.S visited Bn. Hd. Qrs. during evening. Harrassing fire out by 5 of Ind. Bde Front recommenced. 5 S.W. in possession of the enemy. This Carrier arrived through this area. Casualties N.R. C.C.S Sick 15 Nos. 3.O.R's Sick from Hos. 6.O.R's Strength increase 11 O.R. From C.C.S. 3 through. Recreants 2.O.R. to C.C.S.	[sig]
KEMMEL SECTOR	27/8/18	Tues.	A fair day. Dull. C.O visited Coys in line during afternoon. Warning orders Re Relief of Bn. by Bn. 34th M.G.R'S but received. Operation orders No. 54 received (Re Relief of 51 B.P. as reserve Brigade) 21 Coms. & Capts. Part to Tilques Refer as advance parties. A Normal 24 hours on the area. Harrassing fire carried out throughout the night. Casualties 1.O.R. Wounded Sick 15 O.R's. 3.O.R to C.C.S. 2 Ph. Recreants to C.C.S. 10 OR. (2 Ph. Parties) 11.O.R's Sick fathers. 7O.R. Strength Increase Nil. Strength Decrease Nil.	[sig]
KEMMEL SECTOR	28/8/18	Wed.	A fair day. Rain during afternoon & night. Operation Order No. 55 issued Re Relief of Bn. by 34th M.G. R'S Relief of Bn. by 34th M.G. R'S 7.H p.m Commenced. C Coy which in Reserve to reliev'd a Coy 34th M.G.R'S. E Coy embussed at Tilques area at 10p.m. Transport commenced to Tilques area by Route March at 2.0am. A Normal 24 hours on the area. Harrassing fire carried out during night. Casualties Nil. Strength Increase Nil. Strength Decrease Nil.	[sig]
KEMMEL SECTOR	29/8/18	Thurs.	A fine day. C Coy arrived SALPERWICK at 2am CC. Transport arrived SALPERWICK 11am. also Qr Mr & Stores. A Coy Reliev'd in Right Section by a Coy 34th M.G.R'S during night. Qr. Hd. Qrs. reliev'd by B.H.Q. 34th M.G. Bn. Hd. Qrs & Coy embussed at ST OMER at 8am. 10.pm. A Normal 24 hours in the area. Casualties Nil. Sick to Hos. 7.O.R's. Sick from Hos. 1.D. Q.R's known A.C. Camp 10 Off. 5.O.R. Strength Increase Nil. Strength Decrease Nil. To C.C.S.12.O.R. Evacuated from Corps area 13 O.R.	[sig]
TILQUES AREA	30/8/18	Fri.	A fine day. Bn. Hd. Qrs & A Coy arrived SALPERWICK at 9 am. Billets completed 9:30 am. Bn.Hd. Qrs available on CHEER meal SALPERWICK. A quiet day. Further arrivals of Trains during day. D Coy Reliev'd in Regt. Section by a Coy 34th M.G. R'S proceeded to Reserve Billets for the night. Casualties Nil. Sick Nil. Strength Increase Nil. Decrease Nil.	[sig]
TILQUES AREA	31/8/18	Sat.	A fine day. Warning order to move to adjacent area received at Bn. Hd. Qrs. B Coy. Returned in Centre Section by a Coy 34th M.G.R. Moves of B & D Coys to Tilques were cancelled. Both Coys arrive under orders of S.O.C. 12 to Bn. H.Qrs. D.D & B Coys. Drafts arriv'd of Battn. A.& C. Coys. in Tilques. A & D Coys on forward area. Kemmel under orders Q.O.C. 124 A.B.Bde. Casualties Nil. Sick Nil. arm. Kemmel under orders G.O.C. 124 A.B.Bde. Strength of Batt. 48 Officers 849 other ranks.	[sig]

SALPERWICK
1 - 9 - 18.

Ewe Talbot Lieut. Col.
Commanding 41st Bn M.G. Corps.

SECRET.   Copy No. 9

OPERATION ORDER NO. 40.
by
LIEUT.-COL. A. W. TATE.
Commanding 41st Battalion Machine Gun Corps.
Thursday, 1st August, 1918.

To: O.C. "D" Company,
    41st Battalion Machine Gun Corps.

1.   On the early morning of August 3rd, the 35th Division intend to attack and capture the DRANOUTRE RIDGE.

2.   The final objectives to be consolidated are as follows:-
        A line M.34.d.30.45. - M.34.d.88.85., Southern edge of wood in M.35.a. - Trench in M.35.a. and b. - M.35.b.17.20. 70 meter contour - LOCREHOF FARM - M.29.central.

3.   "D" Company, 41st Battalion Machine Gun Corps will co-operate by firing barrage "N" as shown on attached tracing (issued to "D" Company only) from M.30.a.80.45. to M.30.c.92.35.
        8 guns will be employed on this barrage emplaced in the vicinity of M.17.d.85.95.

4.   Guns will take up position on the night of 2nd/3rd August, and will be ready to fire 5 hours before Zero.
        O.C. Company will report "All Ready" to O.C. 35th Battalion M.G.C., who will be at his Headquarters, R.11.c.8.5. by the code word "PONY".

5.   Machine Guns will not commence firing at Zero until Artillery Barrage has actually opened.

6.   On the S.O.S. going up, guns will immediately open on their barrage lines, in accordance with instructions given in Appendix (issued to "D" Company only).

7.   The ordinary S.O.S. Signal will be used by Infantry Brigades in the line in case of attack.
        The 106th Infantry Brigade will be provided with SPECIAL SIGNAL to denote counter attack on the newly captured position.
        This will be in use until 8 a.m. on the day after the attack, when it will be replaced by the ordinary S.O.S. Signal.
        The Normal S.O.S. Signal is a rifle grenade parachute signal bursting into three stars, RED over GREEN over YELLOW.
        The SPECIAL SIGNAL is a rifle grenade signal bursting into three stars, RED over RED over RED.

8.   O.C. "D" Company will send a representative to synchronise watches at 106th Infantry Brigade Headquarters, M.22.a.0.1. at 12 noon on Zero minus 1 day.

9.   Zero hour will be notified later.

10.   ACKNOWLEDGE.

Issued at 9-45 a.m.   Lieut.-Colonel.
1-8-18.   Commanding 41st Battn. M.G.Corps.

Copies to:
        Copy No. 1. 41st Division "G".
             2.   do.   C.R.A.
             3. 123rd Infantry Brigade.
             4. 35th Battalion Machine Gun Corps.
             5. O.C. 106th American Machine Gun Battn.
             6. "   "A" Coy. "   "   "   "
             7. War Diary.
             8. File.

SECRET.   Copy No... 11 ...

OPERATION ORDER NO. 41.
BY
LIEUT.-COL. A. V. TATE,
Commanding 41st Battalion Machine Gun Corps.
Saturday 3rd August 1918.

To: O.C. "A" Company.
     "B"   "
     "C"   "
     "D"   "
Transport Officer.
Quartermaster.
Medical Officer.
O.C. No. 5 Section, Divl. Signal Company.

1.   "B" Company will relieve "C" Company in the Left Sub-Sector on the night of the 5th/6th August.

2.   "B" Company will arrange with "C" Company to send Nos. 1 of guns into the line on the previous night.

       "C" Company will take over the billets vacated by "B" Company, and will be in Divisional Reserve, ready to move forward immediately if required. All Officers of the Reserve Company will reconnoitre this area.

3.   Handing over files, trench maps, periscopes etc., will be handed over on relief.

4.   Completion of relief to be notified to Brigades concerned and to Battalion Headquarters by Battalion Code.

5.   ACKNOWLEDGE.

                                          2nd Lieut. A/Adjutant.
Issued at 3.30 p.m.   for O.C. 41st Batt. M.G.Corps.
3-8-18.

Copies to:
            Copy No. 1. 122nd Infantry Brigade.
                     2. 123rd   "   "
                     3. 124th   "   "
                     4. 41st Division "A".
                     5. Divisional Signal Officer.
                     6. 41st Division "Q".
                     7. 6th Division.
                     8. O.C. 105th American Machine Gun
                                        Battalion.
                     9. War Diary.
                   10. File.
                   11. Spare.

SECRET.   Copy No. 10

OPERATION ORDER NO. 42.
BY
LIEUT.-COL. A.W. TATE.
Commanding 41st Battalion Machine Gun Corps.

To: O.C. "A" Company.
    "B"   "
    "C"   "
    "D"   "

PRELIMINARY INSTRUCTIONS.

1.   In order to straighten the present front line on the left of the Divisional Front :-
       The approximate line N.14.a.50.00 - N.9.d.40.00 will be captured on a date and at a time to be notified later.

2.   The operation will be carried out by the 122nd Infantry Brigade with one Battalion.
       One Company 6th Division will co-operate on the left of the attack, and, inconjunction with the 122nd Infantry Brigade, will advance their present line of posts N.9.d.51.22 - N.9.d.12.22 - N.9.c.9.0 - N.9.c.6.0 to join their present post at N.9.d.40.00 with our left post on the objective.
       The light railway from MILKY WAY JUNCTION - WILLEBEEK JUNCTION (inclusive to 6th Division) will be the dividing line.

3.   The attack will be carried out under a Barrage.
       A strong standing barrage is to be placed on the ground to the right of the objective during the attack, special attention being paid to the Machine Gun emplacements and T.M. positions in the valley of the KLEINE KEMMEL BEEK and on the N. and N.E. slopes of KEMMEL HILL, which can bring fire to bear on the attacking troops.
       During the period preceding the attack the Artillery will obliterate the enemy trench from N.14.b.27.20 to N.14.d.10.80, and will carry out several shoots into the area N.E. Corner of Square N.14.b with a view to destroying the old British and enemy wire in that area, also line of wire running from N.14.b.80.90 to N.15.a.30.40 and any wire round enemy posts which is known to exist.
       These special shoots will be so carried out so as not to betray special activity on any one particular portion of the front.

4.   41st Battalion Machine Gun Corps will co-operate during the attack by concentrating fire on selected areas, and, on our troops reaching their objective, by placing a S.O.S. barrage in front of the new line.
       This S.O.S. barrage will not be fired unless the S.O.S. signal goes up or under the orders of the Brigade Commander.

5.   Location of Batteries and tasks is shown in Appendix.
       The preparation of barrage positions will be commenced and carried out forthwith by the O.C. Machine Gun Companies in whose sector they are situated.

6.   It will be necessary to move up the Machine Gun Company in Divisional Reserve for this operation.

7. All guns will remain laid on the S.O.S. Lines until noon on the day following the operation.
The attack will take place at night.

8. The Date of the Attack and Zero Hour will be communicated later to all concerned.

9. ACKNOWLEDGE.

[signature]

Lieut.-Colonel.
Commanding 41st Battn. M.G.Corps.

Issued at 7.30.p.m.
4th August 1918.

Copies to:-

Copy No. 1. 41st Division "G".
2. C.R.A. 41st Division.
3. 122nd Infantry Brigade.
4. 123rd Infantry Brigade.
5. 124th Infantry Brigade.
6. 6th Machine Gun Battn.
7. C.M.G.O.
8. War Diary.
9. File.
10. Spare.

S E C R E T.　　　　　　　　　　　　　　　　　　　　　　　　Copy......13...

OPERATION ORDER NO. 43.
BY
Lieut.Col. A.W. TATE.
Commanding 41st Battalion Machine Gun Corps.
Monday 5th August 1918.

To: O.C."A" Company.
　　　"B"　　"
　　　"C"　　"
　　　"D"　　"
　　Quartermaster.
　　Transport Officer.
　　Medical Officer.
　　O.C.No.5.Section,Divl.Signal Coy.

1.　　Machine Gun Company 105th American Infantry Regiment and Machine Gun Company 106th American Infantry Regiment, will be attached to 41st Battalion Machine Gun Corps for a period of 6 days commencing on August 6th.

2.　　The attachment will be divided into three periods, each lasting two days.
　　　Period i.　The attachment of a proportion of personnel to gun teams.
　　　　　　ii.　The relief of a portion of the guns in the line.
　　　　　　iii. Relief of complete sections.

3.　　On the night of August 6th/7th, 4 Officers and 81 Other Ranks of the 106th A.I.R.M.G.Company, and 4 Officers and 86 Other Ranks of the 105th A.I.R.M.G.Company (including N.C.O's) will be attached to the three Companies in the line - 106th A.I.R.M.G.Company on the Right, 105th A.I.R.M.G.Company on the Left. Headquarters of O.C. 105th A.I.R.M.G.Coy. will be at Headquarters, Left Company, 41st Bn.M.G.C. and Headquarters of 106th A.I.R.M.G.Coy. at Headquarters of Right Company, 41st Bn.M.G.C.
　　　Three American Other Ranks and a proportion of N.C.O's, will be attached to each of the guns in the line for Period i.

4.　　Company Commanders of 41st Battn.M.G.C. will therefore arrange to send up extra personnel to the line to bring teams up to strength, not less than two other ranks of this Battalion to be at each position.
　　　It will also be necessary to take the guns of the 41st Battalion into the line, and left Company 105th A.I.R.M.G.Coy. will arrange to take up one gun, tripod and spare parts, on account of th a 17th gun now being manned in the Left Sector. This gun can be taken up on one of the limbers of the 106th A.I.R.M.G.Battalion under arrangements to be made direct between Company Commanders.

5.　　Detailed arrangements for the attachment and for guides to meet the incoming detachments have already been made between British and American Companies concerned.
　　　Rations for the first 24 hours will be taken in on the man.

6.　　On the night of August 7th/8th, the guns of the American teams mentioned in Period ii para.2, will be brought up to Company Headquarters in readiness for the following night.

7.　　On the night of August 8th/9th, Period ii. will commence; detailed instructions will be issued later.

8.　　On the night of August 10th/11th Period iii. will commence.

9.　　Arrangements for rations and transport will be made direct between American and British Transport Officers, Quartermaster and Supply Officer.

10　　Transport,Supply Officers Department and details of 105th and 106th A.I.R.M.G.Coys. will move to "B" Echelon, 41st Battn.M.G.C. on the evening of August 6th, and O.C. 105th and 106th A.I.R.M.G Coys. will make their Headquarters with 41st Bn.M.G.C.

11.　　ACKNOWLEDGE.

　　　　　　　　　　　　　　　　　　　　　　　　2nd Lieut.A/Adjutant,
Issued at 6 a.m.　　　　　　　　　for O.C. 41st Battn. M.G.Corps.
6-8-18.
Copies to: No.1. 41st Division "G".　　No.2. 41st Division "Q".
　　　　　　3. 122nd Ifny.Bde.　　　　　4. 123rd Infy Bde.
　　　　　　5. 124th　"　　"　　　　　　6. C.R.E. 41st Div.
　　　　　　7. C.R.A. 41st Div.　　　　　8. O.C. 105th A.I.R.M.G.C.

No. 9. O.C. 106th A.I.R.M.G.Company.
10. C.M.G.O.
11. Left Company (American)
12. Right   "   "
13. War Diary.
14. File.
15. Spare.

SECRET.   Copy..........

OPERATION ORDER NO. 44.
BY
Lieut.-Col. A. W. TATE.
Commanding 41st Battalion Machine Gun Corps.
TUESDAY AUGUST 6th 1918.

To: O.C. "A" Company.
      "B"   "
      "C"   "
      "D"   "

APPENDIX "B" attached.

Reference Operation Order No 42 of this Office dated 4-8-18.

1. The Operation detailed in this Order will take place on the night of August 8th/9th. Zero hour will be notified later.

2. Batteries will move into position at dusk on the night of the 8th instant, and will be ready to fire one hour before Zero, when Officers Commanding Batteries will report all ready to their Group Commanders, who will report to the Officer Commanding Groups (Major A. M. CHALMERS) whose Headquarters will be at Left Machine Gun Company H.Q.

3. 6th Machine Gun Battalion have arranged to co-operate by laying down a S.O.S. barrage line from N.15.b.05.20. to the MILKY WAY - WILLEBEEK JUNCTION Light Railway.

4. Officers Commanding Left and Centre Companies will arrange to dump sufficient S.A.A. at the Battery positions in their area for the operation.

5. Reference para. 7, Batteries will remain in position until noon on the 10th instant, after which, they will return to their Battle Positions and Reserve Position as soon as possible.

6. The Signal for guns to fire, will be the opening of the Artillery Barrage.
   O.C. Groups will arrange to send an Officer to synchronise watches, at 122nd Brigade Headquarters at 9 p.m. on the evening of the 8th and to pass on this time to Group Commanders.

7. Calculations will be forwarded to Major A.M. CHALMERS by the evening of the 7th to Reserve Company H.Q.

8. ACKNOWLEDGE.

                                                      Lieut.-Colonel.

Issued at 8 a.m.   Commanding 41st Battalion M.G.Corps.
7-8-18.

Copies to:
                Copy No. 1. 41st Division "G".
                        2. C.R.A. 41st Division.
                        3. 122nd Infantry Brigade.
                        4. 123rd Infantry Brigade.
                        5. 124th Infantry Brigade.
                        6. 6th Machine Gun Battalion.
                        7. C.M.G.O.
                        8. War Diary.
                        9. File.
                     10. Spare.

SECRET.   Copy No. 11

To: O.C. "A" Company.   O.C. "C" Company.
    Quartermaster.   Transport Officer
    Medical Officer.   O.C. H.Q. Section. Divl. Signal Coy.

                    OPERATION ORDER No.45.
                              BY
                    Lieut.-Col. A. M. TATE.   Cpl Rhodes.
                Commanding 41st Battalion Machine Gun Corps.
                       Friday 9th August 1918.
                    ----

1.   On the night of August 10th/11th, "C" Company will relieve
    "A" Company in the Centre Sector.

2.   As the Americans will be commencing Period iii on the
    same night, it will only be necessary to relieve 8 guns of "A"
    Company, Nos. 6.,7.,8.,13.,14.,15.,16.,10 and 11., and at each
    of these positions there will be 1 American.

3.   The remaining 2 Sections of "C" Company will vacate their Battery
    positions, in accordance with Operation Order No. 44 para 5,
    and return to their "A" Echelon.

4.   "A" Company will take over the billets vacated by "C"
    Company, and will be in Divisional Reserve, ready to move forward
    immediately to occupy the ESTOUVRE LINE if necessary.

5.   "A" Company will detail an Officer to reconnoitre this
    line with an Officer of "C" Company, before relief, and all
    Officers of "A" Company will reconnoitre this line as soon after
    relief as possible.
        The Company in Divisional Reserve is responsible for keeping
    these positions notice boarded and the S.A.A. dumps complete.

6.   "A" Company will relieve the 8 Anti-Aircraft positions at
    ABEELE CROSS ROADS L.27.c.1.9.

7.   Handing over files, trench maps, periscopes etc., will be
    handed over on relief.

8.   Completion of relief to be notified to Brigade concerned
    and to Battalion H.Q. by Battalion Code.

9.   ACKNOWLEDGE.
                                            A. M. Tate
                                            Lieut.-Colonel.
                                        Commanding 41st Battn. M.G.Corps.

Issued at 5.30.p.m.
9-8-18.

Copies to:-   No. 1.   O.C. "A" Company.
                   2.   " "B"   "
                   3.   " 105th & 106th A.I.R.M.G.Corps.
                   4.   " 105th A.I.R. M.G.Corps.
                   5.   " 106th   do.
                   6.   122nd Infantry Brigade.
                   7.   123rd   do.
                   8.   124th   do.
                   9.   41st Division "A".
                  10.   41st Division "Q".
                  11.   War Diary.
                  12.   File.
                  13.   Spare.

SECRET.   Copy..........

OPERATION ORDER NO. 46
BY
LIEUT.-COL. A. W. TATE.
Commanding 41st Battalion Machine Gun Corps.
Sunday 11th August 1918.

To: O.C. "A" Company.   O.C. "B" Company.
    " " "C"   "   "   " "D"   "
    Quartermaster.   Transport Officer.
    Medical Officer.   O.C. No.5. Section, Divl. Signal Coy.
                       104th
1.   "A" and "B" Companies, American Machine Gun Battalion, will be attached to 41st Battalion Machine Gun Corps for a period of 6, days commencing on August 12th.

2.   The attachment will be divided into three periods, each lasting two days.
     Period i.   The attachment of a proportion of personnel to gun teams.
            ii. The relief of a portion of the guns in the line.
            iii. Relief of complete sections.

3.   On the night of August 12th/13th, 4 Officers and 81 other ranks of "A" Company 104th A.M.G.Bn. and 4 Officers and 86 other ranks of "B" Company 104th A.M.G.Bn., (including N.C.O's) will be attached to the three Companies in the line - "A" Company on the Right, "B" Company on the Left. Headquarters of O.C."A" Company, will be at Headquaters, Right Company, and Headquarters "B" Company at Headquarters, Left Company, 41st Battn.M.G.Corps.
     Three American Other Ranks and a proportion of N.C.O's, will be attached to each of the guns in the line for Period i.

4.   Company Commanders of 41st Battn.M.G.C. will therefore arrange to send up extra personnel to the line to bring teams up to strength, not less than two other ranks of this Battalion to be at each position.
     It will also be necessary to take the guns of the 41st Battn. into the line, and "B" Company 104th A.M.G.Bn. will arrange to take up one gun, tripod and spare parts, on account of a 17th gun now being manned in the Loft Sector. This gun can be taken up on one of the limbers of the 105th A.I.R.M.G.Company, under arrangements to be made direct between Company Commanders.

5.   Detailed arrangements for the attachment and for guides to meet the incoming detachments have already been made between British and American Companies concerned.
     Rations for the first 24 hours will be taken in on the man.

6.   On the night of August 13th/14th, the guns of the American teams mentioned in Period ii para.2, will be brought up to Company Headquarters in readiness for the following night.

7.   On the night of August 14th/15th, Period ii will commence; detailed instructions will be issued later.

8.   On the night of August 16th/17th, Period iii, will commence.

9.   Arrangements for rations and transport will be made direct between American and British Transport Officers, Quartermaster and Supply Officer.

10. Transport, Supply Officers Department and details of 104th A.M.G.Battalion, will move to "B" Echelon 41st Battn.M.G.Corps on the evening of August 12th, O.C. 104th A.M.G.Bn. will make his Headquarters with 41st Battn.M.G.Corps.

11. ACKNOWLEDGE.

                                            Lieut.-Colonel.
                                      Commanding 41st Battn.M.G.Corps.

Issued at 4 p.m.
11th August 1918.

Copies to: No.1. 41st Division "G"   No.2. 41st Division "Q"
           3.   122nd Infy Bde.   4.   123rd Infy Bde.
           5.   124th Infy Bde.   6.   C.R.E. 41st Div.
           7.   C.R.A. 41st Div.   8.   O.C. 105th & 106th
                                               A.I.R.M.G.C.
           9.   O.C. 105th A.I.R.M.G.C. 10.   O.C. 106th A.I.R.M.G.C.
           11.   O.C. 104th A.M.G.Battn. 12.   C.M.G.O.
           13.   War Diary.   14.   File.

APPENDIX "B"
GROUP ORGANIZATION CHART.

Reference O.O. Nos. 42 & 44   RIGHT GROUP.   COMMANDED BY Major A.S. HIESHELWOOD.

Battery.	Composition.	No. of Guns.	Commander.	Location.	Targets.	Times From	Times To	Rate of Fire R.P.M.
A.	"A" Company.	1.	2nd Lieut. V.R.BROOKER.	See Appendix "A"	See Appendix "A"	Zero plus 2.	For Zero plus 15. Substitute Zero plus 14.	
						Zero Plus 14.	Zero plus 45.	Harassing fire 1 belt per 10 minutes.
						Zero plus 45.		Cease fire.
B.	"C" Company. "A" "	2. 2.	Lieut. G.L.HALE.	do.	do.	do.	do.	do.
C.	"C" "	4.	2nd Lieut. W.A.KEAN. M.C.	do.	do.	do.	do.	do.

LEFT GROUP.   COMMANDED BY Capt. C.D. LOVERING.

D.	"C" Company "B" "	2. 2.	2nd Lieut. J.C.HOWSIN.	do.	do.	do.	do.	do.
E.	"B" " "C" "	2. 2.	2nd Lieut. L.C.TURPIN.	do.	do.	do.	do.	do.
F.	"C" "	4. 2.	Lieut. D.G.WEBSTER. M.C.	N.7.b.90.41. do.	Track N.15.c.65.85. to CANNON GATE 85.70. Culvert on Plank Road at N.15.d.38.35.	do.	do.	do.

SECRET.   Copy....9...
                        OPERATION ORDER NO. 47.
                                    BY
                        LIEUT.-COL. A. W. TATE.
            Commanding 41st Battalion Machine Gun Corps.
                        Sunday 11th August 1918.
            ─────────────────────────────────

To: O.C. "A" Company.
        "B"   "
        "C"   "

1.   Owing to the likelihood of the enemy attempting to retake the
ground lost by him opposite the Left Brigade Sector, from to-night
until further notice the following Machine Guns will be laid on
S.O.S. Lines on this area.

           Guns.   Location.   Target.
        A. C.15. & 16.   M.12.d.05.80.   N.14.d.18.27. to 25.18.

        B. C.10. & 11.   M.12.c.90.13.   N.14.d.10.35. to 18.27.

        C. L.9. & 10.   N.7.c.88.35.   N.15.c.18.65. to 03.63.

        D. E.11. & 16.)   N.7.a.20.90.   N.15.c.15.53. to 30.25.
           L.13. & 14.)

2.   The Reserve Company ("A" Company.) will move up two guns under
an Officer to occupy a position at N.8.c.70.30. These two guns will
employ direct fire only, and will reserve their fire until a target
presents itself.
        "B" Company will arrange to guide these two guns to the position.
        Rations for the first 24 hours will be taken in on the man,
after which, they will go up with "B" Company rations.

3.   The guns mentioned in para., 1 and 2 will move into position
to-night August 11th, and will remain in until further orders are
received.
        They will be laid on their S.O.S. Lines from dusk until 7 a.m.
after which, they will be able to return to their ordinary battle
positions, at the discretion of the O.C. Company.

4.   Guns will not wait for the S.O.S. Signal, but will open fire
immediately the enemy barrage is put down. It is all important to open
fire immediately.
        Rates of fire: 250 Rounds per minute for four minutes, then
                        150 Rounds per minute for five minutes, and then
                        80 Rounds per minute until the situation clears
                        up.

5.   Counter preparation will be fired by the Artillery at 3-15 and
3-45.a.m. on the morning of the 12th instant.
        Machine Guns will not open fire on these occasions.

6.   Only a small amount of the usual night harassing fire will be
carried out by 1 gun of A and 1 gun of / D Groups, so as not to deplete
the ammunition supply too much. This should be carried out on likely
assembly positions opposite the threatened area. When not carrying
out the night firing, these guns will always be relaid on their S.O.S.
Lines.

7.   ACKNOWLEDGE.
                                                    A.W. Tate
                                                    Lieut.-Colonel.
                                            Commanding 41st Battn.M.G.Corps.
Issued at 7.30 p.m.
11-8-18.
Copies to: No.1. 122nd Infy Bde.   No.2. 123rd Infy Bde.
           No. 3.41st Div. "G".   No. 4.C.R.A. 41st Div.
           No. 5.C.M.G.O.   No. 6.105th & 106th A.I.R.M.G.C.
           No. 7.105th A.I.R.M.G.C.   No. 8.O.C. 106th A.I.R.M.G.C.
           No. 9.War Diary.   No.10.File.
           No.11.Spare.

SECRET.   R.236.   Copy ....

To: O.C. "A" Company.   O.C. "B" Company.
        "C"   "   "D"   "
    Quartermaster.   Transport Officer.
    Medical Officer.   O.C. No. 5. Section Divl.Coy.

            Reference American Attachment.

1.   On the night of August 14th/15th, Period II will commence.

2.   "A" and "B" Companies of 104th A.M.G.Battalion will relieve the following guns of the 41st Battalion Machine Gun Corps.

        "B" Company 104th A.M.G.Bn.   12 Guns.   LEFT SECTOR.
        L.12.,15.,13.,14.,11.,16.,5.,and 6.
        C.7.,8.,13., and 14.

        "A" Company 104th A.M.G.Bn.   12 Guns.   RIGHT SECTOR.
        R. 13.,14.,15.,8.,9.,10.,11., and 12.
        C. 15.,16.,10., and 11.

3.   American teams will consist of 5 other ranks, inclusive of N.C.O's., and 41st Battalion M.G.C. will leave in 1 N.C.O. per team.
        These teams will be under the command of the American N.C.O's.

4.   Surplus personnel will make up the teams of the guns depleted by the adjustment in para.,3 above, so that there will be a greater proportion of British personnel at each position not relieved under the command of British N.C.O's

5.   All guns will be under the command of the British Right, Centre and Left Machine Gun Company Commanders in whose areas they are respectively situated.

6.   Completeion of relief to be reported to Brigades; and to Battalion Headquarters by Battalion Code.

7.   ACKNOWLEDGE.

                                        K Ingle
                                        Capt. & Adjutant.
                            for O.C. 41st Battn. M.G.Corps.

Issued at noon.
13th August 1918.

Copies to:-
            Copy No. 1. 41st Division "G".
                     2.   "   "   "Q".
                     3. 122nd Infantry Brigade.
                     4. 123rd   "   "
                     5. 124th   "   "
                     6. C.R.E. 41st Division.
                     7. C.R.A.   "   "
                     8. O.C. 104th A.M.G.Battalion.
                     9. O.C. "A" Company 104th A.M.G.Bn.
                    10. O.C. "B"   "   "   "   "   "
                    11. C.M.G.O.
                    12. War Diary.
                    13. File.
                    14. Spare.

SECRET. R.257.

To: O.C. "A" Company.
    "B"   "
    "C"   "

    Reference Operation Order No.,47 of this Office dated August 11th.

    All guns at present on the Special S.O.S. Barrage opposite the Left Brigade front will revert to their ordinary duties on the night of August 14th/15th.

    The 2 guns of the Reserve Company that were moved up for the operation will return to their Company on the same night.

    ACKNOWLEDGE.

15th August 1918.   Lieut.-Colonel.
                   Commanding 41st Battalion M.G.Corps.

Copies to ALL Recipients of Operation Order No.47.

SECRET

To: O.C. "A" Company.　　　　O.C. "D" Company.　　　　Copy........
　　Quartermaster.　　　　　　Transport Officer.
　　Medical Officer.　　　　　O.C.No.5.Section Divl.Signal Coy.

OPERATION ORDER NO. 48.
BY
LIEUT.-COL. A. W. TATE.
Commanding 41st Battalion Machine Gun Corps.
Wednesday 14th August 1918.

---

1. On the night of August 15th/16th, "A" Company will relieve "D" Company in the Right Sector.

2. As the Americans will be commencing period ii on the night of August 14th/15th, it will only be necessary to relieve 8 guns of "D" Company, and to relieve the 1 British N.C.O. at the other positions.
   The guns to be relieved are Nos. R.13.,14.,15.,8.,9.,10.,11., and 12. O.C."D" Company will arrange for a guide for each of the positions to be relieved, and O.C."A" Company 104th American M.G. Battalion will arrange with O.C."A" Company 41st Battalion M.G.C. to provide guides for bringing in the relieving British N.C.O., if necessary.

3. The remaining 2 Sections of "A" Company 41st Battalion M.G.C. will be prepared to relieve "A" Company 104th American M.G.Bn. on the night of August 18th/19th.

4. "D" Company will take over the billets vacated by "A" company, and will be in Divisional Reserve, ready to move forward immediately to occupy the WESTOUTRE LINE if necessary, and all Officers of "D" Company will reconnoitre this line as soon after relief as possible.
   The Company in Divisional Reserve is responsible for keeping these positions notice boarded and the S.A.A. dumps complete.

5. "D" Company will relieve the 2 Anti-Aircraft positions at ABEELE CROSS-ROADS L.22.c.1.9.

6. Handing Over Files, Trench Maps, Periscopes etc., will be handed over on relief. Special attention is drawn to Order No. R.238 of this Office dated 13-8-18.

7. Completion of relief to be notified to Brigade concerned and to Battalion H.Q. by Battalion Code.

8. Acknowledge.

　　　　　　　　　　　　　　　　　　　　　Lieut.-Colonel.
　　　　　　　　　　　　　　　　Commanding 41st Battn.M.G.Corps.

Issued at noon
14th August 1918.

Copies to.

　　Copy No. 1. O.C."B" Company.　　2. O.C.104th A.M.G.Bn.
　　　　　　3. 　"　"C"　　"　　　　4. 　"　"A" Coy.　"
　　　　　　5. 122nd Infy Bde.　　　 6. 　"　"B"　　　"
　　　　　　7. 123rd　　"　　"　　　8. 41st Division "G".
　　　　　　9. 124th　　"　　"　　　10. 　"　　"　　　"Q"
　　　　　 11. 30th Division.　　　 12. File.
　　　　　 13. War Diary.　　　　　 14. Spare.

Secret

Copy No. 13

To: O.C. "A" Company.   Quartermaster.   R.245.
       "B"   "   Transport Officer.
       "C"   "   Medical Officer.
       "D"   "   O.C. No 5 Section, Divl. Signal Coy.
    Signal Officer.

Reference American Attachment.

1. On the night of August 16th/17th, Period III will commence. Officers Commanding "A" and "B" Companies 104th American M.G. Battalion, will take over command of the positions detailed in para 2. of Order No. R.236 dated 13-8-18.
They will be under the orders of the G.O.C. Sectors in which their Sections are situated, and to whom they must report on taking over.
The usual daily returns will be rendered direct to O.C. 41st Battalion Machine Gun Corps.

2. The British Officers and N.C.Os. at present at the positions to be taken over will be withdrawn.
The remaining American personnel will remain attached to the gun positions that are not being relieved.

3. Receipts will be exchanged for all tripods, clinometers, ammunition and trench stores taken over on relief, and a duplicate forwarded to this office. All deficiencies must be reported immediately.
American Company Commanders will see that any ammunition expended is replaced, and that the dumps at all positions are maintained.

4. Completion of relief to be reported to Brigades and Battalion Headquarters.

5. ACKNOWLEDGE.

                                Capt. & Adjutant.
Issued at 3.30 p.m.   for O/C. Commanding 41st Battn. M.G. Corps.
15th August 1918.

Copies to: Copy No. 1.   41st Division "G"
                       2.   "   "   "Q"
                       3.   122nd Infy Bde.
                       4.   123rd   "   "
                       5.   124th   "   "
                       6.   C.R.E. 41st Division.
                       7.   C.R.A.   "   "
                       8.   O.C. 104th A.M.G.Bn.
                       9.   O.C. "A" Coy. "
                      10.   O.C. "B" "   "
                      11.   C.M.G.O.
                      12.   War Diary.
                      13.   File.
                      14.   Spare.

SECRET   Copy No......

To. O.C. "A" Company.

OPERATION ORDER No. 49.
BY
LIEUT.-COL. A. W. TATE.
Commanding 41st Battalion Machine Gun Corps.
Saturday 17th August 1918.

PRELIMINARY ORDER.

1. The 30th Division intend to attack and capture the DRANOUTRE RIDGE. The operation will probably take place at night.

2. The final objectives to be consolidated are as follows:-
A line M.34.d.60.45. - M.34.d.88.85., Southern Edge of Wood in M.35.a. - Trench in M.35.a. and b. - M.35.b.17.20. 70 meter contour - LOCREHOF FARM - M.29. central.

3. "A" Company 41st Battalion M.G.C, will co-operate by firing on selected targets in squares M.30.a. and c. and M.36.a. from Zero to Zero plus 30. At Zero plus 30, they will barrage on the line M.30.a.7.2. to M.30.d.1.1. until Zero plus 46.
If the S.O.S. is sent up, they will barrage on this same line

4. 8 guns will be employed on this barrage Nos. R.9. to 16. emplaced in the vicinity of M.17.d.65.95.

5. All Batteries will be ready to fire by Zero minus 4 hours. O.C."A" Company will report all ready to O.C. 30th Battalion M.G.C. whose Headquarters will be with Advanced Divisional Headquarters at LA MONTAGNE by the code word "BLIGHTY".

6. Machine Guns will not commence firing at ZERO until Artillery Barrage has actually opened.

7. Zero day and hour and targets selected will be issued later.
Probable amount of S.A.A. required per gun 6,500.

8. ACKNOWLEDGE.

                                                          for Lieut.Colonel.
                                           Commanding 41st Bn.M.G.Corps.

Issued at 3-30 p.m.
17th August 1918.

Copies to:-
        Copy No. 1 41st Division "G"
                 2. "   " C.R.A.
                 3.124th Infantry Brigade.
                 4.30th Battalion M.G.C.
                 7. War Diary.
                 8. File.
                 9. Spare.

SECRET.   R.295.

                                                      Copy........

To: O.C. "A" Company.

   Referring 41st Battalion M.G.C. O.O. No. 51 paras., 1 and 2.

   Delete target at M.33.a.08.70. and substitute M.30.a.70.20.

   The gap thus formed will be covered by increasing the frontage of the remaining 9 targets so as to cover from M.33.a.08.70 to 60.20.

   Acknowledge.

                                                      K Lage
                                                      Capt. & Adjutant.
18th August 1918.   for O.C. 41st Battn. M.G.Corps.

   Copies to:

         Copy No. 1. 41st Division "G"
                  2. C.R.A. 41st Division.
                  3. 124th Infantry Brigade.
                  4. 30th Battalion M.G.C.
                  5. War Diary.
                  6. File.
                  7. Spare.

SECRET

Copy No. 10

To: O.C. "A" Company.   O.C. "D" Company
    "B" "   "A" " A.M.G.Bn.
    "C" "   "B" "

OPERATION ORDER NO. 50.
BY
LIEUT.-COL. A. W. TATE.
Commanding 41st Battalion Machine Gun Corps.
Saturday 17th August 1918

1. On the night of August 18th/19th, period III of the American Training Programme will end, and British Companies in the line will arrange to relieve the positions at present manned by "A" and "B" Companies 104th A.M.G.Bn.

2. Arrangements must be made between British and American Company Commanders for the American personnel attached to the other positions to rejoin their Companies on the same night, and if necessary, to replace them with British personnel.

3. Details for the procedure of the American Companies on relief will be issued by O.C.104th A.M.G.Bn.

4. The Left Company will continue to occupy number L.17 position and will draw the Training Gun for this purpose.

5. Receipts on handing over will be carefully checked, and any deficiencies immediately reported.

6. Details for the relief are to be made direct between British and American Company Commanders concerned.

7. Completion of relief to be reported to Brigades and Battalion H.Q.

8. ACKNOWLEDGE.

Capt. & Adjutant.
Issued at 3-30 p.m.   for O.C. 41st Battn. M.G.Corps.
17th August 1918.

Copies to:-

Copy No. 1. 41st Division "G".
         2.   "   "   "Q".
         3. 122nd Infy Bde.
         4. 124th   "   "
         5. 123rd   "   "
         6. C.R.E. 41st Division.
         7. C.R.A.   "   "
         8. O.C. 104th A.M.G.Bn.
         9. C.M.G.O.
        10. War Diary.
        11. Quartermaster.
        12. Transport Officer.
        13. Signal Officer.
        14. Medical Officer.
        15. O.C.No. 5. Section Divl Signal Coy.
        16. File.
        17. Spare.

SECRET.   Copy........

To: O.C. "A" Company.
       "C"   "

OPERATION ORDER NO. 51.
BY
LIEUT.-COL. A. W. TATE.
Commanding 41st Battalion Machine Gun Corps.
Sunday 18th August 1918.

Reference O.O. No. 49. Preliminary Instructions.

1.   Targets selected for harassing fire from Zero to Zero plus 50 are shown on attached map.

2.   Rates of fire for "A" targets engaged by 8 gun Battery at M.17.d.65.05.
            Zero to Zero plus 50.   100 rounds per minute.
            Zero plus 50 to Zero plus 46. 100 rounds per minute on
                                          S.O.S. line.

3.   "A" Battery will remain in position until Zero plus 28 hours.

4.   The Centre Company will arrange to co-operate by firing on Targets marked "B" with 2 guns emplaced at M.12.c.90.15. and on Target "C" with 2 guns emplaced at M.12.d.30.50.
       Rates of fire.
       Zero to Zero plus 5.   150 rounds per minute
       Zero plus 5. to Zero plus 15.   80 "   "   "
       Zero plus 15 to Zero plus 45.   Harassing bursts of fire.
       These guns will not have S.O.S. lines for this operation.

5.   Should the S.O.S. signal be sent up by our troops "A" Battery will immediately open fire on its S.O.S. line.
       Rates of fire.   250 rounds per minute for 4 minutes then
                          60 rounds per minute until the situation
                             clears up.

6.   Synchronisation will be carried out at 5 p.m. on Zero minus 1 day at 90th Infantry Brigade H.Q. M.28.a.0.1.
       Zero hour and day will be notified later.

7.   ACKNOWLEDGE.
                                                  K. Logg.
                                              Capt. and Adjutant.
Issued at 6 p.m.   for O.C. 41st Battn. M.G.Corps.
18th August 1918.

Copies to:
           Copy No. 1. 41st Division "G".
                   2. C.R.A. 41st Division.
                   3. 124th Infantry Brigade.
                   4. 90th Battn. M.G.C.
                   5. War Diary.
                   6. File.
                   7. Spare.

S E C R E T   Copy......

To: O.C. "B" Company.   Transport Officer.
    "D" "   O.C. No. 3 Section Divl. Section Coy.
    Quartermaster.   Signalling Officer.
    Medical Officer.

OPERATION ORDER NO. 52.
BY
LIEUT.-COL. A. W. TATE.
Commanding 41st Battalion Machine Gun Corps.
Monday 19th August 1918.
----

1.   On the night of August 20th/21st, "D" Company will relieve "B" Company in the Left Sector.

2.   "B" Company will take over the billets vacated by "D" Company, and will be in Divisional Reserve, ready to move forward immediately to occupy the WESTOUTRE LINE if necessary.

3.   "B" Company will relieve the 2 Anti-Aircraft positions at ABEELE Cross-Roads L.22.c.1.9.

4.   Handing Over Files, Trench Maps, Periscopes etc., will be handed over on relief.

5.   Completion of relief to be notified to Brigade concerned and to Battalion H.Q. by Battalion Code.

6.   ACKNOWLEDGE.

Capt. & Adjutant.
Issued at noon   for O.C. 41st Battn. M.G.Corps.
19th August 1918.

Copies to:

Copy No. 1. O.C. "A" Company.
        2.   "C"   "
        3. 122nd Infantry Brigade.
        4. 123rd   "   "
        5. 124th   "   "
        6. 41st Division "G".
        7. 41st Division "Q".
        8. War Diary.
        9. 6th Division.
       10. File.
       11. Spare.

SECRET.   Copy No. 10

OPERATION ORDER NO. 53.
by
LIEUT.-COL. A. W. TATE.
Commanding 41st Battalion Machine Gun Corps.
Friday, 23rd August, 1918.

To: O.C. "B" Company.
       "   "C"   "
      Quartermaster.
      Transport Officer.
      O.C. No. 5 Section Divl. Signal Coy.
      Signalling Officer.

1.   On the night of 25th/26th August, "B" Company will
        relieve "C" Company in the Centre Sector.

2.   "C" Company will take over the billets vacated by
        "B" Company, and will be in Divisional Reserve, ready
        to move forward immediately to occupy the WESTOUTRE
        LINE if necessary.

3.   "C" Company will relieve the 2 Anti-Aircraft
        positions at ABEELE Cross Roads L.22.c.1.9.

4.   Handing over Files, Trench Maps, Periscopes etc.
        will be handed over on relief.

5.   Completion of relief to be notified to Brigade
        concerned and to Battalion Headquarters by Battalion
        Code.

6.   Attention is called to R.273 of to-day.

7.   ACKNOWLEDGE.

                                        Capt. and Adjutant.
Issued at 1 p.m.   for Lieut.-Colonel.
23-8-18.   Commanding 41st Battn. M.G.Corps.

Copies to:
                Copy No. 1. O.C. "A" Company.
                        2.   "   "D"   "
                        3. 122nd Infantry Brigade.
                        4. 123rd Infantry Brigade.
                        5. 124th Infantry Brigade.
                        6. 41st Division "G".
                        7.   do.   "Q".
                        8. War Diary.
                        9. File.
                       10. Spare.

                    ****

SECRET.

SECRET.

To: O.C. "A" Company.
    "B"   "
    "C"   "
    "D"   "

1.   Infantry Bdes of the Division are being redistributed on the night of the 26th/27th August, so that the front will be held by 2 Infy. Bdes. in the line and one Infy. Bde. in Divisional Reserve.

2.   The new inter-Brigade boundary will run -

   H.13.d.70.25. - H.7.c.4.0. - H.11.b.6.1. - H.5.d.0.1.

   and the inter-group boundary E. of the front line will run from H.27.d.5.0. - H.13.d.70.25.

3.   124 Inf. Bde. will be on the Right in present H.Q.
   123   "   "   "   "   "   "   "   Left   "   "   "
   122   "   "   "   "   "   "   in Divisional Reserve with H.Q. at L.34.a.5.9. behind the Headquarters Area Commandant LAPPE.

4.   This will not affect the present distribution of Machine Guns in the Divisional Area, but O.C. Centre Company will be responsible to both Right and Left Centre Brigade Commanders according to whichever area his guns are in.

                                    Capt. and Adjutant.
                                      for Lieut.-Colonel.
23rd August, 1918.   Commanding 41st Battn. M.G.Corps.

Copies to:

      Copy No. 1.   41st Division "G".
            2.   "   "   "Q".
            3.   C.R.A. 66th Division.
            4.   C.R.E. 41st Division.
            5.   122nd Infantry Brigade.
            6.   123rd   do.
            7.   124th   do.
            8.   War Diary.
            9.   File.
          10.   Spare.

OPERATION ORDER NO. 55.
by
LIEUT.-COL. A. W. TATE.
Commanding 41st Battalion Machine Gun Corps.
Tuesday, 27th August, 1918.

To: O.C. "A" Company.
    "   "B"   "
    "   "C"   "
    "   "D"   "
    Transport Officer.
    Quartermaster.
    Signalling Officer.
    O.C. No. 5 Section, Divl. Signal Coy.
    Medical Officer.

Reference Operation Order No. 54 dated 27-8-18.

Transport Arrangements.

1. August 28th.
   Transport will move to TILQUES Area, staging for the night at RENESCURE.
   Transport of "C" Company will move off to RENESCURE via QUAESTRAELE – OXELAERE – BAVINGHOVE – LE NIEPPE.
   "C" Company "B" Echelon will meet the "A" Echelon at K.35.d.central at 2-45 p.m. under 2nd Lieut. HILLS.

2. August 29th.
   Transport of "A" Company (less "A" Echelon) and Battalion Headquarters will meet at K.35.d.central at 3-15 p.m. proceeding to RENESCURE via QUAESTRAETE – OXELAERE – BAVINGHOVE and LE NIEPPE.
   This party will be under an Officer to be detailed by "A" Company.

3. August 30th.
   "A" Echelon of "A" Company will proceed as in para. 2 under the Senior N.C.O. moving off at 2-30 p.m.

4. August 31st.
   "D" Company, "A" and "B" Echelons and "B" Company (less its "A" Echelon) will proceed to RENESCURE via route as in para. 2 under Lieut. BUTLER, rendezvous at K.35.d.Central at 2-45 p.m.

5. September 1st.
   "A" Echelon of "B" Company will proceed under the Senior N.C.O. as in para. 4 moving off at 2 p.m.

6. Billets to be obtained from Area Commandant RENESCURE to whom Officer should report in advance of column.

7. Normal distances between Units and vehicles as laid down in 2nd Army Area will be maintained throughout.

8. The personnel of the Division will be conveyed to the TILQUES Area by rail and bus in accordance with orders to be issued later.

No kit other than trench bundles can be taken on the trains or busses, and arrangements must be made to send all kit other than this to Transport Lines on the night before relief.

The Officer Commanding the train Company will be in Command of the column in each case.

- 2 -

Supply Railhead changes to LUMBRES on 31st August.

On 29th August supplies for troops proceeding on night 28th/29th will be drawn by M.T. and delivered in TILQUES area.

On 30th August supplies for troops in TILQUES Area and for those proceeding thero on night 29th/30th will be drawn by M.T. and delivered in TILQUES Area.

On 31st August and 1st September supplies for troops proceeding on night 31st/1st will be drawn by M.T. and delivered in TILQUES Area.

On 2nd September the whole Divisional Train will draw by M.T. from LUMBRES.

On 27th August Train will deliver rations for consumption 28th/and 29th to troops proceeding to new area on night 28th/29th.

On 28th August Train will deliver rations for consumption 29th/and 30th to troops proceeding to new area on night 29th/30th.

On 30th August Train will deliver rations for consumption 31st and 1st to troops proceeding to new area on night 31st/1st.

As the transport leaves the day before its unit, arrangements must be made to issue the two days rations to the men on the night before the transport leaves.

Two buses will be at Divisional Headquarters K.24.a, 2.3. at 9 a.m. on August 29th to convey the Packs of the Battalion.

Quartermaster will arrange for two guides to meet these buses at the above rendezvous and conduct them to Quartermaster's Stores.

Baggage wagons will report to units on the morning of the day before they march.

9. All ammunition, petrol tins (in excess of Mobile Establishment), balance of week's allotment of solidified alcohol, gum boots, gas clothing, pack saddles, water tins, and all trench stores will be handed over to the 34th Division on relief and a copy of receipts sent to Divisional Headquarters.

10. All camps and billets will be handed over in a thoroughly clean and sanitary condition.

11. ACKNOWLEDGE.

Issued at 12-30 a.m.
28-8-18.

Capt. and Adjutant.
for Lieut.-Colonel.
Commanding 41st Battn. M.G.C.

Copy to:-
41st Division "G".   41st Division "Q".
122nd Infantry Brigade.
123rd Infantry Brigade.
124th Infantry Brigade.
War Diary.
File.
Spare.

SECRET.   Copy No........

OPERATION ORDER NO. 54.
by
LIEUT.-COL. A. W. TATE.
Commanding 41st Battalion Machine Gun Corps.
Tuesday, 27th August, 1918.

To: O.C, "A" Company.
        "B"   "
        "C"   "
        "D"   "
     Quartermaster.
     Transport Officer.
     Signalling Officer.
     O.C. No. 5 Section Divl. Signal Coy.
     Medical Officer.

1.   The 41st Division will be relieved by the 34th Division.
   Machine Gun Company reliefs will be as follows:-

   1.   Night 28th/29th August.
            "C" Company, in Divisional Reserve, including the
        two Anti-aircraft guns at ABEELE Cross Roads will be
        relieved and will entrain with the 122nd Infantry
        Brigade Group for ESQUERDES sub-area of TILQUES Area.
        Night 29th/30th August.
        "A" Company will be relieved in the Right Sector, and
        on relief, will entrain for ST. MARTIN-AU-LAERT sub-
        area of TILQUES Area.
        Night of 30th/31st August.
        "D" Company will be relieved in the Left Sector.
        Details of further movement will be issued later.
        Night of 31st August/1st September.
        "B" Company will be relieved in the Centre Sector.
        Details of further movement will be issued later.

2.   Nos. 1 of Forward Guns will remain in 24 hours after
   relief.

3.   All copies of Defence Schemes, Aeroplane Photos,
   Trench Stores, Anti-aircraft posts etc., will be handed
   over on relief.

4.   Tripods, belt boxes, range cards etc. will be handed
   over, and receipts obtained for same.
        Company Commanders will inform this office 24 hours
   before relief, of the number of belt boxes that will
   be handed over at each position.

5.   Details of relief, guides and Transport arrangements,
   will be arranged direct between Company Commanders
   concerned.

6.   Train arrangements will be notified later.

7.   Acknowledge.

Issued at 4-30 p.m.   Capt. and Adjutant.
27-8-18   for Lieut.-Colonel,
                                         Commanding 41st Battn. M.G.C.
Copies to:
            41st Division "G".   41st Division "Q".
            C.R.A. 66th Divn.   122nd Infantry Brigade.
            123rd Infantry Bde.   124th   do.
            34th Battn. M.G.C.   27th American Division.
            30th British Division.

41st Battalion Machine Gun Corps

War Diary

for the Month of

September 1918

(Original)

WAR DIARY of 41st BATTN MACHINE GUN CORPS

INTELLIGENCE SUMMARY for SEPTEMBER 1918

Place	Date	Hour	Summary of Events and Information	Remarks and references to Appendices
NIEPPES AREA	1/9/18		A fine day. Transport left SAILLY-SUR-LYS for forward area by March Route at noon. Operation order Nos 56 & 57 issued in connection with relief of 27 American Divn. Bn Hqrs 41st Bn. A normal 24 hours in area. Roll of Officers on strength attached. Strength of Battalion 41 B offrs 8 & 9 other Ranks. Orders for most of Bn to carry forward into area cancelled.	
DICKEBUSCH SECTOR	2/9/18		A fine day. Under orders of 12th Inf Bde. A Coy moved into left sector & relieved a Coy 27 American Divn M.G.s in left Bde Sector. Bn M.G.s in left Bde Sector. On Under orders of 172 Inf Bde. D Coy moved into Sector & relieved a Coy 27 American Divn M.G.s in Right Bde Sector. On relief, the situation was normal. Bn Hd Qn. A & C Coys entrained at St Omer at 5 p.m. detrained at ABEELE at 7 p.m. Bn Hd Qn moved to Hd Qn on arrival. #1 Div Nil Qrs. A & E Coy to Reninck Billets near REMY SIDING. 22bn went to settled by 9 p.m. Relief of American M.G.s completed during the night. Disposition of Bn at m.n. as follows. Bn Hd Qn. B Nichelen Farm. ? Qr M5 SH700 at Point (Sheet 27) L.14.c.6.8. Right Coy (D) Hd Qrs at (Sheet 28) N.1.d.2.0.70. Left Coy Nd Qrs (A) H270 15.30. A & E Coys Reninck Bts at S.19.d.7.7. Situation during 24 hours otherwise, enemy Artillery & M.G. fairly active. Enemy slowly rearrangements of Snipers & M.Gs.	
DICKEBUSCH AREA	3/9/18		A. Fine day. C.O. (2) in Comm to visit all Coys & Bdes Hd Qrs. Positions for Adv Hd Qrs reconnoitred & selected at S 23 d Q 5.05 (NAZER COTTAGES). Orders received during night that Bn will recommence advance at dawn on 4th inst. E Coy moved into left Sector in operation of left Bde by futter downs on 4 inst. E Coy moved into left Sector in Comm of B Coy & Capt Harth 2/in Comm D Coy again for Centre. Maj. Hamilton resumed Comd of B Coy & Capt Harth 2/in Comm b Coy again for Centre. Weather warm. H.V. gunfire active, during 24 hours, chiefly H.V. gunfire active, coming out & around Ypres. Artillerie otherwise.	
DICKEBUSCH AREA	4/9/18		A fine day. C.O. & 15 hrs. to visit Coys & Bdes. during forenoon. Advance continued at Dawn, but was met with stiff enemy resistance, little progress made. Casualties during 1st & 3rd Sept, ncl. dove Wounded 2. O Rs Rank & File wounded 2.0 Rs Rank & File. Strength returns 20 Rs from Base Depot Strength decrease 5 OR to 260. Advanced H.Q. opened at 7 p.m.	
	5/9/18		C.O. visits Bdes & Coys in line. 50 O.R.'s arrived as Draft from Base. Lt Mais Smith left Battn for U.K. to resume Dental Studies. A Coy relieved D Coy in Right Sector on night relief complete by midnight.	

WAR DIARY or INTELLIGENCE SUMMARY

Army Form C. 2118

(Erase heading not required.)

II September 1918

Place	Date	Hour	Summary of Events and Information	Remarks and references to Appendices
DICK F. BUSCH AREA	6/9/18		Fine day. C.O. proceeds up line to Left Bde. also B^T C Coys. The A.M.G.O. calls at H.Q. at 7 p.m.	KT
	7/9/18		Capt Toth posted to B Coy for duty as 2nd in command. C.O. visits Coys in line. C.O. visits advanced H.Q. in a.m. & A.Enklem & Reserve Coy in p.m. making arrangements for relief of B Coy by C to night, complete by 1 a.m.	KT
	8/9/18		Wet. C.M.G.O. visits Rear Bath H.Q. C.O. visits advanced Bath also 1/3 Bde & R^t Coy H.Q. in Tns. 3 O.R.s to C.C.S.	KT
	9/9/18		Wet. C.O. proceeds up line to R^t Coy sectors. Walk 2 I/c to recover the gun position.	KT
	10/9/18		Wet. C.O. visits Coys in line in a.m. 2/Lt Shrimpton up on duty for duty in Tanks to attemp. C.O. proceeds advance to U.K. 2 w/c return to Rear Hq. Visits Coys in line & Reserve Coy in p.m. 'D' Coy relieve 'C' in Left sector tonight. 8 O.R's wounded. 2 proceed to course at Grantham.	KT
	11/9/18		Fine. O.C. visits Right Coy in Front Bde. loves orderly Room at Arnaus Hqs. Lt Totter returning from leave.	KT
	14/9/18		Wet O.C. visits A.Enklem & Reserve Coy at Week. C.M.G.O. calls at H.Q. 'B' Coy relieve 'A' Coy in Right sector tonight. complete 10.15 p.m.	KT
	15/9/18		Fine C.O. visits Left Suffolk Coys & advanced H.Q. Huns to be moved. Casualties 3 O.R.'s wounded & gassed. Team h^t moves to every man in Bath.	KT

WAR DIARY or INTELLIGENCE SUMMARY

Army Form C. 2118

III   September 1918

Place	Date	Hour	Summary of Events and Information	Remarks and references to Appendices
DICKEBUSCH AREA	16/9/18		Tuesday C.O. visits support Coy & Arranges H.Q. and prepares Defence Scheme (M.G.) in p.m.	KF
	17/9/18		Preparing location for M.G. guns and M.G. Defence Scheme. Arrt. Board B. Bns accoutred. Left at Reserve Coy billets in a.m.	KF
	18/9/18		Fine. C.O. visits C.M.G.O. 150 pr Gun Bn T.G. Drawn and 100 prs issued to Coys in line (50 per Coy) C.O. visits Coys in line & support Coys. Drawn w/Offrs in so now stationed H.Q. support & Reserve Coys & M.G. H Echelons of Coys in their new billets.	KF
	19/9/18		C.O. visits Coys in line & to 34 Divn re move & both. On billets. These alloted us already occupied in W/Frank's Coys change ovr billets. 5 M.M. Drawn from Army by "B" Echelon Limbers. 14 Divn M.G. (I Coy) arrive in enemy W/Frank's to billet in place now occupied by "B" Echelon - finds them practically nearly. C.M.G.O. calls at H.Q. Fine. C.O. reconnts. ground wh. O.C. II Coy for enumeration in W/Frank in w/Frank's M. Queens Bn. J.T.O. Wrkg. in re worn Transport. Support Coy employed taking S.A.A. up the line at night.	KF
	20/9/18		C.O. visits B'n "A" Echelon re worn to billets in A'BEELE, also 6 Reserve Coy re demarcation at 3 pm. "B" "D" Coys relieved in their Coy 34 M.G. Bn in Line.	KF
	21/9/18		C.O. attends Staff Conference at Army H.Q. Conference B/C Coys: 10 gnr Afflidavit at Baltic	KF
	22/9/18		H.B. 2.30 pm. C.Y.F. Service 6 pm in Barn at M.G. Batln H.Q.	KF

WAR DIARY or INTELLIGENCE SUMMARY

Army Form C. 2118

September 1918

Place	Date	Hour	Summary of Events and Information	Remarks and references to Appendices
DICKEBUSCH SEE (L)	23/9/18		Wet. C.O. visit transport lines and Coys in trenches.	Wt
	24/9/18		Fine. Coys resting & cleaning up in billets.	
	25/9/18		Wet. 'D' Coy awaiting 123 Bde in demonstration at wire. Cazelles fell. Tomorrow C.O. meets Coy Commanders Conference at H.Q. 5 P.M. Draft A/32 ORs arrivg & 1 Officer (2Lt WARWICK) posted to 'C' Coy	Wt
	26/9/18		Fine. 'B' Coy assisting 123 Bde in Demonstration and D Coy with 123 Bde. C.O. visits all Coys in evening & gave them 0.0.6. Col Tate returns from leave to U.K.	Wt 0.0.6.
	27/9/18		Fine. Preparing to move to AUCKLAND FARM. Coys move with Bde billeted in their respective areas. Battn HQ opens at 5pm in new locality.	
	28/9/18		2nd Army and Belgians attack at 5.30 a.m. 41st Div participate as per ordrs. Good progress made throughout day with casualties light. Very little opposition. Wet—wet.	Wt
LOCK 8 & SPOIL BANK AREA	29/9/18		Fine Div & Batt'n Hq move to LOCK 8 & SPOIL BANK AREA. 'C' 'D' Coys with 124 & 143 Bde in attack. Lt WEBSTER (C Coy) killed, names at night. BUZENEVAL Lays in Reserve.	Wt
	30/9/18		Very wet all day. Receive situation reports from C. Coy who spent having 5 Guns in COMINES. C.O. visits Bdy & B Echelon. Battn Dump full. Gave kit store to be made at AUCKLAND FARM.	Wt

A.W. Tate Lieut Colonel
Commanding 11/21 Battalion Mockingfusiliers

SECRET.   OPERATION ORDER NO. 56.   Copy No......
by
LIEUT.-COL. A. W. TATE.
Commanding 41st Battalion Machine Gun Corps.

To: O.C. "A" Company.
    "B"   "
    "C"   "
    "D"   "
    Quartermaster.
    Transport Officer.
    2nd Lieut. MILLS.
    Signalling Officer.
    O.C. No. 5 Section Divl. Signal Coy.
    Medical Officer.

1.   The 41st Division will relieve the 27th American Division in the Left Sector XIXth Corps as follows:-

1st September.
    124th Infantry Brigade and "B" and "D" Companies, 41st Battalion Machine Gun Corps will move from 34th British Division Reserve Area to 27th American Division Reserve Area.

2nd September.
    "A" and "C" Companies and Battalion Headquarters will move by rail or bus to 27th American Division Reserve Area (ABEELE AREA).
    Details will be communicated later.

Night 2nd/3rd September.
    124th Infantry Brigade and "B" Company, 41st Battn. Machine Gun Corps relieves 105th American Regiment in Left Sub-Sector, Left Sector XIXth Corps.
    123nd Infantry Brigade and "D" Company, 41st Battn. Machine Gun Corps relieves 106th American Regiment in Right Sub-sector.
    Detailed arrangements for the relief to be made between Company Commanders concerned.
    Headquarters of Units of 27th American Division are:-
    105th Infantry Regiment.   H.27.b.7.7.
    106th   "   "   H.31.a.6.9.

Transport Arrangements.

    Transport of "A" and "C" Companies and Battalion Headquarters will march under 2nd Lieut. MILLS, who will command the 2nd Column, including Transport of other Units of the Division, on the afternoon of September 1st.
    Starting Point, Cross Roads, immediately West of ARQUES, 5-15 p.m.
    Transport will proceed via ARQUES - LE NIEPPE and ZUYPTEENE, staging the night at ZERMEZEELE, billets from Area Commandant of that town.
    Details regarding march 2nd instant will be communicated later.
    Supplies for consumption on the 2nd instant will be delivered to Units and issued to men before Transport leaves. Supplies for consumption on the 3rd instant will be delivered by Motor Transport to Divisional Train at ZERMEZEELE on night of the 1st instant and to Units in new area on the 2nd September.

ACKNOWLEDGE.

                                Capt. and Adjutant.
Issued at 10-30 a.m.   for Lieut.-Colonel.
1-9-18.   Commanding 41st Battn. M.G.Corps.

BUSES.

Date.	Unit.	Embus at.	Debus at.	Time dep.	Time arrive	Remarks.
28th/29th.	132nd Bde.H.Qrs. 233rd Fld.Coy.R.E. "C" Coy.M.G.Battn. 1 Coy. Pioneers. Portion Divl.H.Q. Divl.Observers. 158th Fld.Ambce.	Head of column L.S4.d.1.7. Facing South.	ESQUERDES.	10 p.m.	3.0.p.m.	Column consists of 35 lorries. 158th Field Ambulance will be picked up on main STEENVOORDE-CASSEL Road about 1½ kilometres WEST of CASSEL. The last5 lorrys of column will be left vacant for this purpose.

TRAIN

Date	Unit	Entrainment.	Detrainment.	Depart.	Arrive.
29th/30th.	Headquarters and "A" Company, M.G.Battn.	ABEELE.	ST.OMER.	4 a.m. 30th.	9 a.m.
31st/1st.	"D" and "B" Companies M.G.Battn.	ABEELE.	LUMBRES.	4 a.m. 1st.	9 a.m.

SECRET.

OPERATION ORDER NO. 57.
by
LIEUT.-COL. A. W. TATE.
Commanding 41st Battalion Machine Gun Corps.
Sunday, 1st September, 1918.

To: O.C. "A" Company.
    "   "C"   "
    Quartermaster.
    Medical Officer.
    Signal Officer.
    O.C. No. 5 Section, Divl. Signal Company.

1.   Headquarters Personnel, "A" and "C" Companies will move off independently to-morrow the 2nd instant, and will entrain at 3 p.m. at ST. OMER.

        Companies will be at the station, ¾ of an hour before advertised departure of the train.

        Orders as to destination will be given at the Detraining Station.

        2 Lorries will be at SALPERWICK Church 10 a.m. to go to ABEELE Aerodrome.

2.   ACKNOWLEDGE.

                                            [signature]
                                        Capt. and Adjutant,
                                        for Lieut.-Colonel.
Issued at 7-15 p.m.   Commanding 41st Battn. M.G.Corps.
1-9-18.

Copies to:

            Copy No. 1. 41st Division "G".
                2.   do.   "Q".
                3. War Diary.
                4. File.
                5. Spare.

SECRET.   Copy No............

OPERATION ORDER NO. 58.
by
LIEUT.-COL. A. W. TATE.
Commanding 41st Battalion Machine Gun Corps.
Thursday, 5th September, 1918.

Ref. Maps.
    1/10,000 Sheet 28 S.W. 2.
    1/20,000 Sheet 27 N.E.
    1/20,000 Sheet 27 N.W.

To: O.C. "D" Company.
    " " "A" "

1.-   The present Front occupied by 122nd and 124th Infantry Brigades will be taken over on the night 5th/6th September by 123rd Infantry Brigade and a Battalion of 124th Infantry Brigade, as follows:-
    (a) The present front line Battalion of 122nd Infantry Brigade will be relieved by a Battalion of 123rd Infantry Brigade.
    (b) The 26th Bn. Royal Fusiliers to be placed at the disposal of G.O.C. 123rd Infantry Brigade, will extend to their left, relieving the 10th Bn. "Queens" R.W.Surrey Regt, and occupy the front system of the present Left Brigade Sector.
    (c) A Battalion of 123rd Infantry Brigade will be placed in Support just in rear of VIERSTRAAT SWITCH, about MAJOR'S POST and CAPTAIN POST.
    The remaining Battalion of 123rd Infantry Brigade will be in Brigade Reserve about Squares N.10.a. and b.
    (d) Headquarters 123rd Infantry Brigade will be established at H.31.a.6.9.
    (e) Command of Brigade Sub-Sectors will pass from 122nd and 124th Infantry Brigades respectively, to G.O.C. 123rd Infantry Brigade at 6 a.m. 6th September.

2.-   On relief 122nd Infantry Brigade will be disposed,
        Headquarters at G.14.c.2.4.
        1 Battalion at G.20.c.5.9.
        1 Battalion about HOOGRAAF G.26.c.
        1 Battalion about LIJSSENTHOEK L.24.c.

    124th Infantry Brigade (less 1 Battalion) will be disposed,
        Headquarters WALKERS FARM H.27.b.6.7.
        1 Battalion MEDOC FARM G.36.a.2.7.
        1 Battalion G.24.b.6.8.

3.-   On the night of 5th/6th September, "A" Company, 41st Battalion Machine Gun Corps will relieve "D" Company in the Right Sector.
    "D" Company, on relief, will be in Divisional Reserve, and will occupy the billets vacated by "A" Company.

4.-   Belt Boxes and Tripods will be left in the line, and before handing over positions, personnel of "D" Company must see that the personnel of "A" Company thoroughly understand their positions and the general situation.

5.- Completion of relief to be reported to Brigade and Advanced Battalion Headquarters.

6.- ACKNOWLEDGE.

Issued at 4-30 p.m.
5-9-18.

Capt. and Adjutant.
for Lieut.-Colonel,
Commanding 41st Battn. M.G.C.

Copies to:-

Copy No. 1. 41st Division "G".
2. do. "Q".
3. O.C. "B" Company.
4. " "C" "
5. Quartermaster.
6. Transport Officer.
7. Signalling Officer.
8. O.C. No. 5 Section Divl. Sig. Coy.
9. Major J. MUHLIG, M.C.
10. 122nd Infantry Brigade.
11. 123rd Infantry Brigade.
12. 124th Infantry Brigade.
13. War Diary.
14. File.
15. Spare.
16. C.R.A.

SECRET. Copy No. 13.

OPERATION ORDER NO. 59.
by
LIEUT.-COL. A. W. TATE.
Commanding 41st Battalion Machine Gun Corps.
Sunday, 8th September, 1918.

To: O.C. "B" Company.
    " "C"   "

1. "C" Company will relieve "B" Company in the Left Sub-Sector, to-night September 8th and on relief, "B" Company will go into billets at G.19.b.70.70. and be in Divisional Reserve with "D" Company.

2. Tripods and Belt boxes etc. will be taken out by "B" Company, but all bulk S.A.A. will be handed over.

   Details of relief will be arranged direct between Company Commanders concerned.

3. All information as to situation, enemy movement, work in hand and contemplation, will be handed over by "B" Company before relief.

4. Completion of relief to be reported by wire to 123rd Infantry Brigade and to Battalion Headquarters.

5. ACKNOWLEDGE.

Issued at 3-30 p.m.
8-9-18.

Capt. and Adjutant.
for O.C. 41st Battn. M.G.Corps.

Copies to:
Copy No. 1. 41st Division "G".
      2.   do.   "Q".
      3. C.R.A. 41st Division.
      4. 122nd Infantry Brigade.
      5. 123rd   do.
      6. 124th   do.
      7. O.C. "A" Company, 41st Battn. M.G.C.
      8.   "   "D"   "   do.
      9. Quartermaster.   do.
     10. Transport Officer.   do.
     11. Signal Officer.   do.
     12. 35th Battn. M.G.Corps.
     13. War Diary.
     14. File.
     15. Spare.

******

To: 41st Division "G".
 do. "Q".
 122nd Infantry Brigade.
 123rd Infantry Brigade.
 124th Infantry Brigade.
 Signal Officer.
 O.C. "A" Company.
     "C"   "
     "D"   "
 Quartermaster.
 Transport Officer.
 O.C. No. 5 Section, Divl. Signal Coy.

   Reference Operation Order No. 89 of to-day.
   The billets of "B" Company will be at ZEALAND FARM
 G.16.a.00.38.

                                           K Rogers
 8th September, 1918.   Capt. and Adjutant.
                                     41st Battn. M.G.Corps.

SECRET.   Copy No..........

OPERATION ORDER NO. 60.
by
LIEUT.-COL. A. E. TATE.
Commanding 41st Battalion Machine Gun Corps.
Tuesday, 10th September, 1918.

To: O.C. "C" Company.
    "   "D"   "

1.   "D" Company will relieve "C" Company in the Left Sub-
Sector, on the night September 12th/13th and on relief,
"C" Company will go into billets at L.23.b.6.7. and be in
Divisional Reserve with "B" Company.

2.   Details of relief will be arranged direct between
Company Commanders concerned.

3.   All information as to situation, enemy movement, work
in hand and contemplation, will be handed over by "C"
Company before relief.

4.   Completion of relief to be reported by wire to 123rd
Infantry Brigade and to Battalion Headquarters.

5.   ACKNOWLEDGE.

                                            [signature]
Issued at 9 p.m.
10-9-18.   Capt. and Adjutant.
                                           41st Battn. M.G.Corps.

Copies to:

        Copy No. 1. 41st Division "G".
             "   2.   do.   "Q".
             "   3. C.R.A. 41st Division.
             "   4. 122nd Infantry Brigade.
             "   5. 123rd Infantry Brigade.
             "   6. 124th Infantry Brigade.
             "   7. O.C. "A" Company, 41st Battn. M.G.C.
             "   8.   "   "B"   "   do.
             "   9. Quartermaster.   do.
             " 10. Transport Officer.   do.
             " 11. Signal Officer.   do.
             " 12. O.C. No. 5 Section, Divl. Signal Company.
             " 13. 35th Battn. M.G.Corps.
             " 14. War Diary.
             " 15. File.
             " 16. Spare.

SECRET. Copy No............

OPERATION ORDER NO. 61.
by
MAJOR J. MUHLIG, M.C.
Commanding 41st Battalion Machine Gun Corps.
Thursday, 12th September, 1918.

To: O.C. "A" Company.
      "B"   "

1. "B" Company will relieve "A" Company in the Right Sub-Sector, on the night September 14th/15th and on relief, "A" Company will go into billets at G.16.a.00.56. and be in Divisional Reserve with "C" Company.

2. Details of relief will be arranged direct between Company Commanders concerned.

3. All information as to situation, enemy movement, work in hand and contemplation, will be handed over by "A" Company before relief.

4. Completion of relief to be reported by wire to 122nd Infantry Brigade and to Battalion Headquarters.

5. ACKNOWLEDGE.

12-9-18.
Issued at 12 noon.

Capt. and Adjutant.
41st Battn. M.G.Corps.

Copies to:-

    Copy No. 1. 41st Division "G".
           2.   do.   "Q".
           3. C.R.A., 41st Division.
           4. 122nd Infantry Brigade.
           5. 123rd   do.
           6. 124th   do.
           7. O.C. "C" Company. 41st Battn. M.G.C.
           8. " "D" "   do.
           9. Quartermaster.   do.
         10. Transport Officer.   do.
         11. Signal Officer.   do.
         12. O.C. No. 5 Section, Divl. Signal Company.
         13. 54th Battn. M.G.Corps.
         14. War Diary.
         15. File.
         16. Spare.

****

To: O.C. "A" Company.
    "   "B"   "
    "   "C"   "
    "   "D"   "
======================

1. The following system will come into force from the night of 13th/14th September.

   One Company in Forward System Right.
    "   "   "   "   "   Left.
    "   "   "   Support with Headquarters at ZEALAND FARM, G.15.a.00.55.
    "   "   "   Reserve with Headquarters at L.23.b.6.7. or L.18.c.9.0.

On relief in the line by "B" Company, "A" Company will move to Reserve Billets and become Divisional Reserve. "C" Company will move into Support Billets complete with "A" Echelon Transport and will come under orders of G.O. C.Support Brigade.

Support Company will be ready to move forward with Transport (Wheel and Pack) at short notice.

Although Companies will occupy the same sectors in the Forward System this will ensure all Companies taking their turn in Support.

O.C. Support Company should report at Headquarters Support Brigade on moving into Support.

An amended Schedule of Reliefs will follow.

K Fr__
Capt. and Adjutant.
for 41st Battn. M.G.Corps.

Issued at 8-30 p.m.
13-9-18.

SECRET.

Copy No........ 15

41st Battn. Machine Gun Corps Operation Order No. 62.

1. In conjunction with 41st Division Order No. 271 the Battalion will take part in the attack of which details have been given verbally to all concerned.

2. The Battalion will be disposed as follows :-

   Battalion Headquarters. ZEVECOTEN. G.35.d.8.2.
   (with Divisional Headquarters).

   "C" Company.   Under orders of G.O.C. 124th Inf. Bde.

   "D"   "   "   "   "   "   123rd   "   "

   "B"   "   ) Divisional Reserve.
   "A"   "   ) (in event of one Company being placed
                   under orders of 122nd Inf. Bde. that
                   will be "B" Company.)

   "B" Echelon Transport   ) AUCKLAND FARM.
   Rear Battalion Headquarters.)

3. (a). A Contact Aeroplane will fly along the front of attack about 1 hour after Zero and thereafter every clock hour.

   (b). A Counter Attack Aeroplane will patrol the front from Zero plus 40 minutes onwards and will signal the development of an enemy counter attack by giving a red parachute flare.

4. The repair of the following roads to take Horse Transport will be undertaken by R.E. as soon as possible after Zero.
                MIDDLESEX ROAD.
   SHRAPNEL CORNER - VERBRANDENMOLEN ROAD.

5. All Brigade Headquarters will be in communication with Divisional Headquarters by buried cable.

6. As the approach march to forming up lines may be impeded by wire, all wire cutters will be carried.

7. Men employed on XIX Corps Liaison Patrol work will be operating in the Corps Area. Each man of the patrol will be furnished with a pass and will wear a yellow and white shoulder strap.
   They should be furnished with any information they ask for and should be given every assistance possible.

8. All ranks should be warned against entering dugouts, pillboxes and shelters until they have been examined by the Tunnellers.

9. Instructions re moves and routes will be issued later.

10. ACKNOWLEDGE.

Issued at............
25th September, 1918.

Major.
Commanding 41st Battn. M.G.Corps.

Copies to:-

                                                                  No. of Copies.

Copy No. 1.	Commanding Officer.	1.
2.	2nd-in-Command.	1.
3.	O.C. "A" Company.	2.
4.	" "B" "	2.
5.	" "C" "	2.
6.	" "D" "	2.
7.	Transport Officer.	1.
8.	Quartermaster.	1.
9.	Medical Officer.	1.
10.	O.C. No=5 Section, Divl. Signal Coy.	1.
11.	War Diary.	2.
12.	File.	1.
13.	Spare.	2.

                                          ==*=*

SECRET.   Copy No. 10

41st Battalion Machine Gun Corps Instruction
No. 1 to accompany 41st Battalion Machine Gun
Corps Operation Order No. 62.

1.   Units therein mentioned will move on J - 1 Day in
accordance with attached March Table.

2.   The following distances will be maintained on the line
of march:-

   (a). For Serial Nos. 7 - 9 - 10.

         200 yards between Companies and Units of
         equivalent road space.

         200 yards between Units and their Transport

         20 yards between each six vehicles of
         Transport.

   (b). For Serial No. 6.

         100 yards between Platoons or Units of equivalent
         road space.

         100 yards between each six vehicles of Transport.

                                              Major.
Issued at..........
26th September, 1918.   Commanding 41st Battn. M.G.C.

Copies to:
             Copy No. 1. Commanding Officer.
                     2. 2nd-in-Command.
                     3. O. C. "A" Company.
                     4. "   "B"   "
                     5. "   "C"   "
                     6. "   "D"   "
                     7. Transport Officer and
                        Quartermaster.
                     8. Medical Officer.
                     9. O.C. No. 5 Section,
                        Divl. Signal Company.
                    10. War Diary.
                    11.   File.
                    12. Spare.

==*=*

MARCH TABLE TO ACCOMPANY INSTRUCTION NO. 1.

Divisional Serial No.	Unit.	From.	To.	Starting Point.	Time.	Route.	Remarks.
6.	"C" Company, 41st Battn. Machine Gun Corps.	G.35.d.6.7.	BRANDHOEK - VLAMATINGE AREA.	Road Junction G.34.b.3.0.	7-5 p.m.	Cross Roads. G.29.b.50.55. - Road junction. H.13.b.2.0.	Coming under orders of G.O.C. 124 Bde. on arrival of Bde. in New Area.
7.	123rd Inf. Bde. Group. (includes "D" Company 41st Battn. M.G.Corps.)	HOOGRAAF AREA.	OUDERDOM and DOMINION CAMP AREA.	CONDIMENT CROSS. G.32.d.	7-20 p.m.	RENINGHELST Road junction G.34.b.3.0. - Cross Roads G.29.b.50.55.	"D" Company will move under orders issued by 123rd Inf.Bde.
9.	122nd Inf. Bde. Group. (includes "B" Company 41st Battn. M.G.Corps.	ABEELE AREA.	HOOGRAAF AREA.	—	—	Cross Roads L.33.c.2.4.	"B" Company will move under orders of 122nd Inf. Bde.
10.	"A" Company, 41st Battn. M.G.Corps.	L.24.c.8.0.	HOOGRAAF AREA.	—	—	Cross Roads L.33.c.2.4.	"A" Company will march under orders of G.O.C. 122nd Inf. Bde.
—	Battalion Headquarters.			MERMEY CROSS ROADS.AREA. G.23.a.central.	} } }	Starting Point, Route and Time will be notified later to those concerned.	
—	"B" Echelon Transport and Stores.			AUCKLAND FARM.	} }		

SECRET.

Copy No... 15

War Diary

41st Battalion Machine Gun Corps Administrative
Instructions issued in connection with 41st
Battalion Machine Gun Corps Order No. 6.

1. The following is issued in conjunction with 41st Division Administrative Instruction No. 43.

2. Accommodation allotted to Units whilst in Corps Reserve will be in accordance with attached Table "A".

3. Transport.

   (a). 1st Line Transport of Machine Gun Battalion will be divided into 2 Echelons (as per organisation table already issued). The "A" Echelon will during operations be controlled by the Machine Gun Company concerned, the "B" Echelon by Machine Gun Battalion.
   Mounted or cycle orderlies from "B" Echelon will be sent to Battalion Headquarters at a time to be notified later.

   (b). A mounted orderly from the S.A.A. Section D.A.C., will report (at a time to be notified later) to Headquarters Machine Gun Battalion.

   (c). Companies will arrange for the formation of a Pack Train for carriage of ammunition as part of their "A" Echelon.

4. Ammunition.

   Companies will arrange with Staff Captain' Brigade' with whom they are working for any Rifle Grenades, Ground Flares Red, or 1" Very Lights Red and White they require.

   Any S.A.A. required for Pack Train will be drawn from Divisional Dump at G.27.d.9.3. but when operations commence all drawing should be through Mobile Echelons and S.A.A. Section, D.A.C.
   There are dumps of S.A.A. and Grenades which may be drawn on in case of emergency in 35th Division Area at:-
   BEDFORD HOUSE.   I.26.a.9.4.
   WOODCOTE HOUSE.   I.20.c.5.2.
   RAILWAY CUTTING. I.20.d.1.9.
   In 14th Division Area at:-
   VIJVERHOEK.   H.29.b.1.1.

5. Supplies.

   At Zero hour each man will be in possession of one day's complete ration and his Iron Ration.

   Supplies will be delivered by the Divisional Train to "B" Echelon 1st Line Transport and by "B" Echelon 1st Line Transport to Units daily.
   Machine Gun Companies who it is anticipated may be East of the line VOORMEZEELE - ZILLEBEKE LAKE on the first night of operations will arrange a suitable meeting place for guides for "B" Echelon Transport before operations commence.

   Solidified Alcohol will be issued under arrangements to be notified later.

- 2 -

6. Water.

Table "B" shows existing Water Points in 35th Division Area and any information which is available as to the supply in the area now occupied by the enemy.

Regimental Medical Officers will take with them their Water Testing Apparatus and any wells which may be discovered will be tested by them before use.
A notice showing result of test dated and signed by Testing Officer will be put over all sources of water so dealt with.

7. Medical.

The Light Echelon of Field Ambulances will collect and evacuate casualties from Regimental Aid Posts.
Main Dressing Stations at VLAMATINGE and BRANDHOEK.
Heavy Sections of Field Ambulances will be located at HILLHOEK but will be ready to move forward at 24 hours notice.
Trench Foot Soap and Powder will be available for issue from each Field Ambulance.
Every man will carry one pair of dry socks on his person.

8. R.E. Material.

No Forward Dumps will be formed. Enemy material should be used and the location of any dumps of material reported to Battalion Headquarters.

9. Ordnance.

Division Ordnance Store will remain in its present position.

10. Provost Instructions.

Straggler Posts will be established. Prisoners will be sent to 35th Division Cage at H.15.d.9.0. until a more forward cage is established. Strict instructions will be given to prevent roads being blocked to traffic by prisoners.
Coming back mounted men and troops who can move off the roads will do so in order to free the roads for wheeled traffic.

11. Veterinary.

An Advanced Collecting Post will be formed at H.13.d.5.4. No. 52 Mobile Veterinary Section will be at L.28.c.2.7.

12. Roads and Tracks.

A map showing Roads and Tracks on the Front and those which it is intended to extend is being circulated separately. A copy should be in possession of every Officer or N.C.O. in charge of Transport.

15.   **Disposal of Details, Surplus Kits and Packs.**

    (a). Battalion will go into action as near as possible to minimum strength laid down in OB 1919/14/6/18 as amended by OB 1919/7/7/18.
Specialist N.C.O. Instructors will not be taken into action.

    (b). Officers and Battalion Surplus Kit will be despatched to the Divisional Reception Camp in charge of any details who may be sent there.

    (c). In connection with sub-paras. (a) and (b) above, Kits Packs, Blankets etc. will be stored as under on morning of Zero day:-

        All Companies at their respective Company Headquarters as situated on morning of Zero day.
"B" Echelon Transport will collect from Company Headquarters on same morning and bring same to AUCKLAND FARM.
Men detailed by Companies to remain out of action will take care of their respective Company Stores.

Issued at............
25th September, 1918.

                        Major.
                  Commanding 41st Battn. M.G.Corps.

Copies to:-

                                      No. of Copies.

Copy No.			
1.	Commanding Officer.		1.
2.	2nd-in-Command.		1.
3.	O.C. "A" Company.		2.
4.	"	"B" "	2.
5.	"	"C" "	2.
6.	"	"D" "	2.
7.	Transport Officer.		1.
8.	Quartermaster.		1.
9.	Medical Officer.		1.
10.	O.C. No. 5 Section, Divl. Signal Company.		1.
11.	War Diary.		2.
12.	File.		1.
13.	Spare.		2.

==*=*

ADDENDUM 1.   Reference para. 5 SUPPLIES.
        Solidified Alcohol will be issued to Machine Gun Battalion for distribution to Companies as under:-
        1st Day, "C" Company.) 150 ozs. per Company.
                "D" ")
        2nd Day. All Companies. 150 ozs. per Company.

==*=*

Amendment No. 1 to 41st Battalion Machine Gun Corps
Administrative Instructions issued in connection with
41st Battalion Machine Gun Corps Operation Order No. 62.

TABLE "A".

Battalion Headquarters.	For ZEVECOTE G.88.d.8.0. road HERSEY CROSS. G.95.c. central.
"C" Company.	For LAURENCE CAMP. G.11.c.8.6. road CATTERICK CAMP. G.11.d.

26th September, 1918.

                                            Major.
                            Commanding 41st Battn. M.G.Corps.

Issued to all recipients of O.O. 62.

TABLE "A".

Unit.	Location.	Remarks.
"B" Echelon Transport and Rear Battalion Headquarters.	AUCKLAND FARM. G.17.d.5.5.	Includes Quartermaster's Stores etc.
Battalion Headquarters, C.O., Adjutant and small staff.	ZEVECOTEN. G.35.d.8.2.	In vicinity of Divl. Headquarters.
No. 5 Section, Divl. Signal Coy.	ZEVECOTEN. G.35.d.8.2.	With Battalion Headquarters.
"C" Company.	LAURENCE CAMP. G.11.c.5.6. (coming under orders of G.O.C. 124th Inf.Bde.)	
"D" Company.	DOMINION CAMP. G.25.b.8.5. (coming under orders of G.O.C. 125rd Inf.Bde.)	Transport with Companies. Water Carts and Field Kitchens will move to AUCKLAND FARM. G.17.a.5.5. when Companies leave area.
"A" Company, "B" "	In present 125rd Inf. Bde. Area as far as possible. (In Reserve) with 122nd Inf. Bde.	
H.Q. 124th Inf. Bde. " 125rd " " " 122nd " "	G.18.b.6.7. DOMINION FARM. G.24.a.3.5. HOOGRAAF CAMP.	
Adv. Parties 124 Bde. " " 125 " " " 122 "	Group report to Area Comndt. " " " " " " " " " "	BRANDHOEK. G.11.a.6.5. DICKEBUSCH. G.22.d.2.5. LAPPE. L.34.a.8.8.

TABLE "B".

(a). Water Supply in the Divisional Area is as follows:-
    Water Cart Refilling Points.   TIPPERHOEK. L.28.c.5.4.
                                    HOOGRAAF.   G.31.b.2.3.

Map Location.	Nature.	Surroundings.	Fit or Unfit for drinking.	No. of scoops reqd.	Supply.
G.23.c.central.	Pump.	Good.	Fit.	1.	Fair.
G.12.c.2.7.	"	"	"	1.	Good.
A.D.S. Long Barn.	"	Fair.	"	2.	Poor.
G.23.d.2.3.	"	Good.	"	1.	Good.
G.25.b.9.5.	"	"	"	2.	Fair.
G.27.a.4.0.	"	Fair.	"	2.	Fair.
G.27.d.2.4.	"	"	"	1.	Good.
G.27.a.7.3.	"	Good.	"	2.	"
G.24.d.2.6.	"	Fair.	"	2.	"
H.19.c.3.5.	"	Good.	"	2.	"

Water from all these points require boiling or chlorinating.

Water Supply 55th Division Area.

Water Cart Refilling Points.   WATCH CORNER. G.15.b.1.7.
                                VLAMERTINGE. H.2.d.9.4.

(b).
Water Tanks filled by Light Railway at H.18.c.8.1.
                                       H.24.a.9.5.
                                       I.19.b.1.3.

(c).
It is understood that a Sterilizing Lorry will be sent to I.20.b.0.5. as soon as the situation permits.

(d).
Wells used to exist in enemy territory at the following points but must not be used before they are tested.

    I.31.c.40.30.   O.5.c.95.10.   O.10.b.10.40.
    I.31.c.30.40.   I.33.c.80.85.   O.9.d.35.25.
    O.3.a.80.70.   I.32.d.85.20.   I.33.a.50.00.
                     I.29.c.50.50.

Shallow Bore Holes.

    BOULT SOMMES.   I.30.a.70.15.
    HEDGE WOOD.   I.30.b.40.30.
    LARCH WOOD.   I.29.c.10.90.

A795

#1st Battalion Machine Gun Corps

War Diary

— for the Month of —

October 1918

Original.

Army Form C. 2118.

WAR DIARY 41 Batt. M.G.C.
INTELLIGENCE SUMMARY.
(Erase heading not required.)

October 1918.

Place	Date	Hour	Summary of Events and Information	Remarks and references to Appendices
SPOIL BANK AREA	1/10/18		Fine. With Bdes and 'A' Echelon re returns. An attacker 'B' Echelon establishes at J.3.2.D. (Map 28). Good progress made with attack, temporary check on left.	KF
	2/10/18		Fine. 2 W/S much 'A' Echelon. Renewed attack by XIX & II Corps launched at 2 a.m. between MENIN & WERVICQ. D Coy with 123 Bde, 'B' Coy with 1/4, A.T.O. with 1/4. Reports to date (28/9/18 - 2/10/18) 3 O.R. killed 31 wounded.	KF
	3/10/18		Fine. C.O. proceeds up the line to A, B & C Coys, Dwy Htg & 101 M.G. Batt'n. 41st Div. take over from 29th. Tonight Lt. BETTS reports for duty, posted 'A' Coy.	KF
PHELEVELT	4/10/18		Fine early. Batt. Htg. move to PHELEVELT (J.24.d.31.) Division move to J.14.a.3.3.	KF
	5/10/18		Fine. P.O.C. holds conference at noon. C.O. visits A Coy in J.M. B Coy (A.Echelon) have twenty four kills by shell fire. Number fire commences at midnight.	KF
	6/10/18		Fine. D Coy & M Coy, 101 M.G.C. proceed to rest area near REMY. C.O. holds conference. A E Coys at Batt. Htg. 123 Bde moves also to be relieved. Blanket (Spare ones) sent up from B Echelon to Coys. 34th M.G. Batt'n where 8 D Coy's guns completed by 9.30 p.m. (Capt. GODFREY) report tonight. Take over from Capt. CRUICKSHANK. New M.O. (S.O.K.)	KF
	7/10/18		Fine. B Coy moves to rest. With new D Coy.	KF
	8/10/18		Fine. Greatest aerial activity. C.O. visits Corps at rest & 1/3 Bde. B Echelon transport to come moving Battn stores from HUCKLAND FARM to Du Rauphen Camp ABEELE 35th Div. will take over present Battn Htg and Kinel Draft of 50 O.R.s arrived. B' (to 92 W Y58100) D.D. & L. London, E.C. [printed] Killed ministration for finnishstick awards to 4 officers & 13 O.R.s sent to Dn. Htg.	KF

WAR DIARY 41 M.G.C.
INTELLIGENCE SUMMARY
Army Form C. 2118.

October 1918

Place	Date	Hour	Summary of Events and Information	Remarks and references to Appendices
GHELUVELT	8/10/18 (cts)		C Coy moved to bivouac & and D Coy return and are in Divisional Reserve.	
	9/10/18		Fine. O.C. 101 M.G. Batta. called at Battn. HQ. C Coy mls 1×3 Bde. Draft of officers & O.R. O.C. mls D Coy who to relieve A Coy in the Line tonight.	
	10/10/18		Fine. O.O. Embusing all night moved out 7.2.a.m. 2 officers LT FELLS 92/M Middx. regt and 30 O.R.s joined and reported to A.T.B. Coys. also draft of 30 O.R.s	OO 542
	11/10/18		Fine O.C. 101 M.G. Batta. mls. C.O. in view.	
	12/10/18		Batta. HQ. move to J.14.c.14.95.a. 7.a.m. Capt. O'M TOVEY to report to Framlingham for 1st Duty also 2/Lt KNIGHT and 2/Lt PORTER. B Coy relieving D Coy in the trenches.	
			Sevel Inspects. Lt OSBOURNE to attacks to the Battn.	
	13/10/18		Wet. A.T.C. Coys return in R 1×4 Bde Firm rest billets. Bdes taking up accounts positions tonight.	
	14/10/18		Fine & windy early. Enemy attack at 0535. 34 Bns. left 41 wounded and 35 on Fire. 2 Coys. 101 M.G. Batta. attached all machines gunning about 100 prisoners night C.O. mls B Echelon & O/C 101 M.G.C. called at Battn. HQ. 2nd Lt 34 kd 2nd Lt called re	
	15/10/18		Fine. C.O. mls B Echelon & O/C 101 M.G.Batta. tonight. Very few troubling Ist Bde also relieving tonight. relieving C Coy. 41 M.G.Batta. tonight very few troubling	
DADIZEELE	16/10/18		Wet. B Echelon mls to ASHMORE FARM area (DADIZEELE) Coys move with Bdes. Casualties for date (4-16th) 1 killed 11 wounded.	
	17/10/18		Fine. Batta HQ move to MOORSEELE.	
	18/10/18		Fine. C.O. in Corps rep'ter 230/c. F.M.O. wounded (shell) Bn. found remain attacked. XIX Corps Today will battle with MOORSEELE tomorrow. A Coy casualties 4 killed 37 wounded.	

WAR DIARY 41 M.G.C.
INTELLIGENCE SUMMARY
October 1918

Place	Date	Hour	Summary of Events and Information	Remarks and references to Appendices
COURTRAI area	19/10/18		Fine. Battn. H.Q. move to new billet in MOORSEELE.	KT
	20/10/18		Wet. Battn. H.Q. & B Echelon move to HEULE. A & B Coy move to Bde and C'S'unit Int Bde. 41 Div H.Q. move to POSSELHOEK.	KT
	21/10/18		Wet. Battn. H.Q. were asking orders in Cleaning up HOOPE, settled in at 11 p.m. when in farm. B Echelon to instruction hill S.27 d.	KT
	22/10/18		Wet - Moved Battn H.Q. to Walshult of COUTRAI, During attack of MOOSHE CHATEAU. 2nd Lt +BARRITT wounds near crossing 76.	KT
	23/10/18		Fine. C.O. visits Bdes. B Echelon move to WALLE in early morning.	KT
	24/10/18		Fine. C'mds. Bde & Bn. 41 Div taken [?] Bn 7 not attacking. 5th Lt [?] 135 Bde arrive. 55 a remainder [?] being reorganised [?] & [?] 2nd attack returns from [?] also 1st Lieut's from hospital, to B Coy & 2nd Lt FISHER posted to B Coy	KT
	25/10/18		Fine. Attack resumed by 1.—XIX—X Corps at 0900. Together LESCAUT forceline up to Pause line gained. Capt. THORPE attends T.G.M. as member.	KT
	26/10/18		Fine. C.O. visits Corys in am. billetting party spent morning Hqrs COURTRAI. at 7.30. Division is being relieved by 35th Div. H.Q. & C & D Corys and billets in COUTRAI. A&B at EVANDALIE Both Maps GASTON moves from billet line.	KT
	27/10/18		Fine. Following appointments to take effect fum 15 Sep Capt. HARTLEY to command A Coy, Capt. LOSRING 2i/c, D Coy Capt. LINDSAY 2i/c B Coy. A & B Coy move to HILL in COUTRAI Reception Camp move to LEDEGHEM.	KT
	28/10/18		Fine. C.O. holds Conference at 10 am at Battn Hqrs re promotion. Henry kits & stores expected from Reinforcem Camp at [?] C.O. attends Conference at Div Hq. 4.30 pm.	KT

Army Form C. 2118.

WAR DIARY 41 M.G.C.
or
INTELLIGENCE SUMMARY. October 1918 IV
(Erase heading not required.)

Instructions regarding War Diaries and Intelligence Summaries are contained in F.S. Regs., Part II. and the Staff Manual respectively. Title pages will be prepared in manuscript.

Place	Date	Hour	Summary of Events and Information	Remarks and references to Appendices
COOTRAI	28/10/18	(CD)	2/Lt. FRANZMAN and PLOYER join Batt'n & are posted to "B" and "C" Coys.	—
	29/10/18		Fine. Coy's resting and cleaning up. "C" Coy handed Capt Cruickshanks (M.O) 12/7/16	KT
	30/10/18		Fine. Major CHALMERS and Capt THORPE moves on leave. Batt'n C.O's orders at 9:15 am. Baw D.Coy allots Batt. Coys Intelli Schemes.	KT
	31/10/18		Meeting. G.O.C. Infach. Battlion & reviewed at 10 a.m. "A" & "B" Coys prepare to go with 2nd + 3rd Inf Brigade attacks to in 8/10 + 1/11 in three in am.	KT

Wm Fake
Fredk. [?], Colonel
Commanding 41st Battalion
Machine Gun Corps.

SECRET.

WAR DIARY

To O.C. A Coy   Transport Officer
       B "   O.C. Advanced B Ech.
       C "   Signal Officer
       D "

Operation Order No 63
by
Lieut. Col. A.W. Tate
Cmdg 41 Bn Machine Gun Corps.

1. On the night of 7/8 October 123 Infantry Brigade is relieving 124 Infantry Brigade in the line.

2. On the same night A Coy 41st Bn Mn MGC. will relieve C Company 41st Bn MGC who will occupy area vacated by "A" Coy and be in Divisional Reserve.

3. On October 8th "D" Coy at present in rest with 122 Brigade will embuss at 14.00 at HOOGRAFF CABARET and debuss at YPRES SQUARE relieving 'C' Coy in Divisional Reserve. C Coy will embuss at YPRES Square at 15.30 and take over billets vacated by D Coy.

4. On the night 9th/10th D Coy will relieve A Coy in the line and

O.O. (3 Ch)

4. A Coy will come into Divisional Reserve.

5. On Oct 10 by 10th B Company will relieve A Coy and A Coy will go into rest. Details will be arranged between Companys Concerned later.

6. On night of 10/11th B Coy will relieve D Coy in the line, D Company coming into Divisional Reserve.

7. On October 12th A and C Companies will rejoin 122nd Infantry Brigade.

8. Details of reliefs to be arranged between Company Commanders Concerned.

9. The 2 Companies of the 101 Bn. M.G.C. will remain in the line as at present.

10. ACKNOWLEDGE

K. Nagle
Capt & Adjutant
for Lieut Col
Comdg 41 M.G. Corps

Copies 1. 41 Div G.
2. 41 Div Q.
3. 122 Inf Bde
4. 123
5. 124
6. OC 101 Bn MGC

SECRET.   Copy No. ....

OPERATION ORDER NO. 64
by
LIEUT.-COL. A. W. TATE.
Commanding 41st Battn. Machine Gun Corps.
Thursday, 10th October, 1918.

To: O.C. "A" Company.
    "B" "
    "C" "
    "D" "
Quartermaster.
Transport Officer.
Medical Officer.
Signal Officer.
O.C. No. 5 Section, Divl. Signal Company.

1.   Second Army are to attack on a day (J) and at an hour (H) which will be intimated later to all concerned.

2.   41st Division will attack with 34th Division on the Right and 35th Division on the Left.

    Each Division will attack on a one Brigade Front.
    122nd Infantry Brigade will lead, followed by 124th Infantry Brigade.
    123rd Infantry Brigade will be in Divisional Reserve.

3.   <u>Action of the Infantry.</u>
    124th Infantry Brigade with Headquarters at K.20.c.30.95, will be formed up in its assembly position sixty minutes before (H) and will commence moving forward in rear of 122nd Infantry Brigade at (H). When 122nd Infantry Brigade halts on the line of the 2nd pause of the barrage 124th Infantry Brigade will close up under the barrage, pass through 122nd Infantry Brigade, advance immediately the barrage lifts, and continue through to the Final Objective.
    The Final Objective will be consolidated immediately and patrols will be pushed forward well in advance of it.
    123rd Infantry Brigade will commence moving forward at seventy five minutes after (H) and will halt about Squares K.29.d. and K.30.c. They will be prepared on receipt of orders, to relieve 124th Infantry Brigade, on the Final Objective, and to continue the work of consolidation and patrolling.
    They will also be prepared on receipt of orders to operate in the area of the Division on our Left.

4.   <u>Action of the Artillery.</u>
    The attack will start under a creeping barrage which will move forward at the rate of 100 yards in two minutes, and will continue to the limit of range. There will be an extra pause of 15 minutes after every 1500 yards. The barrage will come down two minutes before (H), the first lift and the Infantry advance will be at (H).
    A proportion of smoke shell will be fired in the barrage as far as first "pause", to blind the enemy

- 2 -

and to assist the Infantry for Direction.

A proportion of smoke shell will also be fired along the 1st and 2nd "pause" lines to indicate this to the Infantry.

When the barrage moves forward from 2nd "pause line" it will be continued to N. and S. Grid Lines between Squares L.53. and L.55., when the barrage will cease: before it ceases, a final burst of smoke will be fired to indicate to the Infantry that no further fire will be forthcoming.

Two rounds of Thermite Shell will be fired at each lift of the barrage - one round when the barrage first lifts and one round one minute later - to denote the Southern Boundary of the Division on our left.

At the pauses of the barrage, one round of Thermite will be fired to mark the pause and one round a minute during the first five minutes of the pause.

5. Action of Machine Guns.

101st Battalion Machine Gun Corps (less two Companies) will be attached to 41st Division for the operation. Each of these Companies will man 12 guns.

6. The advance of the Infantry will be assisted by a Machine Gun Barrage, laid down by "B" and "C" Companies, 101st Battalion Machine Gun Corps and "D" Company, 41st Battalion Machine Gun Corps.

Instructions for the carrying out of this Barrage and the areas to be barraged are being issued separately.

On completion of their tasks these Companies will revert as follows:-
"D" Company, 41st Battn. M.G.C. to 125rd Infantry Bde.
"B" and "C" Companies, 101st Battn. M.G.C. to Divisional Reserve, as ordered from Divisional Headquarters.

7. "A" and "C" Companies, 41st Battalion Machine Gun Corps will be attached to 124th Infantry Brigade, and will come under the orders of the Brigade Commander on returning from the rest area on the 15th instant.
"B" Company, 41st Battalion Machine Gun Corps will be attached to 123nd Infantry Brigade, and will relieve "D" Company in the line on the night of the 12th/13th, and will be under the orders of the Brigade Commander on completion of relief.
"D" Company, 41st Battalion Machine Gun Corps, as in para. 6 above, will join 125rd Infantry Brigade at a location and time that will be intimated later to O.C. "D" Company, from which hour they will be under the orders of the Brigade Commander.

8. Communications.
(a). On J minus 1 day at 6 p.m. the Machine Gun Report Centre, which will be in telephonic communication with Battalion Headquarters at J.14.b.40.95. will be established at K.29.c.9.9. All messages for transmission will be handed in there.

(b).   At (H) hour on J day, O.C. No. 5 Section with a detachment of signallers will proceed to JOHNSTON FARM (K.33.a.3.5.) where a Forward Report Centre will be linked up with the Report Centre mentioned in para (a).

During this time, reports will still be handed in at the Rear Report Centre.

(c).   Company Commanders will be advised when the Forward Report Centre is established, and messages will then be handed in at this location.

(d).   As the attack progresses the Forward Report Centre will advance to KNIGHTS FARM (L.53.b.4.3.) which point will be the final Headquarters of the 124th Infantry Brigade.

(e).   Company Commanders will be advised immediately a Report Centre opens.

(f).   Four pigeons will be delivered to the Machine Gun Report Centre daily.

(g).   4 Runners will run forward from the Report Centre to Companies with messages coming from the rear.

(h).   Endeavours will be made to connect "A" Echelons on to the Divisional System.

(i).   Priority messages can be sent from all Infantry Brigades by wireless.

It is of the greatest importance that Company Commanders should keep in close touch with their Brigades and Battalion Headquarters and keep them informed of the situation, casualties, requirements etc.

Issued at. 10:00
11-10-18.

Capt. and Adjutant,
41st Battn. M.G.Corps.

Copies to:-

Copy No. 1.   41st Division "G",
         2.   do.   "Q",
         3.   122nd Infantry Brigade,
         4.   123rd Infantry Brigade,
         5.   124th Infantry Brigade,
         6.   101st Battn. M.G.Corps,
         7.   War Diary,
         8.   File,
         9.   Spare.

SECRET.   Copy No........

Administrative Order No. 1 issued in connection
with 41st Battalion Machine Gun Corps Operation
Order No. 4.

1.   S.A.A.
            The supply of S.A.A. throughout the operations will
       be through normal mobile channels of "A" Echelons 1st
       Line Transport and S.A.A. Section D.A.C. as in the last
       operation.
            The Orderly from the S.A.A. Section will be
       with Advanced "B" Echelon during the operation.
            The dump from which S.A.A. will be drawn
       throughout the operation is situated at J.20.c.3.4.
            A forward dump will be formed at H.30.d.6.9.
       by the 123rd Infantry Brigade as an initial reserve
       for the two attacking Brigades.
            A dump of 100,000 rounds S.A.A. has been formed
       at J.20.c.3.4. for the use of the barrage guns of
       101st and 41st Battalions Machine Gun Corps.

2.   SUPPLIES.
            Instructions will be issued to Battalion
       Quartermaster direct.

3.   MEDICAL.
            Trench Foot Precautions.
            Trench Foot Soap and Talc Powder can be drawn
       from Forward Field Ambulances on demand.
            All ranks will carry a spare pair of socks.
            Arrangements will be made to keep a supply of
       clean socks at Advanced "B" Echelon for exchange with
       a similar number sent down from the line, if
       necessary.
            The Battalion Medical Officer will see that all
       men's feet are attended to before proceeding to the
       line.

4.   R.E. MATERIAL.
            Divisional R.E. Dump is at J.30.c.6.9.
            German Dump exists at K.29.d.1.7.

5.   VETERINARY.
            No. 52 M.V.S. will be at H.16.d.1.1. with an
       Advanced Collecting Station at I.10.c.3.4.

6.   ORDNANCE.
            D.A.D.O.S. Store is at MERSEY CROSS.
            Ordnance Refilling Point for Units in the Forward
       Area is at ECOLE, I.9.c. at 15.00 hours daily.

7.   DISPOSAL OF SURPLUS KITS.
            Surplus Kit, packs, greatcoats and blankets of
       "A" and "C" Companies will as far as possible be sent
       to the Divisional Reception Camp before moving to
       Forward Area.
            Any greatcoats, blankets, kits etc. which are with
       Companies in the Forward Area and are not required in
       action, will be collected and dumped previous to H hour

at the dump of the Brigade to which Companies are attached.

K Trager.
Capt. and Adjutant.
41st Battn. M.G.Corps.

11-10-18.

Issued to all recipients of 41st Battn.
Machine Gun Corps Operation Order.
No. 64.

SECRET.   Copy No.......

Amendment No. 1 to 41st Battn.
Machine Gun Corps Operation
Order No. 64.
----

1.   The barrage will open at H - 5 minutes instead of
H - 3 minutes.

2.   The Machine Gun Barrage will therefore open at H - 5
minutes, and Barrage Instructions and tracing issued with
Operation Order No. 64 will be amended accordingly.

3.   The signal for the Machine Guns to open fire will be
the opening of the Artillery Barrage.
        The rate of fire will be 30 rounds per gun per minute.
        In addition to the amount of ammunition required to
fire the barrage, 1000 rounds S.A.A. will be kept at each
gun position as a reserve.
        There will be one petrol tin of water for each gun.

4.   Batteries will be in position at H - 3 hours on J
day, and will report all ready to Headquarters, 41st Battn.
M.G.C. by wiring the code word "COAL".

5.   Watches will be synchronised at 123nd Infantry Brigade
Headquarters (K26C40.30) after mid-day on J - 1 day.

6.   ACKNOWLEDGE.

Issued at.. 2400   Capt. and Adjutant.
12-10-18.   41st Battn. M.G.C.

Copies to all recipients of 41st Battn.
Machine Gun Corps Operation Order
No. 64.

SECRET. Copy No.......

Amendment No. 1 to 41st Battn.
Machine Gun Corps Operation
Order No. 64.

1. The barrage will open at H - 5 minutes instead of H - 2 minutes.

2. The Machine Gun Barrage will therefore open at H - 5 minutes, and Barrage Instructions and tracing issued with Operation Order No. 64 will be amended accordingly.

3. The signal for the Machine Guns to open fire will be the opening of the Artillery Barrage.
   The rate of fire will be 30 rounds per gun per minute.
   In addition to the amount of ammunition required to fire the barrage, 1000 rounds S.A.A. will be kept at each gun position as a reserve.
   There will be one petrol tin of water for each gun.

4. Batteries will be in position at H - 3 hours on J day, and will report all ready to Headquarters, 41st Battn. M.G.C. by wiring the code word "COAL".

5. Watches will be synchronised at 122nd Infantry Brigade Headquarters (K26c 40.30) after mid-day on J - 1 day.

6. ACKNOWLEDGE.

Issued at..14.00. Capt. and Adjutant.
12-10-18. 41st Battn. M.G.C.

Copies to all recipients of 41st Battn.
Machine Gun Corps Operation Order
No. 64.

Reference 41st Battn. M.G.C. Operation Order No. 64.
para. 6.

Tasks for the M.G. Barrage Guns are as follows:-

1. "D" Company, 101st Battn. M. G. Corps.   Coy.H.Q. K22d7585
   6 gun Battery at K.35.c. 75.93

No. of guns.	Target.	Time.
(a). 3.	K.35.b.56.00. to K.35.d.62.62.	Zero - 2 to Zero.
(b). 3.	K.35.d.62.62. to K.35.d.70.22.	Zero - 2 to Zero plus 6.

   Above guns lift -

| (a). .. | K.35.d.70.22. to Q.5.b.30.85. | Zero to Zero plus 12. |
| (b). .. | Q.5.b.30.85. to Q.5.b.38.52. | Zero plus 6 to Zero) plus 12.) |

   6 Gun Battery at K.35.d. 15.84.

| (a). 3. | K.35.c.10.95. to K.36.c.20.57. | Zero - 2 to Zero plus 4. |
| (b). 3. | K.36.c.10.55. to K.36.c.20.13. | Zero - 2 to Zero plus 10. |

   Above guns lift -

| (a). .. | K.35.c.29.13. to Q.6.a.40.78. | Zero plus 4 to Zero) plus 16.) |
| (b). .. | Q.6.a.45.92. to Q.6.a.55.55. | Zero plus 10 to) Zero plus 16.) |

---

2. "C" Company, 101st Battn. M.G. Corps.   Coy.H.Q. K25d 25.75
   3 4 Gun Batteries at.. K.31.b.51.62   K.31.b.60.78. K.31.b.70.90.

   Frontage of Target 360 yards.

No. of guns.	Target.	Time.
12.	K.35.d.55.15. to K.35.d.65.80.	Zero - 2 to Zero plus 5.

   Lift to -

| | K.36.c.02.00. to K.36.c.13.70. | Zero plus 5 to Zero) plus 14.) |

---

3. "D" Company, 41st Battn. M.G. Corps.   Coy.H.Q. K26d95.05
   2 8 Gun Batteries on line K.34.a.80.80. to K.28.d.80.70.
   Frontage of Target 480 yards.

No. of guns.	Target.	Time.
16.	K.35.d.80.70. to K.36.a.65.25.	Zero - 2 to Zero plus 2.
Lift to -	K.36.c.56.40. to K.36.d.37.95.	Zero plus 2 to Zero plus) 18.)
Lift to -	K.36.d.45.05. to K.31.c.50.60.	Zero plus 18 to Zero) plus 45.)

==*=*=*

PART 1 OF 2

SECRET.

MACHINE GUN

"B" Coy H.Q.
101ST BN. M.G.C.

"C" COMPANY
101ST. M.G. BATN.

"D" COY H.Q.
101ST. BN. M.G.C.

NOTE.—(1). These traces are intended to facilitate the communication of information as to the position of targets, which have been located on a squared map.
(2). The squares on this trace are 500 yards in length on the 1/10,000 scale, 1,000 yards in length on the 1/20,000 scale, and 2,000 yards in length on the 1/40,000 scale.
(3). The squares on the trace are fitted to the squares of the map showing the targets, which are then drawn on the trace. Sufficient letters and numbers must also be added to enable the recipient to place the trace in the correct position on his own map. A little detail may also be traced, but this is not essential. The name and scale of the map to which the trace refers must be always given. The trace can be used for the 1/10,000, 1/20,000, or 1/40,000 scale.

G.S.G.S. 3025.

Tracing taken from Sheet 28. N.E.
of the 1: 10,000 map of

Signature

Date 12.10.18

PART 2 OF 2

ARRAGE.

23　　　　　　　24

"B" Coy. 101ST Bn. M.G.C.

Identification Trace for use with Artillery Maps.

35　　　　　　　36
ZERO - 2 TO ZERO × 5
ZERO - 2 TO ZERO + 14.
ZERO - 2 TO ZERO + 2
ZERO + 2 TO ZERO + 18
ZERO - 2 TO ZERO
ZERO - 2 TO ZERO + 4
ZERO + 18 TO ZERO + 45.
ZERO - 2 TO ZERO + 6
ZERO - 2 TO ZERO + 10
ZERO TO ZERO + 12
ZERO + 4 TO ZERO + 16
ZERO + 6 TO ZERO + 12　ZERO + 10 TO ZERO + 16.

Q

SECRET.

To: O.C. "A" Company.
    "B"   "
    "C"   "
    "D"   "
    Transport Officer.
    Signal Officer.
    O.C. No. 5 Section, Divl. Signal Coy. R.E.
    Medical Officer.

1.   The XIXth Corps in conjunction with II Corps on the Left, will resume the attack in a North Easterly direction on October 31st.

2.   On night 31st October/1st November, 122nd Infantry Brigade with "A" and "B" Companies 41st Battn. Machine Gun Corps will relieve the portion of the 35th Division from the Southern Corps Boundary as far North as Square P.29.

3.   On night 1st/2nd November, 124th Infantry Brigade with "C" and "D" Companies, 41st Battn. Machine Gun Corps will probably be required to carry out an additional relief of the 35th Division, North of Square P.29.

4.   Arrangements under which Machine Gun Companies will rejoin their Brigades will be issued later.

5.   ACKNOWLEDGE.

                                        Capt. and Adjutant.
30-10-18.   41st Battn. M.G.C.

Copies to:-

    41st Division "G".
        do.   "Q".
    122nd Infantry Brigade.
    124th   do.

                ==*=*

To: O.C. "A" Company.
    " "B"   "
    " "C"   "
    " "D"   "
    Transport Officer.
    O.C. No. 5 Section, Divl. Signal Coy. R.E.
    Battn. Signalling Officer.
    Regimental Sergeant Major.

The Divisional Commander will inspect the Battalion to-morrow morning 31st October, at 9-30 a.m.

Companies will parade in the field immediately South of the CAVALRY BARRACKS.

Guns will be mounted in front of Companies (locks in): spare part boxes will not be brought on parade.

The Regimental Sergeant Major will arrange for the Company Markers to be in position by 9-15 a.m.

Headquarter's Personnel will parade at Battalion Headquarters under the Adjutant.

The Battalion Transport, under the Transport Officer, will parade at 10 a.m.

Dress:- Drill Order, Box Respirators and Steel Helmets to be worn.

Any bathing parades will not be cancelled for this parade, but will be carried out as usual.

Parade States to be rendered to Battalion by 9 a.m. 31st October.

ACKNOWLEDGE.

                                    Capt. and Adjutant.
30th October, 1918.   41st Battn. M.G.C.

41st Battalion A. I. Corps

War Diary

— for —

month ending 30th November 1918

WAR DIARY or INTELLIGENCE SUMMARY

Army Form C. 2118

Place	Date	Hour	Summary of Events and Information	Remarks and references to Appendices
Courtrai	Nov 1		Fine day. Adjutant went on leave. C-B Companies came under the orders of 124 Bde at 9AM. A+B Coys relieve two companies of the 33rd M.G. Batt. The night of 1/2nd Nov C+D companies went into the line. Strength of Battn. 44 officers 721 ORs	A762 NKW
Courtrai	Nov 2		Fine day. Brigade moved to St Louis area. Battn HQrs moved from Courtrai to Sweveghem. CO went to a conference at 124 BDE at 13.30 hours. B Echelon moved into area I.32 (Sheet 29)	NKW
SWEVEGHEM	Nov 3		Fine day. CO reconnoitred for new HQrs in vicinity of St Louis. Batt HQ moved at 16.00 hours to H.16.b.5-2 (near Deerlyck). 2/Lt McNair of A Coy went sick, also Lieut Vokes of D Coy evacuated to C.C.S. both influenza. Several cases in Battn.	NKW
DEERLYCK area	Nov 4		Fine day. Regt Sergeant Major went on 14 days engagement leave. A.B.C. Coys came out of the line to Harlebeke and Vichte area. D Coy remains with 123 Bn in line in barrage positions Q.14.c.c. Slightly gassed cases. Capt Lowery of D Coy wounded in arm.	NKW
"	Nov 5		Wet day. CO went to Dine, also visited 101 Battn and 124 BDE. Lieut Smalley of D Coy went on leave. B Coy training in H.12.d.9.8 attd 124 BDE.	NKW
	Nov 6		Bn. day doing army exercises at intervals. CO went to conference at Dine.	NKW OO 65
	Nov 7		Tuesday. D Coy arrived by lorry on bus. B Echelon moved to J.21.a.28. Dine. The following men were awarded Military Medals 107776 Pte G.C. Jones, 327155 H. Dodds, 123385 O. Halmer	NKW

RICHTIE Field, Lieut Adjutant

WAR DIARY of 1st Bn MACHINE GUN CORPS

INTELLIGENCE SUMMARY

for NOVEMBER 1918

Army Form C. 2118.

Place	Date	Hour	Summary of Events and Information	Remarks and references to Appendices
DEERYCK	8/11/18	—	A fine day. Body of 5 off & 86 O.Rs Joined Bn from Base Dépôt. A quiet 24 hours. Major Nulty returned from leave. Report received during night of enemy retirement from line of River SCHELT. Preparations for attack cancelled. Orders received to move to KIERCHM on 10th inst.	MN
KIERCHM	9/11/18	—	A fine day. C Coy crosses the Scheldt. Owing to enemy's speedy without incident, occupy MEERSCHE. A quiet 24 hours.	MN
KIERCHM	10/11/18	—	A fine day. Bn HQ Moved to KIERCHM during forenoon. C & 2 C Coys proceeded MEERSCHE during afternoon. Companies within forward unit Batts to whom they were attached. A quiet 24 hours.	MN
KIERCHM SCHOORISSE	11/11/18	—	A fine day. News received during morning that the Armistice had been signed & that hostilities would cease at 11 hours on 11th inst. Bn HQ Qm mkrs to SCHOORISSE during afternoon. A Coy moved to NEDERBRAKEL, B & C Coy to NIEUKERQUE. C & S SCHOORISSE & Dt NEDERBRAKEL. B Echelon Transport moved to SCHOORISSE. A quiet transmit 24 hours.	MN

WAR DIARY

41st Bn Machine Gun Corps
INTELLIGENCE SUMMARY for NOVEMBER 1918

Army Form C. 2118

Place	Date	Hour	Summary of Events and Information	Remarks and references to Appendices
NEDERBRAKEL	12/11/18		A fine day. Bn Hd Qrs moved to NEDERBRAKEL during forenoon. A & D Coys moved to bivouac of GRAMMONT. C & B Coy remained at Limmerghen. A quiet 24 hours. No signs of enemy, who has retired a considerable distance.	
NEDERBRAKEL	13/11/18		A fine day, cold. Situation normal. Both reserve stationary. C, B & D Coys moved to Grammont during forenoon.	
NEDERBRAKEL	14/11/18		A fine day. B Coy moved to PATICHE area with 122 9 B.D. A quiet 24 hours. Disposition of Bn as follows: Bn Hd Qrs NEDERBRAKEL. B Echelon SCHORISSE. A Coy Grammont SCHENEVEKES. B Coy PATICHE & SARLARDINGE. D Coy at TRIPPEN.	
NEDERBRAKEL	15/11/18		A quiet day. C.O. to Conference at Div Hd Qrs during forenoon. B Echelon moved to NEDERBRAKEL. Coy M.O. Conference at Bn Hd Qrs during afternoon. The following awards have been notified. Awarded the M.C. 2/Lt R. STEAD, 2/Lt J. KNIGHT, Lieut A.C. LINDSEY, Lieut G.D. LOVERING. The D.C.M. 10543 Sgt (A/CSM) Evans, AD 53342 Sgt Vaney S, 143981 Sgt HAZLETON & W.10771 Pt S. M'GREVY, 67639 Pt Radcliffe W.12300 Pt Monk W 277.7 Pt Sergeant 88961 Pt Tattersall R. 17640 Sgt Meyneg, 11031 Cpl Bencow J. Awarded the M.M. 10443 Sgt (A/CSM) Evans AD 53342 Sgt Vaney S, 143981 Sgt HAZLETON & W.10771 Pt A. MAGGET, 11299 Pt S. M'GREVY, 67639 Pt Radcliffe W.12300 Pt Monk W 277.7 Pt Sergeant 88961 Pt Tattersall R. 17640 Sgt Meyneg, 11031 Cpl Bencow J.	

WAR DIARY or INTELLIGENCE SUMMARY

Army Form C. 2118

1st Bn M.G. Corps

(4th Month of November 1918)

Place	Date	Hour	Summary of Events and Information	Remarks and references to Appendices
Neerpelt	16/11/18		A fine day. Bn Hd Qrs & C Coy remained at Neerpelt. A quiet 24 hours in area. O/C Signal Section RE reported Bn Report Cny.	
Neerpelt	17/11/18		A fine day, Still Morning. Divine Service between Bn Hd Qrs & B Coy attended "Thanksgiving" service in the NEDERBRAKEL CHURCH, thro G.O.C. Div inspected Bn on arrival BGr Gr troops on the square before marching into Church. He gave a short address. Lt Col Cw T who was in command of the 2nd Brigade. Preparations made for the following advance to the German frontier. Operation order No 66 issued. So far as concerned a quiet 24 hours in the area.	A/201
Nederbrakel	18/11/18		A fine day, cold. Bn Hd Qr group convoys to Bn Hd Qrs, B & C Coy move by Route March to GRIMMINGE. Remainder en Route No. A & D Coy moved with 12th & 17th Bdn Groups respectively. Bn Hd Qrs B & C Coy moved under orders of E.R.A. Command'g Bn Hd Qr Group. A quiet 24 hours en route to Bn	O.O. 66
Grimminge	19/11/18		A dull day. Rain set in towards day. Spent cleaning up & inspect'g gear. C O to Brig during afternoon. A quiet 24 hours and Brucke M.G. left Bn Hd Qrs to take charge of 18 KRR. temporarily	

WAR DIARY of 4th P.S. Bn Machine Gun Corps

Army Form C. 2118.

INTELLIGENCE SUMMARY
(Erase heading not required.)

Month: NOVEMBER 1918

Instructions regarding War Diaries and Intelligence Summaries are contained in F. S. Regs., Part II. and the Staff Manual respectively. Title pages will be prepared in manuscript.

Place	Date	Hour	Summary of Events and Information	Remarks and references to Appendices
GRIMNICOURT	21/11/18		A fine bright day. General S. Lefroy S. Maget Brig. & 1st PBF attended the Bull. Off. & B.G. Coy moved to Approximation during afternoon & from 21/10/18 the other Coy.s still remain billeted in the former areas. A quiet 24 hours.	A/1
APPREGNIES	22/11/18		A fine day, rifle for HL Off. for the Chatham Sports of C during the afternoon. Detached NCOs & men to return this a.m. A quiet 24 hours.	A/1
SARS-LA-BRUYÈRE	22/11/18		A fine day. All C.O. Walker Rowell's command returned with exception of Div. H.Q. troops & Thirty D.B.M.T. returning during evening. A quiet 24 hrs.	A/1
SARS-LA-BRUYÈRE	23/11/18		A fine day. C.O. & Rowell Cpt. starting for H.Q. BEF. & 5 Offrs. arrive from Base Depot. A Posth. ? Conf. of Offrs. A quiet 24 hours. No wind.	A/1
SARS-LA-BRUYÈRE	24/11/18		A fine dull wet day. Offrs. temperance service in hut & for August. No event ? return.	A/2
SARS-LA-BRUYÈRE	25/11/18		A quiet day C.O.L. Quiet return to base Tommy service at A.M. during wee. G.O.C. Dy Admirers Meeks Calling to all Party on HM.	A/2
SARS-LA-BRUYÈRE	26/11/18		QI Group on the Cunningham's Battefront Classic a quiet return	A/2

WAR DIARY / INTELLIGENCE SUMMARY

Army Form C. 2118.

41st Bn Machine Gun Corps

Month of November 1918

Place	Date	Hour	Summary of Events and Information	Remarks and references to Appendices
SAINT GERMAIN	26/11/18		A fine day. Night very disturbed. Aeroplanes. Memo orders Bn Movements. A Coy & RHQ's during November. A guns unsuccessful Patrol.	MG
SAINT GERMAIN	27/11/18		A wet day. Rain throughout the day. 1/Lt & Lt Mr Ramsey reported from U.K. A guns 24 hours in the area.	MG
SAINT GERMAIN	28/11/18		A fine day. CO visited B Coy during the afternoon. A guns 24 hours in the area.	MG
SAINT GERMAIN	29/11/18		A fine day, cold. A guns unsuccessful 24 hours in area. Strength of Batt. 14 officers, 832 other Ranks. Disposition of Batt. Bn HQ The Chateau SAINT BERGEN. A Coy Vanère B Coy APPELTERRE, C Coy APPELTERRE, D Coy S.E of GRAMMONT. Since the cessation of hostilities in 11 Nov the weather has been great & unsettled.	MG

LIEUT. COL.
COMMANDING 41st BATTALION
MACHINE GUN CORPS

SECRET.   Copy No. 10.

OPERATION ORDER NO. 65.
by
LIEUT.-COL. A. V. TATE.
Commanding 41st Battalion Machine Gun Corps.
Thursday, 7th November, 1918.

To: O.C. "A" Company.
    "B" - "
    "C"   "
    "D"   "
    Transport Officer.
    Signal Officer.
    O.C. No. 5 Section, Divl. Signal Coy.
    Medical Officer.
    O.C. C Coy. 10th Battn. M.G.Corps.

1.   On a date and at a time which will be communicated later to all concerned, the XIX Corps will force the passage of L'ESCAUT in conjunction with the X Corps on the right.
      All preparations will be put in hand forthwith and be completed by midnight 10th/11th November.

2.   (a). The front of attack of the 41st Division will be from Point Q.21.b.0.5. to Q.10.central.
      (b). Right Division boundary Q.21.b.0.5. to Q.30.d.5.0. thence due East.
           The boundary with the VII French Corps runs due East from Q.10.central.
      (c). First Objective of the 41st Division will be Q.30.d.5.0. through Q.34.b.8.6. to Q.12.a.0.0.

3.   The attack on the 41st Division Front will be carried out by 124th Infantry Brigade on the Right, and 122nd Infantry Brigade on the Left.
      Inter-Brigade Boundary Q.15.b.85.50. - Q.17.c.30.85. - Q.34.b.8.6.
      55th Division is attacking on the Right of the 41st Division.

4.   The operation will be carried out in two phases as follows :-

Phase 1.
      The passage of L'ESCAUT and deployment of the attacking troops along the line of the railway on the right bank.
      This phase will probably commence about 2½ hours before "H" and will be carried out under a creeping artillery barrage.
      Covering parties of Infantry will first cross the river in boats, and when these parties have established themselves, foot and pontoon bridges will be thrown over for the remainder of the Infantry to cross.

Phase 2.
      The advance under a creeping barrage from the line of deployment to be
      It is clearly understood that the objective line given is not meant to terminate the operation, but merely this phase. Brigades will push on beyond this objective if possible.

- 2 -

The Barrage will come down at "H" 200 yards in advance of the line of the railway; first lift will be at "H" plus 5 minutes, and rate of advance 100 yards in three minutes.

5. Action of Machine Guns.

(a). For this operation "C" Company, 101st Battalion Machine Gun Corps will be attached to 41st Division, and come under the orders of O.C. 41st Battalion Machine Gun Corps.
"A" Company, 41st Battalion Machine Gun Corps, will be attached to 124th Infantry Brigade.
"B" Company, 41st Battalion Machine Gun Corps will be attached to 123rd Infantry Brigade.
"C" and "D" Companies, 41st Battalion Machine Gun Corps, and "C" Company, 101st Battalion Machine Gun Corps will be employed on barrage tasks, to cover the passage of the Infantry over the River, and the advance to the Railway (Phase 1).

(b). "D" Company, 41st Battalion Machine Gun Corps will be in position approximately along the line Q.5.c.0.0. – Q.5.d.4.9. to bring intense fire to bear along the front of HERSCHE village, afterwards lifting to the Railway and searching the intervening ground.
On completion of their task, "D" Company will be attached to 123rd Infantry Brigade, and O.C. Company will arrange direct with the Brigade the details for his Company to join the Brigade. They will be prepared to move forward with their Brigade to exploit the success of the operation.

(c). "C" Company, 41st Battalion Machine Gun Corps will be in position approximately along the line of the PAROCHIEBEEK from Q.14.a.0.2. to Q.9.c.0.5. and will bring fire to bear within the boundaries of the 124th Infantry Brigade on the line of the Railway, afterwards lifting to 400 yards forward of the Railway, searching the intervening ground on route, and will thereafter search the ground between 400 and 800 yards forward of the Railway, until the commencement of Phase 2, when they will fire at the limit of range (2,800 yards) until "H" plus 5.

(d). "C" Company, 101st Battalion Machine Gun Corps will be in position approximately along the line Q.9.c.4.4. – Q.9.d.9.9.
Their task will be the same as that detailed in para (c), but within the boundaries of the 122nd Infantry Brigade.

(e). Details of lines of fire and times to lift will be issued later.

(f). On completion of their tasks, "C" Companies, 41st and 101st Battalions Machine Gun Corps will come into Divisional Reserve and will be prepared to move forward immediately on receipt of orders to reinforce or relieve the forward Companies.

(g). Company Commanders concerned, will arrange to reconnoitre and prepare battery positions and dump the necessary ammunition in readiness, in accordance with orders already given verbally. They will report to Battalion Headquarters

- 3 -

as soon as possible the exact positions selected.

6. Companies will move into forward billets on the 9th instant, and into their battle positions on the night of the 10th/11th.

During the day of the 10th, care must be taken not to betray the concentration of troops in the area to hostile aircraft and kite balloons.

7. O.C. No. 5 Section, Divisional Signal Company will establish a Forward Report Centre at J.35.c.3.3., and will arrange for communications with the Headquarters of Barrage Companies, Brigades, and Battalion Headquarters.

Arrangements will be made to push forward this Report Centre in the event of the operation being successful.

Every endeavour must be made to keep in close touch with all Companies.

8. ACKNOWLEDGE.

Issued at 19.00
7-11-1918.

Lieut.-Colonel.
Commanding 41st Battn. M.G.Corps.

Copies to:-
Copy No. 1. 41st Division "G".
2. do. "Q".
3. do. C.R.A.
4. 122nd Infantry Brigade.
5. 123rd Infantry Brigade.
6. 124th Infantry Brigade.
7. O.C. 101st Battalion M.G.Corps.
8. 55th Division.
9. VII French Corps.
10. War Diary.
11. File.
12. Spare.

To: O.C. "B" Company, 41st Battn. M.G.Corps.
Major J. MUHLIG, M.C.   do.

A Thanksgiving Service will take place in NEDERBRAKEL CHURCH on the 17th instant. The Rev. W. FIELD senior non C. of E. Chaplain and the Rev. C. S. DUNN acting Senior C. of E. Chaplain will officiate.

"B" Company, 41st Battn. Machine Gun Corps and Battalion Headquarters will attend the service.

Dress :- Drill Order, Braces and Pouches, Rifle.

The band of the 18th K.R.R.C. will attend.

The following will be the programme :-

11.15 a.m.   Markers from each unit report at Church to Divisional Staff Officer.

11.30 a.m.   Troops march on to the markers on the Main Square.

11.45 a.m.   Divisional Commander rides on parade and is received by a General Salute.
             The Divisional Commander will then address the troops.

12 noon.   Troops enter the Church.

12.15 p.m.   Service.

Troops march home on leaving church about 12.45 p.m.

November 15th 1918.

Lieut.-Colonel.
Commanding 41st Battn. M.G.C.

Diary

Reference attached.

1. Battalion Headquarters will parade as strong as possible at 11.10a.m. Place of parade Headquarters Billet Yard.

2. O.C. "B" Company will arrange for his Company to arrive at Battalion Headquarters at 11.20 a.m.

3. Sergt. Barnett, Battalion Headquarters is detailed as marker for 41st Battn. Machine Gun Corps. He will report to a Divisional Staff Officer at NEDERBRAKEL CHURCH at 11.15 a.m. He should know the total numbers of Officers and Other Ranks of 41st Battn. Machine Gun Corps on parade.

4. "B" Company will be sized before marching off from their billets.

November 16th 1918.

Major.
41st Battn. M.G.Corps.

Parade States by 10·30 from "B"

SECRET.

OPERATION ORDER NO. 66.
by
LIEUT.-COL. A. W. TATE.
Commanding 41st Battn. Machine Gun Corps.
Sunday, 17th November, 1918.

Ref. Maps TOURNAI and BRUSSELS 1/100,000.

1. In accordance with the terms of the Armistice, the occupied portions of FRANCE, BELGIUM and LUXEMBERG are to be evacuated by the enemy by 26th November, 1918. A further withdrawal East of the RHINE will take place on a later date.

2. The Second Army, consisting of the Cavalry Corps (less one Division) II, III, XXII and Canadian Corps will begin its advance to the German Frontier on the 17th November. The Cavalry Corps will cover the advance, and will be followed by the Canadian Corps on the Right and II Corps on the Left, one day's march in rear.

3. On 17th November, the Cavalry Corps will advance through the present Outpost Line by the following roads, RENAIX - ELLEZELLES - LESSINES.

4. 41st Division will march on 18th November. 41st Battn. Machine Gun Corps (less "A" and "D" Companies) will move with the Divisional Headquarter Group according to attached march table.

5. Billeting parties, consisting of 1 Officer, 1 N.C.O. and 1 man per Company, and 1 Officer and 1 N.C.O. from Battalion Headquarters will rendezvous on November 18th at GRAMMONT Railway Station at 08.00.
Parties should be mounted or on cycles, be fully armed and equipped and in possession of a map.
Location of Company Headquarters will immediately be forwarded to Battalion Headquarters.

6. Supply rendezvous on November 18th will be GRAMMONT Railway Station at 12 noon.
Lorries will remain with Units for which they are working, during the night; units will be prepared to ration and accommodate the drivers.

7. The advance from the line to be reached on 18th November, will probably be continued on the 20th, 21st, 22nd, 23rd and 24th, a halt being made on the 24th and 25th November, the forward move being recommenced on the 26th November.

8. Battalion Headquarters Guard for the 18th will be found by "B" Company, and will be mounted two hours after arrival in billets.
The Guard for the 19th will be found by "C" Company and mounted at 16.00.

9. CANTEEN.
An Advanced Divisional Canteen will open daily after the march is completed, at Divisional Headquarters, from where units can draw. The stock available is of course limited by the question of Transport.

10. BATHS.
Baths will be opened in each group area during each halt period. Clean clothes will be supplied as transport permits.

11. Attention is drawn to the following points :-

- 2 -

MARCH DISCIPLINE.
Must be the object of special attention, and Company Commanders are reminded that they are responsible for maintaining it and supervising it.

(a). Halts will take place from 10 minutes to every clock hour - to the clock hour, whatever time units may have passed the starting point.
Company Commanders should synchronise their watches so that men are ready fallen in at the clock hour, and the whole column steps off together.
The Battalion Signal Officer will be responsible for obtaining signal time each day and Companies can obtain it from him.

(b). At all halts, the road must be cleared instantly, the men falling out on the right of the road.
A warning will be given to Transport a few minutes before each halt, so as to enable them to pull well in to the side of the road when the order to halt is given.

(c). No Officers or Other Ranks will march alongside the column but must be in the intervals. If they have occasion to pass from front to rear of a portion of the column they will do so on the right hand side.

(d). Any personnel marching with Transport will be in formed bodies.

(e). No arms or equipment may be placed on Transport and no man may ride on a Transport vehicle except driver and mate, without the permission of an Officer.

(f). On pave roads, lorries and cars must be given way to and not turned off the pave.

(g). Troops will march with rifles slung over one shoulder; arms will be sloped on the command "March to attention", but this command will only be given on arrival in billets, and as a compliment on passing the Brigade, Divisional, Corps or Army Commanders for the first time on any day.
Marching through towns and large villages, troops will be given the command "March to Attention with Arms slung" when all rifles will be slung on the left shoulder, marching in all other respects as when marching are "Attention".

(h). Falling Out Reports will be rendered to Battalion Headquarters at the end of each day's march.

12. DRESS.
Leather Jerkins may be worn UNDER THE EQUIPMENT, or carried rolled on the belt at the discretion of the Group Commander.
The Waterproof sheet will be carried on the man, ready to put on in the event of rain.

13. ACKNOWLEDGE.

Issued at 4-20 p.m.
17-11-18.

Lieut.-Colonel.
Commanding 41st Battn. M.G.Corps.

Copies to:
O.C. "B" Company.
" "C" "
Major J. MUHLIG, M.C.
Transport Officer.
War Diary.
File

MARCH TABLE.

Unit.	From.	To.	Starting Point.	Time.	Remarks.
Battalion Headquarters, "B" Company. Battalion Headquarters Transport. (In above order).	MEURKRAKEL.	SANTBERGEN - CANTONMENT AREA.	Cross Roads 400 yards W. of MEURKRAKEL Station.	09.00.	To follow 19th Middlesex Regt.
"C" Company.	SARLANDINGE.	do.	SARLANDINGE.	10.00.	Will march independently from SARLANDINGE to destination.

Note :- Units will break off from the column and proceed to their Billeting Areas at the road junction ½ mile South East of SANTBERGEN CHURCH.

1st AMENDMENT TO 41st BATTN. MACHINE GUN CORPS
ORDER NO. 66.

TRANSPORT.

The detail of lorries and G.S. Wagons will be amended as follows :-

For first three days of march -

Machine Gun Bn. H.Q.   1 lorry in lieu of 2 G.S. Wagons.
Machine Gun Coy.
   attd. 124th Inf. Bde. 1   "   "   "   " "   "   "

G.S. Wagons are confirmed for -

Machine Gun Bn. H.Q.   1.
Machine Gun Coy.
   attd. 123rd Inf. Bde.   2.

Remainder of G.S. Wagons will not be available for first three days.

                                                 Lieut.-Colonel.

17th November, 1918.   Commanding 41st Battn. M.G.Corps.

Copies to:-

                  O.C. "B" Company.
                   "   "C"   "
                  Major J. MUHLIG, M.C.
                  Transport Officer.
                  War Diary.
                  File.

App 10

War Diary
for
December
1918.

41 M.G.C.

WAR DIARY of 41st Bn. MACHINE GUN CORPS

Army Form C. 2118.

INTELLIGENCE SUMMARY

(Erase heading not required.)

for Month of **DECEMBER 1918**

Place	Date	Hour	Summary of Events and Information	Remarks and references to Appendices
ANTOING	1/12/18		A fine day. C.O. to Division. Warning order re move received. Companies carry out training & sport. Dispositions of Battn. remain as here-to-fore. Q.M. received unit from U.K. A quiet uneventful 24 hours in area. Strength of Battn. 47 officers 832 O.R.s	JM
– do –	2/12/18		A fine day, cold wind. C.O. visited B & C Coys during forenoon. 21 Corps to Mingoval during afternoon. A quiet uneventful 24 hours in the area.	JM
– do –	3/12/18		A fine day, mild. C.O. visited A & C Coys during afternoon. Divisional football competition commenced. B Coy played Brit. Signal Coy in Semi Final. Result A draw. Training of Companies continued. A quiet uneventful 24 hours in the area.	JM
– do –	4/12/18		A mild day, dull & rainy. Corps M.G.O. 10th Corps visited HQ during forenoon. Training resumed. A quiet 24 hours in the area.	JM
– do –	5/12/18		A fine day. Mild & bright. C.O. 16 Corps H.Q. Coy during afternoon & evening. Draft of 69 Other Ranks arrived from Base Depot & taken on strength. A quiet uneventful 24 hours in the area. Strength of BC 47 Off. 873 O.R.s	JM
– do –	6/12/18		A fine day. Quiet. C.O. visited B & C Coy during forenoon. Detailed instructions re Move received. Probable date of Move noted as 11th inst. A quiet 24 hours in the area. Training resumed.	JM
– do –	7/12/18		A fine day. C.O. visits Division & 19 Middlesex Regt. at Wavrechain. Horses to Corps. Court of Enquiry held at 'C' Coy billet re fire, and at 'A' Coys billet re ——. H.Q. Corps Operation order no. 67 issued re Move to New area. A quiet 24 hours in the area.	JM

WAR DIARY of 141st BN. MACHINE GUN CORPS

INTELLIGENCE SUMMARY for DECEMBER 1918

Army Form C. 2118.

Place	Date	Hour	Summary of Events and Information	Remarks and references to Appendices
SANTBERGEN	8/12/18		A fine day, light winds. 2/Lieut Madel Enters Crewe unit. Training resumed. Capt Cruickshank MID Offr. reported Battalion from 18 KRRC. A quiet 24 hours in the area.	
— do —	9/12/18		A dull day, rain throughout the day. Adjutant to Vians to attend a F.S & M.G. quiet 24 hours in the area.	
— do —	10/12/18		A fine day. Temperature mild. Training resumed. A quiet 24 hours in the area. C. O. visits Division 2/r Command & A Coy re Court of Inquiry.	
— do —	11/12/18		A fine day, mild. Preparations made for move to new area. Two drafts in A Coy in connection with operations. Lieut MURPHY joins B's & posted to A Coy as Tps Offr. A quiet 24 hours in the area. Battn formed part of B.H.Q. group for purposes of move.	
— do —	12/12/18		Dull wet day, heavy rain. Bn Moved by Road March to ENGHIEN. Arrive new area at noon. Reverulte Rd. A quiet 24 hours.	
ENGHIEN	13/12/18		A fair day, slight Rain. March Resumed. Bn Marching to HAL. Bn arrived mounts the Bn marched as a Batten Bn Billettes above Station as HAL. arriving at 12.30 pm. Casualties nil. A quiet 24 hours.	
HAL	14/12/18		A fine day, March resumed. Bn. Marching to BRAINE L'ALLEUD HQrs & 3 Coys billettes in BRAINE L'ALLEUD. A Coy being billetted at the LION of WATERLOO. Men took advantage of the opportunity to acknowledge Battlefield & Panorama. A quiet 24 hours. 16 Casualties N.L.	

WAR DIARY of 41st Bn Machine Gun Corps

INTELLIGENCE SUMMARY

Month of DECEMBER 1918

Army Form C. 2118.

Place	Date	Hour	Summary of Events and Information	Remarks and references to Appendices
BRAINE L'ALLEUD	15/12/18		A fine day. Battn Remained in BRAINE L'ALLEUD. Troops visited the field of WATERLOO & POUSSEUX during the day. A quiet uneventful 24 hours. Casualties Nil. Strength of Battn 48 Offrs 872 Other Ranks.	
— do —	16/12/18		A dull day. Slight Rain during day. Preparations made for resumption of March. A quiet uneventful 24 hours in above area.	
— do —	17/12/18		A cold day during forenoon. Battn left BRAINE L'ALLEUD at 9 am & proceeded by Route March to MARBAIS. Via QUATRE BROS. Arrived & Billeted by 2 pm. A quiet 24 hours.	
MARBAIS	18/12/18		A cold wet day. Continued Rain throughout 24 hours. Battalion left MARBAIS. Got 9 am & proceeded by March Route to TONGRINNE. Arrived & Billeted by 12 noon. A quiet 24 hours in the Area.	
TONGRINNE	19/12/18		A fine day. Very cold & windy. Battalion left TONGRINNE at 8.15 am proceeding by March Route to DHUY. Arrived by 2 pm. A quiet 24 hours.	
DHUY	20/12/18		A cold day. Rain throughout the day. Battalion left DHUY for COUTHUIN area by Route March. Moving at 12.30 hour Leaving Skeleton Bn Hd Qrs started at ENVOZ Chateau & Village. A quiet 24 hours.	
COUTHUIN	21/12/18		A fine day. C.O. visits Divison during forenoon & Coy during afternoon. Orders received Commencing Demobilisation of Certain Companies engaged settling down in billet area. A quiet 24 hours in the area.	

WAR DIARY of H 1st Bde Machine Gun Corps

INTELLIGENCE SUMMARY

Month of DECEMBER 1918

Place	Date	Hour	Summary of Events and Information	Remarks and references to Appendices
COUTHIN	22/12/18		A fine day. C.O. visited all Coys during forenoon. Companies engaged cleaning up & fitting. Room after the March. A quiet 24 hours in the area. 16 Canadian O.C. Sick N.I.L. Strength of Bdes H.Q. Officers 57/2, other ranks	A/S
—do—	23/12/18		A dull day. Rain tonight at intervals throughout the day. Companies engaged cleaning up etc for Xmas. A quiet 24 hours in the area. 15 Coy ordered to arrange that a certain number of O.Ranks etc. would proceed at 8 p.m. HERON & not leave the return until 3.0 p.m. next day. C/p came accompanied by LADVIR for rest & recreation.	A/S
—do—	24/12/18		A dull day. Winds & Rain throughout the day. C/p recommenced from AMIENS with the No occupation by D Coy. Ranks arranged. Singing parts returned from LADVIR. Sick N.I.L. It was arranged by Coys for Companies Xmas dinner tomorrow. The S/C Rev. good amount of goodstuffs for demobilization left the Battalion this day, proceeding to Corps base at Pont de Commineu for demobilization to Britain.	A/S
—do—	25/12/18		Extra Xmas Campagnat Service. A quiet 24 hours in the area. A fine day. Cold & bright. Morning O/C visited men of HQrs B & D Coys at Dinner hour. All Ranks had a successful Xmas day. Another party of O/Ranks left the Battalion for demobilization. Sick N.I.L.	A/S
—do—	26/12/18		A quiet 24 hours in the area. Festivities— A fine day. Cold & bright. A party of 8 HQ seniors, Men left Battalion for demobilization. N.C.Os visited dinner of C Coy & A Coy. B Coy more the HERON to LADVIR during forenoon. Strength of the Coy 7x12 Other Ranks.	A/S
—do—	27/12/18		A quiet 24 hours in the area. No further casualties. Sick N.I.L. A fine day. Cold & bright. Rain Winds during the night. A quiet 24 hours in the area. O.C. visited Coys visited the HQrs during forenoon. Coys Carried out cleaning up during day.	A/S
—do—	28/12/18		A holiday. Wind & Rain throughout this day. C.O. visited Companies HQrs during afternoon. Companies carried out indoor training. A quiet 24 hours in the area. Sick N.I.L. Casualties N.I.L.	A/S

WAR DIARY OF 1ST BATTN. MACHINE GUN CORPS

INTELLIGENCE SUMMARY

for Month of DECEMBER 1918

Army Form C. 2118.

Place	Date	Hour	Summary of Events and Information	Remarks and references to Appendices
Couruvil	29/12/18		A cold, windy day. Rain throughout the day. Companies resumed training. A quiet 24 hours in the area. Scott Nos. to available RRs. Strengths of Battalion 40 Offrs 748 ORs.	WT
—do—	30/12/18		No change in the weather. Orders received to complete demobilization of Cradesmen to be sent to concentration camp by 31st Dec. Imperial M.G. Units (Army Sv. Regg) instead Personnel Foreman Sick & Conv. at work. 20 O.Rs left Bn for Dunferries Station & quiet 24 hours in the area. Sick 1 Offr 33 OR Dunferries accidents injuries & pers from this front.	W
—do—	31/12/18		A fine day, inclined to Rain. Companies carried out training during the day. Bn Team of 19th Mx Regt at Rugby football during the afternoon. Results drawn. A quiet 24 hours in the area. Sick Capt Lovering & Lay to C.C.S. Cramelles Nm. Strength of Battalion 45 Offrs 768 Other Ranks. Resumé for December 1918. The weather has been unsettled. Rains were carried out under very trying climatic conditions. Very little chance of getting down to work owing to the changing of area & settling down. Stats of health of the battalion has been very satisfactory. On the whole a very quiet period.	M

31-12-18.

E. W. Tate Lt Col.

Comdg 1st & 2nd Bn M.S. Corps

41st Battalion Machine Gun Corps

War Diary

For the Month Ending

January 31st 1919

41st BATTALION.
MACHINE GUN
CORPS.

WAR DIARY of 41st Batt MACHINE GUN CORPS

INTELLIGENCE SUMMARY

for MONTH of JANUARY 1919.

Army Form C. 2118.

Place	Date	Hour	Summary of Events and Information	Remarks and references to Appendices
COUTHUIN	1/1/19		A fine day. Cold & bright. Companies carried out Training Programmes during forenoon. Sports & Recreation during the afternoon. Parties organised by Coys to visit LIEGE & NAMUR. (It is quiet 24 hours with the area.) Inspection of Baths arranged at 1st an, followed. B/c H.Q Qrs & Spares at TRIEUX. A Coy underwent. Senrs A Coy at ENVOZ. C Coy at COUTHUIN, D Coy at LAVOIR. Further arrangements all connected with Telephones. C-o visited C & B Coys during forenoon, also visited Divisional Strength of Companies on 1st A Coy. (Major R.S. HARRIS/Comdg) 10 Officers 178 other Ranks. B Coy (Major A. HARRISON Comdg) 9 Officers 178 other Ranks. C Coy (Maj A.M. CHALMERS Comdg) 11 Officers D Coy (Major N.F. GADSDON Comdg) 8 Officers 172 other Ranks, Total Strength 44 offs 768 O.Rs. SickHis. Bronchitis Nm. A quiet 24 hours in the area.	
-do-	2/1/19		A fine day, except for occasional showers of rain. C.O. & party from B.Hd attended lectures on Wild Animal life during the afternoon. Training resumed by Companies. Meeting of Representatives for the forming of a Battalion Concert Troupe. Discussion steps for formation of a Good Rugby Team undertaken. Plenty of material at present rather crude & unrefined. Sick. Nic Bronchitis Nm. A quiet 24 hours in the area.	
-do-	3/1/19		A fine day. L.O. visited Division during forenoon. Leapt. Krango departed to Special leads to U.K. Companies Resumed Training during to the continues difficulty in obtaining boots for the battalion is in a condition that utterly forbids unnecessary walking or Route Marching by the men. Courses arranged with Artillery & Div Train to Farm men so drivers to replace those leaving 2 Officers 38 Other Ranks joined Battn from 10th Reception Camp which arrived at HUY from COURTRAI this day Head Qrs played B Coy at football. A very good & exciting game, Orders received for release of Students & Teachers who see education one for the Post Prelum Army. A quiet & normal 24 hours in the area. Sick I.O.R. to field Ambulance. Bronchitis Nm. Capt G. is Lovering D-Coy to C.C.S. Was obey / March off Kruger	

WAR DIARY of 41ST BN MACHINE GUN CORPS

INTELLIGENCE SUMMARY

for Month of JANUARY 1919.

Army Form C. 2118.

Place	Date	Hour	Summary of Events and Information	Remarks and references to Appendices
COUTHUIN	4/1/19		A fine day, although there is steady falling, down to 28. It very unusual. Rugby match with 19 M.G. Regt cancelled. Warning orders were received moved to Camp. 2 offs + 38 O.Rs reported Bn from Reception Camp. arriving at 11th Qrs at 1am. Coys allotted to Bns for operations as follows. A Coy to 12 R. Bn 13 Coy. to 15/22 Bn, 5c Coy to 12/23 Bn. C Coy to 15/14 Bn. 6 Co as Reserve. to Coys orders to collect a dump of 19 German M. Gs from the Chateau. HUGGORYNE. abandoned by the enemy. Coys resumed Training during the forenoon, sports during the afternoon. Sick N. 6 Casualties N. Strength of Bn 45 offs 779 O.Rs. During the forenoon, sports during the afternoon of Bn was carried out by Board M&S Committee	MR
COUTHUIN	5/1/19		A dull day, inclined to Rain. C.O. visits Battalion during the forenoon. Parts of 5 O.Rs left for 11th & 12th Army Schools of Instruction. Parts of 6 R. for Demobilisation. (5) left the Battalion. Orders Received from the Q.R.S the WORLD. 12 R.M. Note awarded the D.S.O. London Gazette 1-1-19. Coys resumed Training. A quiet 24 hours and still no RSM.	MR
COUTHUIN	6/1/19		A fine day, very cold wind. Sunny & bright. Another party of O. Rs left Battn re 10 time serving soldiers under Col Loving of 2 years & over to complete. Lt CRUICKSHANK departed for Cologne to take Charge (6) of Repatriated Prisoners of War. Conference resumed Training. A very quiet 24 hours with the arms. Sick N. 2 O.Rs to Field W. Casualties nil. Demobilisation Reception Camp N. Huy. Disposition of Battn as for 15th January 1919.	MR
COUTHUIN	7/1/19		A very fine day. Bright + lovely quite warm. C.O. visited Divisions at VILAMONT in connection with more Bombing, Rodman Training Competition in conduct of A & D Coys during forenoon of School, August 2nd Runs in this area. Still a great difficulty in obtaining Boots for Coys & Wartshirts. Cigars had war in this week the usual weekly issue of tobacco & cigarette failed. 2 Officer + 13 other Ranks joined Bn from Base Depot (Lieut Stevenson & 2/Lt REFKSD). Slight alteration made in war programme, this day. Sick Nil. Casualties Nil. A very quiet 24 hours in this area. Orders through off strength no: of Canadian Ordinance whom are returning in Cologne Bridge – Accession to C.C.S. Strength of Battalion 48 officers 764 other Ranks. Inspection of Battalion as heretofore, Canadians proceeding very slowly just on present. A great shortage of Transport Drivers – the Battalion the effect of which is also b felt.	MR

WAR DIARY of N[o] 12 BATT[n] MACHINE GUN CORPS
or INTELLIGENCE SUMMARY

(Erase heading not required.)

Army Form C. 2118.

For Month of JANUARY 1919.

Place	Date	Hour	Summary of Events and Information	Remarks and references to Appendices
COUTHUIN	8/1/19		A fine day. Mild & Foggy. Companies resumed Training. Stores, Sports & Recreation during afternoon. C.O. visited Wireman during forenoon & afternoon. O very quiet 2nd hand in this arrival. S.n.R. 2. O.Rs to F.A. Casualties Nil. Received (B) Coy Football Match – Coy Reveille Result B 4 – C 1 goal.	Nil
COUTHUIN	9/1/19		A cold, windy day. Rain at intervals during this day. C.O. departed at 8am for COLOGNE to take over from 1st Canadian Division. 2i/c in Command. 2½ Ardennes during the forenoon to draw Battalion Pay for Current day moved to Corps dump. Removed. 3 Column & 1 hand sensal men left Batt[n] for demobilization & imprisoned with a training during the day. Recreation carried out during the afternoon. Sick Nil. Casualties Nil. Very few ≥ hours in this area. Preparations made for Moving.	Nil
COUTHUIN	10/1/19		A fine day. Very cold but bright. Companies Resumed Training. Ridge 4 in Morning & Sports left for Concentration Camp during forenoon under Command of Capt Hindley. Very heavy at Ris H.L. Quarters Moved ½ Entraining Jan 11th. Sick Nil. Casualties Nil. A quiet sun in this area. Preparations made for Entraining.	Nil
COUTHUIN	11/1/19		A fine forenoon. Rain during the afternoon. Heavy snowfall tonight. Personnel for No. Coys A & C Coys proceeded by Route March to HUY & there entrained for GERMANY. Troop Train N[o] H2 at 13.30 hours arrived at 12.0m H.L. Guns. Transport proceeded to ARDENNE by Route March & entrained for GERMANY. Train leaving at 13.30 hours. 32 hunks belonging to A Coy were left at HUY Station as they could not be got on to the train. B & D Coy (A, S.J.C. Coy & Gr H.L. Gun) reached this GERMAN-BELGIAN frontier at 9.30 hours, at a place named HERBESTHAL. Drinks were exchanged. Belgian for Boche & after a wait of 2 hours the train left for COLOGNE. A quiet uneventful journey throughout this night. Sick Nil. Casualties Nil.	Nil
EN ROUTE COLOGNE	12/1/19		A fine day. Mild & Foggy. Troop Train No. 174 with B & D departments at HOFFNUNGSTHAL at 10 hours, Corps da-trained & marched to their respective Billeting areas. B Coy (attached to 122 Bde) to MENZLINGEN, D Coy (attached to 123 Bde) to WAHLSCHEID, N[o] 181 train with N[o] H.Q. Coy. A & C Coy & moves of Coy GR EISEL for at 6.30 hours at the Personnel of Double Coys & C Coys detrained & proceeded to ENSIN & PORZ respectively, N[o] Train Arrived at HOFFNUNGSTHAL at 11 hours, Remainder detrained & proceeded to ENSIN & PORZ. On arrival at ENSIN, it was noticed to march Bn H.Q. Coy to MARIENBURG & COLOGNE. Move completed at 17 hours. Sick Nil. Casualties Nil. Reached strength of Bn. 44 officers 750 other Ranks.	Nil

D. D. & L., London, E.C.
Wt. W4745/1253 750,000 4/17 Sch. 52 Forms/C2./614

Army Form C. 2118.

WAR DIARY of 1st BATTALION
or MACHINE GUN CORPS
INTELLIGENCE SUMMARY.

(Erase heading not required.)

for Month of JANUARY 1919

Place	Date	Hour	Summary of Events and Information	Remarks and references to Appendices
COLOGNE	13/1/19		A very fine day, except for slight rain during Sunday. Remainder of Battalion settled down in Billets during the MARIENBURG Infantry Barracks. A Coy (with 12 in Pdr.) at IMMENTEPPED, B Coy (with 123 Pdr.) at MENZINGEN, D Coy (with 193 Pdr.) at WAHNSCHIED, C Coy (unattached) at PORTZ. Short transport in Barracks with 1st Divn. C.O. visited Divisional H.Q. at ZOLA LAGER during the afternoon. A quiet 24 hours in the area. Movement of inhabitants quiet and respectful. Section in Casualties Nil.	
-do-	14/1/19		A very fine day, mild & bright. C.O. visited C Coy during the forenoon. Arrangements made for supplying of Companies & administered Instructing rounds. Lt. Hanson & Coy to head C. Many children in the city. A quiet & normal 24 hours in the Area. Section in Casualties Nil. Reports received from Companies of things a/c to C.H.Q. Reported no Billeted comfortably & good. Several men demobilized which are to be replaced.	
-do-	15/1/19		A fine day. Mild & dry. C.O. visited Battn during the forenoon, no issues to be found. 12 re N.C.O.s are Commander. Jan Battn Tickets for Relief's which is got at of Head Major T. Martin M.C. assumed command of Battalion vice Lt. Col. A.B. Todd to leave U.K. A quiet 24 hours in the area. Sect 25 & A Cashes Nr. Nl.	
-do-	16/1/19		A fine day. Mild & dry. Despatch (No. 1 3 O.Rs who were granted Crown in Germany (French) arrived terminated Relain duty for Major afternoon & Several O.R's arrived Concentration Camp at Bonn not yet received clear the Conference of Coy Commander at Bn HQ during the afternoon Several O.R's Elected present officer arrived. parade on 20 pers of Bank men received for the Battalion at 2 years 2 hours down in the afternoon, consisted of Officers and from the afternoon a strength of 1 Officer (Lt R.M.D.) & 70 Privates & been demobilized to Coy some day. Such M. Casualties Nil. Major N F S HORSON arrived Belgian Cross du ... etc.	
-do-	17/1/19		A fine day. Mild & dry. Company arranged Training on the New afternoon Limited General Sports. Supply of Boots began to arrive for the Battalion. But the Condition Nor. C Coys 24 hours in the area.	

WAR DIARY of 41st BATTALION MACHINE GUN CORPS

Army Form C. 2118.

INTELLIGENCE SUMMARY

(Erase heading not required.)

for JANUARY 1919

Place	Date	Hour	Summary of Events and Information	Remarks and references to Appendices
COLOGNE	18/1/19		A fine forenoon, mild. Slight rain during the evening. Major Chatwood K.O.H. over Duties of Tanks M.A.S. & Porz. Companies resumed training in this area. Lectures, Supplies & Clothing & Boots beginning to arrive. A quiet 24 hours in the area. Batt. Hm. Casualties Nil. Strength of Batt. 45 offrs 819 O.R. P.C.K.	—
—do—	19/1/19		A fine day, rather dull. Election day in Cologne. No excitement. Voluntary Parties Leave to Brussels, 1st leave held during the forenoon. S.& K.N. Casualties Nil. A very quiet 24 hours in the area. C.O here during the forenoon.	—
—do—	20/1/19		A fine day, very mild. Companies resumed Training. Recreation during the afternoon. A quiet 24 hours in the area while Batt. Hm. Casualties Nil. Strength of Batt. 45 offrs 865 O.R.	—
—do—	21/1/19		A fine day. Mild & Bright. Lieut J.E. Regrave Reported from Leave to U.K. A heavy day in Br. Officers Companies Resumed Training. A quiet 24 hours in the area. Casualties Nil. Sick Nil.	—
—do—	22/1/19		A fine day, very cold. Slight frost. Companies resumed Training. Capt Ridley C Coy & Lieut U.K. A very quiet 24 hours in the area. Sick Nil. Casualties Nil.	—
—do—	23/1/19		A cold day. Snow fell during the afternoon. At West 15 Fixed Cashiers to draw Batts. Pay in forenoon. Companies Resumed Training. C.O. visited C Coy at Porz during the afternoon. A ferry P.O.A. Quiet 24 hours in the area. Casualties Nil. Sick Nil. Coy officers & Possible Otr. S. Arms Coys Pay. Strength of Batt. 45 offrs 820 Orks. Ranks. Disposition of Batts. as per list. Re: no change.	—
—do—	24/1/19		A fine day, cold & bright. Companies resumed Training. 15 Cot. Brown 12 E Surrey Regt Visited Batt. during the afternoon. A quiet 24 hours in the line. Sick 2 O.R. Casualties Nil.	—
—do—	25/1/19		A fine day, cold snow fell on the Rhine during the forenoon. Companies Resumed Training. Lieutenant H Sick Nm. Casualties Nm. Strength 45 offrs 808 Other Ranks of 2 Reserves for Demobilisation. 2 pm – more Order received for C Coy to Move to Kalk. A quiet 24 hours in the Area. Disposition of Camp & its Headquarters.	—

Army Form C. 2118.

WAR DIARY of 141st BATTn MACHINE GUN CORPS.

INTELLIGENCE SUMMARY.

(Erase heading not required.)

for Month of JANUARY 1919.

Instructions regarding War Diaries and Intelligence Summaries are contained in F. S. Regs., Part II. and the Staff Manual respectively. Title pages will be prepared in manuscript.

Place	Date	Hour	Summary of Events and Information	Remarks and references to Appendices
COLOGNE	26/1/19		A fine day, very cold & bright. Companies voluntary Physical Drill & Games during forenoon. Recreation during afternoon. Preparation for the go to Belgium. E Coy recommenced Italian and Malta reservists men to all areas 24 hours notice. The subject to new area live wire from Ghent to U.K. but no orders yet received up to present & no notification as to extension of leave or demobilisation. Sick Nil. Casualties Nil. O.C. P.M., Q.M. & R.O. visited E Coy. A very quiet 24 hours. Heavy falling snow during the night.	JMc
—do—	27/1/19		A cold day. Snow fell all throughout the day. Notification received extending leave to the Regulars for Demobilisation. Fresh attributes for Demobilisation received from Division. O.C. Coy visited Provost M. 2 O.Rs left for Demobilisation during the forenoon. A quiet 24 hours in the area. Sick 1 O.R. (2 has returned to Duty 10 O.Rs Casualties Nil.	JMc
—do—	28/1/19		A cold day, snow fell at intervals throughout the day. E Coy moves from Porz to Kalk during forenoon. O.C. & 2 M.G.O. & 16 O.Rs left the Batt. for Demobilisation. Chests Wallises & Rugging Warning order ready for move to C Coy to Deutz. Received A & B Coy received training & Reconnaissance of area. Sick Nil. Casualties Nil. A quiet 24 hours in the area.	JMc
—do—	29/1/19		A mild day, bright. A party of 2 Officers (Lt Steven and Lt Br Mc. Pherson) & 45 other Ranks left the Batt for Demobilisation. Remained training. Lt Potter took over the duties of Q.M. vice Lt Mc. Pherson. Sick Nil. Casualties Nil. A very quiet 24 hours in the area.	JMc
—do—	30/1/19		A fine day, cold & bright. Orders received for preparation of everything for demobilisation. Expeditious reservists and heavy and remainder duties of Adjutant. Conference. Resumed Training. A quiet 24 hours in the area. Sick 1 O.R. Casualties Nil.	JMc
—do—	31/1/19		A fine day. Companies recommenced training. D Coy moves from Mauslied to Deutz during forenoon. Adjutant 2 LT. knows the area. Sick Nil. Casualties Nil. Strength of Batt. 40 Officers 773 Other Ranks. Composition of Battalion as follows Batt. Hd.Qrs. MARIENBURG, COLOGNE, A Coy IMMEKEPPEL, B Coy MUNZTHAUSEN, C Coy KALK D Coy DEUTZ	JMc

In the field 31-1-19.

[signed] Commanding 141st M.G. Bn. M.G. Corps.

41st Bn. H.G.C.
A.507.

To: O.C. "A" Company.
       "B"   "
       "C"   "
       "D"   "
Quartermaster.
Medical Officer.
R.S.M.
H.Q. Transport Sergt.
Signalling Sergt.

MARCHING ORDER.

    41st Division will relieve a Canadian Division at the COLOGNE Bridgehead.

    The Division will move to COLOGNE by Strategical Trains commencing 6th instant.

    Order of move, 124th Inf. Bde., 122nd Inf. Bde., 123rd Inf. Bde., one Brigade per diem. Date of move of Battalion Headquarters not yet known. Advanced parties of all Companies to be held in readiness.

    Companies will be attached to Brigades as follows, unless otherwise ordered.

        122nd Inf. Bde.   "B" Company.

        123rd "   "   "D"   "

        124th "   "   "A"   "

"C" Company will move with Headquarters Group.

ACKNOWLEDGE.

Issued at 11.00 hours.   Lieut.-Colonel.
4th January, 1919.   Commanding 41st Battn. M.G.C.

Copies to:

        Copy No. 1. 41st Division "G".
                2.   do.   "Q".
                3. 122nd Infantry Brigade.
                4. 123rd Infantry Brigade.
                5. 124th Infantry Brigade.
                6. War Diary.
                7. File.
                8. Spare.

41st Bn. M.G.C.
A.347.

To: O.C. "A" Company.
    "   "B"   "
    "   "C"   "
    "   "D"   "
    Quartermaster.
    Medical Officer.
    R.S.M.
    H.Q. Transport Sergt.
    Signalling Sergt.

WARNING ORDER.

41st Division will relieve a Canadian Division at the COLOGNE Bridgehead.

The Division will move to COLOGNE by Strategical Trains commencing 6th instant.

Order of move, 124th Inf. Bde., 122nd Inf. Bde., 123rd Inf. Bde., one Brigade per diem. Date of move of Battalion Headquarters not yet known. Advanced parties of all Companies to be held in readiness.

Companies will be attached to Brigades as follows, unless otherwise ordered.

    122nd Inf. Bde.   "B" Company.
    123rd "   "   "D"   "
    124th "   "   "A"   "

"C" Company will move with Headquarters Group.

ACKNOWLEDGE.

Issued at 11.00 hours.   Lieut.-Colonel.
4th January, 1919.   Commanding 41st Battn. M.G.C.

Copies to:
        Copy No. 1. 41st Division "G".
             2.   do.   "Q".
             3. 122nd Infantry Brigade.
             4. 123rd Infantry Brigade.
             5. 124th Infantry Brigade.
             6. War Diary.
             7. File.
             8. Spare.

SECRET.

41st Battalion Machine Gun Corps Administrative Instruction No. 1.

1. The Division will entrain for Germany in accordance with attached Schedule (A).
   Trains will be Strategical Trains composed of -

   1 Officers Coach.
   52 Covers. (Each truck is registered to carry 50 men but trains have been arranged at about 40 men per truck).

   15 Flats.

   Baggage and Supply Wagons will travel loaded with Units reporting to Units by 4.0 p.m. the day before entrainment.

2. Transport will be at the Station three hours, and personnel one hour before scheduled time of departure of train. As the Canadian Division will be detraining from the same trains, care must be taken to leave approaches to trains clear.
   No loading will be commenced until the Canadian Units are clear of the train and approaches, and the trucks cleaned out.

3. Entrainment will be supervised by the D.A.Q.M.G.
   Detrainment will be supervised by the A/D.A.A.G.
   Each Brigade, the R.A., and 19th Middlesex (for other units) will appoint Entraining and Detraining Officers who will be responsible for the entraining and detraining of all units of their Brigade or Group.

4. Before arriving at Detraining Station, Os.C. all trains will tell off a party of 2 Officers and 50 O.Rs to detrain vehicles. Detrainment will not commence until R.T.O. or Detraining Officer has been consulted.

5. SUPPLIES.
   Units will entrain with unexpired portion of the days rations plus one days rations on the man. Supply Wagons will contain a further days rations.

   Water Carts will be filled before entrainment.

   On arrival in New Area, Units will draw rations from 1st Canadian Divisional Train until 41st Divisional Train arrives.

   Railhead in new area will be ROSRATH.

   6/EXTRA TRANSPORT.

6. **EXTRA TRANSPORT.**

The following lorries will report to Battalion at 8.0 a.m. on the day they entrain to carry surplus baggage, Blankets, etc. to entraining station :-

    Machine Gun Battalion.   2 lorries.

7. In both this and the 1st Canadian Divisional Area, the nearest Field Ambulance of either Division will accept sick and casualties until reliefs are completed. Canadian Field Ambulances are situated as follows :-

    No. 1 Canadian Field Ambulance.   WAHN.
    No. 2   do.   URBACH.
    No. 3   do.   COLNVINSST.

7. Mobile Veterinary Sections in either area will accept sick horses of either formation until the relief is complete.

8. 41st Divisional M.T. Company will move by road under arrangements to be notified later. Until the arrival of 41st Divisional M.T. Company in Canadian Divisional Area, the 1st Canadian Division will assist units on arrival with mechanical transport, and 41st M.T. Company will assist Canadian Units arriving. The necessary arrangements will be made between Detraining Officers and Divisional Headquarters "Q".

9. **DIVISIONAL RECEPTION CAMP.**

Divisional Reception Camp will remain at HUY until further orders, but any personnel arriving at HUY will be despatched as early as possible to COLOGNE Area.

10. **BATHS.**

All Baths will close down on 9th instant and re-open as early as possible on arrival in new areas.
Baths Officer will be at WAHN.

11. **CANTEEN.**

Divisional Canteen will close on 9th instant and re-open on 15th instant in the new area at WAHN.

12. Instructions re Advance Parties are being issued separately.

13. ACKNOWLEDGE.

January 5th 1919.

Lieut.-Colonel.
Commanding 41st Battn, M.G.Corps.

Distribution :-

```
O.C. "A" Coy. 41st Battn. M.G.Corps.
 "   "B"  "              do.
 "   "C"  "              do.
 "   "D"  "              do.
Quartermaster.           do.
Medical Officer.         do.
R.S.M.                   do.
H.Q. Transport Sergt.    do.
Signalling Sergt.        do.
41st Division "Q".
War Diary.
File.
Spare.
```

==*

PROGRAMME FOR ENTRAINMENT OF 41st BATTALION MACHINE GUN CORPS.

Scheduled time of departure of trains will be advised by wire as received.

Date.	Train No.	Entraining Station ANDENNE. Units.	Train No.	Entraining Station HUY. Units.
Jan. 11th.	17.	H.Q., M.G. Battalion. "A" Company, M.G.Battalion. "B" " " "	18.	"C" Company, M.G.Battalion. "D" " " "

Possible Detraining Stations:- HOFFNUNGSTHAL. COLOGNE - EISELTOR. BENSBERG.

Others to be notified later.

Composition of remaining trains will be notified later.

==*=*=*

To: O.C. "A" Company.
    "B"   "
    "C"   "
    "D"   "
    Quartermaster.
    R.S.M.
    Signalling Sergt.
    H.Q. Transport Sergt.

A.422.

Wallet

1. All S.A.A. not in belts will be dumped at the Quartermaster's Stores by mid-day on the 10th instant, and a receipt obtained from the Quartermaster, who will report the total amount to this office by 6 p.m. on the 10th.

    "B" Company will provide a guard from 7 a.m. on the 11th instant, who will remain until relieved by the Canadians, and will then proceed by next train to TROISDORF Station.

2. From January 7th inclusive, Supply Wagons of Units will join their Units at the Entraining Station three hours before departure of the train, and not the day previous.

3. All Companies will send Advance Parties, consisting of one Officer and three Other ranks by the train which leaves HUY at 11.40 hours on the 8th. Battalion Headquarters will send Sergeant Mount and two Other ranks. On arrival, advance parties will report to A/D.A.A.G. HOFFNUNGSTHAL STATION for instructions.

4. On arrival at Detraining Station, Companies will immediately proceed by march route to their ultimate destinations.

    Battalion Headquarters.   ENSEN.
    "A" Company.   IHME - KEPPEL.
    "B"   "   MENZLINGEN.
    "C"   "   PORZ.
    "D"   "   WAHLSCHEID.

                                            Lieut.-Colonel.
                                Commanding 41st Battn. M.G.Corps.

7th January, 1919.

To: O.C. "A" Company.
　　　　"B"　　　"
　　　　"C"　　　"
　　　　"D"　　　"
　　　Quartermaster.

Reference move to Germany, the following will be the allotment of Transport for each train.

1.- 　　No. 17 Train.　　　　　　　　　　　　No. 18 Train.

"B" Company.　　　　30 axles.　　　"A" Company.　　　　29 axles.
"D"　"　　　　　　　29　"　　　　　"C"　"　　　　　　 29　"
　　　　　　　　　　　　　　　　　　1 Supply Wagon.　　　2　"
2 Supply Wagons.　　 4　"　　　　　1 Baggage Wagon.　　　2　"
1 Baggage Wagon.　　 2　"　　　　　1 H.Q. Mess Cart.　　 1 axle.
1 H.Q. Water Cart.　 1 axle.　　　 1　"　Maltese Cart.　 1　"
1 H.Q. G.S. Wagon.　 2 axles.　　　2　"　G.S. Limbers.　 4 axles.
　　　　　　　　　　　　　　　　　　1 Italian Cart.　　　 1 axle.

　　　Total.　　　　68 axles.　　　　　　　Total.　　　　69 axles.

2.-　　Proportion of Headquarters Transport will move off with Company Transport of "B" Company, and proportion with "C" Company.
　　　Headquarters Transport Sergeant will ensure that they report to Transport Officers of their respective groups in sufficient time to join their columns.
　　　Sergeant Sherwood will be with No. 18 train.

3.-　　Battalion Headquarters personnel will parade at 12.00 hours and will march to HUY Station under the command of R.S.M.
　　　Dress for Headquarters, valises containing great coats.

4.-　　Commands.

　　　Major N. F. GADSDON will be O.C. No. 17 Train.
　　　Major A. McD. CHALMERS, M.C. will be O.C. No. 18 Train.

5.-　　Beyond the ordinary Transport personnel and brakesmen there should be no need to send parties to entrain vehicles and animals.

　　　　　　　　　　　　　　　　　　　　　　　Major.
10th January, 1919.　　　　　　　　　　　　　 41st Battn. M.G. Corps.

Diary

To: O.C. "A" Company.
　　　 "B"　　"
　　　 "C"　　"
　　　 "D"　　"
Quartermaster.

41st Division "Q" wire received 4 p.m. reads.

Reference Detraining Station.
Trains No. 17 and 18 to HOFFNUNGSTHAL AAA H.Q. and "C" Company personnel detrain COLN EISEL TOR NOT COLN BONN TOR.

　　　　　　　　　　　　　　　　　　　Major.
10-1-1919.　　　　　　　　　　41st Battn. M.G.Corps.

41st Batt Machine Gun Corps. Vol 1.

War Diary

for the Month of

February 1919

Army Form C. 2118.

WAR DIARY of 41st BATTALION MACHINE GUN CORPS

or

INTELLIGENCE SUMMARY.

(Erase heading not required.)

for Month of FEBRUARY 1919.

Instructions regarding War Diaries and Intelligence Summaries are contained in F. S. Regs., Part II. and the Staff Manual respectively. Title pages will be prepared in manuscript.

Place	Date	Hour	Summary of Events and Information	Remarks and references to Appendices
COLOGNE	8/2/19		A fine day. Mild & Bright. Companies Resumed Training. Recreation during the afternoon. C.O. to Board during the afternoon. Sick parade — All officers & Men strength of Battn. 38 offrs 732 other ranks. Inspection of Baths in Winterpohl.	
—do—	9/2/19		A fine day. Mild & Bright. C.O visited during the forenoon. Divine Service during forenoon. Recreation during afternoon. Sick Nil. Casualties Nil. A quiet 24 hours in the area.	
—do—	10/2/19		A fine day. Mild & Bright. Companies Resumed Training. C.O visited Coy's. during forenoon. Sick Nil. Casualties Nil. A quiet 24 hours in the area.	
—do—	11/2/19		A fine day. Mild & Bright. Held Trouble Hours. Companies Resumed Training. C.O visited A & B Coys & H.Q.S. 12–1pm. Recreation afternoon. Sick Nil. Casualties Nil. A quiet 24 hours in the area. Strength of Battn. 37 offrs 732 Other Ranks.	
—do—	12/2/19		A fine day. Mild & Bright. Companies continue to Training. Recreation during afternoon. C.O visited Div. Canteen & R.E. during afternoon. A quiet 24 hours in the area. Sick 1 offr. 1 other rank. Inspection of 10th and 18th R.W.	
—do—	13/2/19		A fine day. Good Weather continues. Companies Resumed Training. A quiet 24 hours in the area. C. visited Divisional Area during forenoon.	
—do—	14/2/19		A fine day. Good Weather continues. Companies Resumed Training. A quiet 24 hours. Sick Nil. Casualties Nil. Capt Cruikshank M.O Reported for Duty from Detachment.	
—do—	15/2/19		A fine day. Good Weather continues. Mild. Companies Resumed Training. C, O & C visited all day during the day. Sick Nil Casualties Nil. A quiet 24 hours in the area.	
—do—	16/2/19		A fine day. Mild & Bull. Companies attended Divine Service during forenoon. C.O visited 122 Bde with intention of Recreation area during forenoon. Sick Nil Casualties Nil. Strength of Bn. 37 offrs 732 OR. A quiet 24 hours in the area.	

Army Form C. 2118.

WAR DIARY of 41st BATTN
or
INTELLIGENCE SUMMARY. MACHINE GUN CORPS

1st Month of FEBRUARY 1919

(Erase heading not required.)

Instructions regarding War Diaries and Intelligence Summaries are contained in F. S. Regs., Part II. and the Staff Manual respectively. Title pages will be prepared in manuscript.

Place	Date	Hour	Summary of Events and Information	Remarks and references to Appendices
Conroyé	1/2/19		A fine day. Cold at night. Troops came Recreation Training & Reconnaissance of areas. A very quiet 24 hours in the area. Sick Nil. Casualties Nil. Q Party of 18 other Ranks left Bn. Details during the forenoon. Major Backett & Harvey Ridge B. Rifle Regt on 152 Divn et cetera Inspections of Battn. Phi Nil. Qr MARTEAVO Convoys A Coy IMMEUPER (3 days RAMBERCOU C Coy KAIN, B Coy DEUTZ. Strength of Battn. 40 officers 446 other Ranks	MH
- do -	2/2/19		A fine day. Held Church Parade. Companies Resumed Training & Reconnaissance & Areas. Capt W. Thorpe assumed Command of B Coy and Major Attenborough Rifle Brigade Part of 2 Mar (Major Name Illeg.) D20 other Ranks left for demobilization. Sick Nil. Casualties Nil. A quiet 24 hours in the area.	MH
- do -	3/2/19		A fine day. Very cold at night. Companies Resumed Training. A quiet 24 hours in the area. Capt. Officer Hoeitch. C & A Coy in communication with R.E. at Telephone Communication Sect. Strength of Battalion (35 officers 630 other Ranks actually present).	MH
- do -	4/2/19		A cold day. Snow fell strongly part of the day. Lt Col AWG also arrived from leave & tre wounds Command of the Battalion being forwarded. Companies Resumed Training. Sick Nil Casualties Nil. A quiet 24 hours in the area.	MH
- do -	5/2/19		A fine day. Mild. A Bugle Party of 8 O.R. Proceeded to Concentration Camp for Demobilization. Batman. Resumed Training. A quiet 24 hours. War. (W.O./1/2/11 & Thomas joined Battn for BCCC. C.O. attended a Conference as to R.I. Nil Gr during the forenoon. Sick Nil Casualties Nil.	MH
- do -	6/2/19		A fine day. Mild & Bright. Parties of 5 Ors Proceeded to Demobilization Camp for Demobilization. 680 Officers. Em Nil. Qr during the forenoon. Sick Nil. Casualties Nil. A quiet 24 hours the Battn Strength of Battn. 36 officers 735 other Ranks.	MH
- do -	7/2/19		A fine day. Warm & Bright. Demobilization of Battn Temporarily Ceased owing down to Manoeuvres Training & Recreation. C.O.t Adjutant visited all Companies during the day Companies Resumed Training & Recreation. Sick Nil. Casualties Nil. A quiet 24 hours in the area.	MH

WAR DIARY of 41st Bn MACHINE GUN CORPS

Army Form C. 2118.

of

INTELLIGENCE SUMMARY.

(Erase heading not required.)

1st FEBRUARY 1919.

Place	Date	Hour	Summary of Events and Information	Remarks and references to Appendices
COLOGNE	17/2/19		Wet in forenoon. C.O. visits 123 Bde & requests line with G.O.C. D.A.A.G. visits C & D Coys to arrange extra accommodation. 2nd i/c visits Adely Room & runs.	RF
	18/2/19		A fine day. C.O. visits 7th Bde & requests line with G.O.C. 2/c departs for U.K.	RF
	19/2/19		Dull day. C.O. visits left Bde sector requests funct. Dog belongs to the Master despatches to M.V.S. for U.K. Supply officer (Nt i Coy Train) calls at Battn Hq.	RF
	20/2/19		C.O. visits 123 Bde & reconnoitres line with G.O.C. Half of O.R.s arrive and are billeted. Corps a quiet day. 1st draft takes over improved.	RF
	21/2/19		Tuesday. C.O. visits Division & repeats Hq billets at Barracks also Transport. Wet. Battalion play 1st round in Soccer Tournament v 19 Middlesex Regt. win 3-0 M.C. Coys ground.	RF
	22/2/19		Naval parades also training carried out in morning by Coys. Fine a quiet day. Divine Service at Barracks MARIENBURG 09.30 hrs	RF
	23/2/19		Fine day. Usual training carried out & the Corps continue reconnoitring lines & fortifications.	RF
	24/2/19		Fine day. D.A.A. & Q visits D Coy & fix up billets. Return to review area. C.O. attached 18 O.R.s. to work to re-enlist. M.O. Rees inspects.	RF
	25/2/19		Fine day CO proceeds with OC A Coy morning line. OC Div'l HT.M. proceeds to RATH- NEUHAR unsuccessful.	RF
	26/2/19		Fine day CO & Adjt move from DEUTZ to RATH-NEUHAR unsuccessful. D Coy returns.	
	27/2/19		Showery day. C.O. interviews with Divisional Commander OC 1st Inf Bde 503 of Batt'n. On 7th Feb at HQ & explain scheme & meet/instructors.	RF
	28/2/19		Showery Commands 5 O.R.s 123 Bde sector plus line work Divisional Commander 26/2/19 717 O.R.s	RF

LIEUT. COL
41st BATTALION
MACHINE GUN CORPS

41st Battalion
Machine Gun Corps.
War Diary
for the Month of
March 1919

To H.Q. London Division

41st BATTALION,
MACHINE GUN
CORPS.
No. A/3.3.8
Date 2/4/19

WAR DIARY
or
INTELLIGENCE SUMMARY

Army Form C. 2118.

41st Battn M.G.C.

MARCH 1919

(Erase heading not required.)

Place	Date	Hour	Summary of Events and Information	Remarks and references to Appendices
COLOGNE	1/3/19		A fine day. Coys carry out training. C.O. visits D.I.T.Hq. Summer time commences at midnight. Aldrock hut available from 23.00 hrs. M.O. hears weekly material inspection of Batt. Hq.	Kf.
	2/3/19		A fine day. C.O.t.S.r. Divine service at Barracks 09.30 hrs.	Kf.
	3/3/19		Meeting held at runs of coms of Batt. Canteen. S/Sgt Troeung's found to be an officer from each Coy per cent - Applnt G. Harris, it slade proceeds on leave.	
	4/3/19		Very wet. C.O. visits 123 Bde & goes over section with Bde Major. Coy's woke up after rifle ranges & carry on training.	Kf.
	5/3/19		C.O. & Q.M. visit all Coy's kindest. Kensafert.Co, C.O. hears case for Orderly Room at Coy Hqs.	
	6/3/19		Wet. C.O. visits A.M.G.O. Div.H.q. Duty H.q. Officers play soccer match v Cavalry Div. at Bonn & lose 6-0.	Kf.
	7/3/19		C.O. visits G.O.C. 10 o'rs & goes o'rs 123 Bde - central sector of line. Strength of Batt. actual present 30 officers 629 O.R.	
	8/3/19		C.O. visits B Coy & Judges Gun Team Competition run from out of each Coy - won by N°2 section. C.O. calls at D Coy.	Kf.
	9/3/19		Fine. Major Grierson arrives this afternoon to take over command of Batta from C.O. who proceeds on leave to PARIS tomorrow.	
	10/3/19		Dull. Major Grierson attends D.O.C. Conference at Div.Hq. at 10 o'hrs. C.O. attd. training.	
	11/3/19		Fine day. C.O. visits 123 Bde sector.	
	12/3/19		Fine. 1 OR repatriated from 11th Batta. C.O. attd. 1 OR 2 were ORs rehouses for 1 year.	Kf.

WAR DIARY or INTELLIGENCE SUMMARY.

Army Form C. 2118.

4/ Bn M.T.G.C. (London Division)

MARCH 1919.

Place	Date	Hour	Summary of Events and Information	Remarks and references to Appendices
COLOGNE	13/3/19		C.O. and Adjutant visit all Coys. C.O. allocates 1 Cpl & 40 O.R.s to Pte. Stacey R.l Battalion officers 35 and 70 O.R.s. a Thursday Coys carry out training of 1 Coy Recruits. Sports meeting in p.m. Capt. Dowling Wilkinson & shoemaker play Rugger for 41 Div.	KT
	14/3/19		Fine. C.O. visits D Coy. After lunch, inter-Coy Soccer matches continue. 41st Div. v. the known in # London Div. from 16 Kings.	KT
	15/3/19		Fine C.O. visits B Coy & goes over gun positions in Deutz etc. Seats Lodges report known to Div.	KT
	16/3/19		Fine. Divine Service in Barracks at 09.30 hrs. Football match in p.m.	
	17/3/19		Showery. Sydney in afternoon. C.O. signs 14 allegations from a finally approved Draft waiting to arrive, notification of arrangements re this cancelled, reinforcements arriving from Strasburg	KT
	18/3/19		C.O. visits 733 Bde & goes over section. 1 Sgt Cook reports for duty from 4th Div	
	19/3/19		Adjutant attends court-martial re Pte Pickering. C.O. visits C Coy in afternoon.	
	20/3/19		Coys despatch advance party draft of arrivals from WHITE CITY COY DEUTZ	
	21/3/19		to go to return from leave (travel). C.O. attends funeral of Major CUNNINGHAM - ADC. to G.O.C. at 11.00 hrs. (full military honours). It's Slade reports from leave (UK).	
	22/3/19		C.O. holds orderly room 09.30. Patients before a/c Coy by Hd Wing on "how many kilos the army fuses Reason" all arranged out of stopes during to strike in UK.	KT
	23/3/19		Lt POTTER leaves Balta 16 stat. for duty in A.P.M. Staff X Corps. M.O. visits C Coy and cinema show by Her butts.	
	24/3/19		Draft of 15 N.C.O.s tour arrive from 8th Batt M.G.C. posts despatches to Corps C.O. O visits	KT

Army Form C. 2118.

WAR DIARY
or
INTELLIGENCE SUMMARY.

(Erase heading not required.)

41st Battn.
M.G. Corps.
MARCH 1919

Place	Date	Hour	Summary of Events and Information	Remarks and references to Appendices
COLOGNE	24/3/19 25/3/19		C Coy & Bn. Qrmstr. arrangements re moving to BENSBERG. 4 Officers (Major TRATT - Lt. FORBMAN - Lt. STOREY - 2/Lt. DUDD[?]N) report from S.R.M.G.C. for duty & are posted to Coys. Col. Jackson A/H.Q.O. Visits H.Qrs. and sees C.O.	N.T.
	26/3/19		C Coy move from KALK to BENSBERG. Completed move at 1300 hrs. Funeral of Cpl CRIPPS at 14.15 hrs. 10.00hrs. C.O. and A/mbulance inspect A-B+D Coys. at 7 pm re Inspection by F.O.C. 0.0.66. sent out to A+T D Coys. re relief on 29th inst.	0.0.66.
	27/3/19		G.O. inspects C+D Coys with Transport at NEUMAR: A Coy at THUM: KEPPEL - Bat. at EIPEN. met C.O. Neill. C Coy at BENSBERG. C Coy sent XP. 30 O.Rs. on fatigue.	N.T.
	28/3/19		Snowing. 50 O.Rs. & Officers (Lt. HOWE & SANGER) Demobilised. 14 Officers report for duty from St. Battn. Care posted to Coys - 4 to A - C+D & 2 to B. B Coy sent 1 Off & 30 O.Rs. on truck hire w/ R.E. use.	N.T.
	29/3/19			N.T.
	30/3/19		Snowing. Col LINDSAY arrived at Battn HQ to take over Battn on 11/1/19 5 O.Rs. (+ drivers) reported for duty from 103 Battn. C.O. & Col LINDSAY visit all Coy's & Brigades. Lt. HODGSON reports at Battn HQ as Assistant Adjutant. Adjutant visits A Coy at NEUMAR 4pm & takes summary of evidence (PETHASTHORN)	N.T.
	31/3/19		Strength of Battn. 48 Officers 501 O.Rs. (present)	N.T.

[Signature] Lieut. Col.
COMMANDING 41st BATTALION
MACHINE GUN CORPS

M.G.C.A/89

To:- Officers Commanding,
    "A" Coy,
    "B" "
    "C" "
    "D" "

    The General Officer Commanding London Division will inspect the 41st Machine Gun Battalion, on Thursday 27th inst.

    Companies will parade with Transport.
Dress :- Drill Order.
Times and locations of parades as under :-

Company.	Location.	Time.
"C" & "D".	HEUMAR. Map ref. COLOGNE. Sheet 4. 1/25000. Area of Ground immediately East of STACHELSHAUSCHEN.	09.30 hours.

Senior Officer present will command parade.

"B".	NEAR BLEIFELD. Map Ref. W. 37.75. OVERATH. 1/25000.	11.15 hours.
"A".	IMMEKEPPEL. Map Ref. OVERATH. 1/25000. F.58.28.	12.15 hours.

    The Divisional Commander will be received with a General Salute.

    Parade States to be at Battalion Headquarters by 08.00 hours, on 27th inst.

25th March 1919.
H.R.W.

Captain and Adjutant,
41st Batt. M.G. Corps.

Copies to:-
    "G" London Div.
    122nd, 123rd & 124th Inf Bdes.
    File.

SECRET.

To:- O's C. "A" Coy,   Quartermaster.
         "B" "   Signalling Officer.
         "C" "
         "D" "

41st BATTALION MACHINE GUN CORPS. O.C. 66.

March 26th 1919.

Reference Maps. Sheets No 2845, and 2846.

(1). On March 28th, the 123rd Infantry Brigade will relieve the 124th Infantry Brigade in the Left Sector of the Divisional Front.

(2). On March 29th, "D" Company, 41st Bn. M.G.C., attached to 123rd Infantry Brigade, will relieve "A" Company, 41st Bn. M.G.C., attached to 124th Infantry Brigade.
   Relief to be completed by 12.00 hours, and reported to Battalion and Brigade Headquarters.   Details of Relief to be arranged between Companies concerned.

(3). Billet and Barrack Stores, e.g. Paillasses, Beds, Tables, Forms, etc., will not be removed, but will be handed over in situ, receipts being given and taken.

(4). Supplies will be delivered to Units under the existing arrangements for delivery of supplies to Units in the various sub-areas.
   Outgoing formations will be careful to explain any special arrangements in force for delivery of supplies by Passenger train.

(4)ᵃ. Lorries for the conveyance of blankets and surplus stores will report as under :-

Date.	No.	To Report at.	Time.
25th Mar.	8 lorries.	H.Qrs, 23rd Middlx. REFRATH.	08.00.
25th "	8 "	H.Qrs, 17th R.Fuslrs. VOLBERG.	After dumping baggage of 23rd Middlx Regt.
28th "	3 "	H.Qrs, 123rd Bde. KALK.	07.00.
28th "	4 "	H.Qrs, 2/4th Queens. KALK.	07.00.
28th "	4 "	H.Qrs, 11th Queens. KALK.	07.00.
28th "	3 "	H.Qrs, 124th Bde. HOFFNUNGSTHAL.	After dumping baggage of 123rd Inf Bde H.Qrs.

/4.Instructions

(4a) Cont'd.

Date.	No.	To Report at.	Time.
28th Mar.	4.Lorries.	H.Qrs, 23rd R.Fuslrs. LINDLAR.	After dumping baggage of 11th Queens.
29th "	4 "	H.Qrs, 26th R.Fuslrs. ENGELSKIRCHEN.	After dumping baggage of 2/4th Queens

(5). All plans of work in hand or proposed, etc., will be handed over on relief.   Defence Scheme
All Guns, Bolt boxes, Stores etc., will be taken with Companies, and not handed over on relief.

(6). Companies will apply direct to their Brigades for any extra transport that may be required

Companies will move by March Route.

(7). From 18.00 hours, March 28th, to 18.00 hours, March 29th, "A" Company, 41st Bn. M.G.C., will be attached to 123rd Infantry Brigade, and "D" Company, 41st Bn. M.G.C., will be attached to 124th Infantry Brigade.

(8). ACKNOWLEDGE.

Lieut-Colonel,
Commanding, 41st Batt. Machine Gun Corps.

Distribution :-   Copies to :-

London Division "G".
"   "   "Q".
"   "   Signal Coy.
122nd Infantry Brigade.
123rd   "   "
124th   "   "
C.R.E.
A.D.M.S.
S.S.O.
War Diary.
File.

41st Battalion Machine Gun Corps

War Diary

For the Month of

April 1919

To: H.Q. London Division

41st BATTALION.
MACHINE GUN
CORPS.

War Diary

O.C.C. A/980

To:- O.C. "A" Coy,   Q.M. 41st Bn.M.G.C.
     "B" "   Signalling Officer, 41st Bn.M.G.C.
     "C" "
     "D" "

WARNING ORDER.

The 123rd Infantry Brigade will relieve the 124th Infantry Brigade in the Left Sector of the Divisional Front on a date to be notified later, probably during the week commencing March 23rd.

This Relief will apply to the Machine Gun Companies attached to the above mentioned Brigades.

21st March 1919.
H.R.W.

Lieut-Colonel,
Commanding,
41st Batt. M.G.C.

Copies to :-

122nd Infantry Brigade   )
123rd   "   "   )
124th   "   "   )
London Division Signal Coy,)   For information.
London Division "G"   )
London Division "Q"   )

WAR DIARY or INTELLIGENCE SUMMARY.

Army Form C. 2118.

(Erase heading not required.)

Place	Date	Hour	Summary of Events and Information	Remarks and references to Appendices
COLOGNE	APRIL 1.		COL. G. M. LINDSAY D.S.O. (D.I.M.G.O. 1st Army) takes over command of the Battalion from LT. COL. A.M. TATE, D.S.O., who becomes 2 i/c in command of the Battalion. All Companies paraded. C.O. & 2 i/c demobilisation.	out out
	2.		C.O. & 2 i/c went "A" Co. in the morning in connection with certain men of the Coy. & demobilisation. LT. E. A. DULLAN, "B" Co. reports to Batt. HQ. for duty as Batt. Accountant.	out
			T/Major F. M. ARKLE reported for duty, and posted to "A" Co. LT. N. D. WEATHERHEAD reported & posted to "B" Co. C.O. & Second in Command sent forward on left Batt. area of Centre Brigade.	out
	3.		C.O. visits II Army L.G. Training (Capt. & Sergt. and) D.I.M.G.O. II Army.	out
	4.		2 Officers 23 O.R. demobilised. (Major GADSDEN & Capt. LINDLEY M.C. "D" Co.) Shenkly/Batt. 49 Officers	out
	5.		7/6 O.R. 2 i/c visited "B" Co. & received Education Scheme and Major Butt. Batt. Education Officer.	out
	6.		C.O. & 2 i/c visited 122 Inf. Brigade in morning & lunched with "D" Co. in connection with Billets	out
			C.O. & 2 i/c visited Batt. lamp, but unsuccessful. Returned round 4th Section of Line of Residence. LT. N. D. WEATHERHEAD "B" Co. reported to take over Batt. R.G. post. Posted also 3 days Instructions for A.C. & D. Companies.	out
	7.		C.O. visits D.I.M.G.O. II Army in morning re depts of Transport, demobilisation etc. C.O. & 2 i/c attend "B" Co. Sports in afternoon. LT. WEATHERHEAD commences training Instructors for Batt. R.G. School.	out
	8.		C.O. & 2 i/c visit "A" Co. in morning. C.O. inspects Company & Billets, and addresses the Company. LT. CRANFIELD reports for duty and takes over unpost "C" Co. at BENSBERG.	out
	9.		C.O. attends Conference at Div. H.Q. LT. F. SMYTH reported for duty and posted to "C" Co. Introduction C.O. & G.H.Q. that the mark of Cosa Ms TATE has been transferred to the new returns for Latex, and that he is	out
	10.		C.O. & 2 i/c visit "B" Co. C.O. inspects Company & addresses all ranks.	out
	11.		Capt./Adjt. R. G. FRAZER demobilised. Duties of Adjutant taken over by LT. C.T. HODGSON. O.C. 2 i/c.	out
	12.		available for immediate demobilisation.	out

Army Form C. 2118.

WAR DIARY
or
INTELLIGENCE SUMMARY.
(Erase heading not required.)

Instructions regarding War Diaries and Intelligence Summaries are contained in F. S. Regs., Part II. and the Staff Manual respectively. Title pages will be prepared in manuscript.

Place	Date	Hour	Summary of Events and Information	Remarks and references to Appendices
COLOGNE	APRIL 14.		C.O. inspects 'D' Co on arriving in afternoon, visits 'B' & 'C' Companies and discusses entries for the Inter-unit Shew at MAYENCE.	
	15.		Informed that the Bath may concentrate in Camp at HEUSSER. Meeting of Company Commanders at Battn HQ to admit all Battalion accounts, and to discuss syllabus for MAYENCE show.	
	16.		C.O. reconnoitres column left of Divisional Rear Army Manoeuvres with G.O.C. 123 Brigade. 2/Lts H.D.TREVOR, R.A.DEEGAN, T.A.BRANTSHAW, A.K. BROOKS & S.A. DASTERR report for duty with the Battalion and go forward to Contingtin. CAPT. W.CRUICKSHANK (M.C.) proceeds on leave. Strength of Battn. 57 Officers 755 O.R.	
	17			
	18		Lt Colonel Falk D.S.O. proceeded to England unmatched.	
	19			
	20			
	21		C.O. & adjt. visited 'A' Co	
	22		C.O. Major Brownphey M.C. attended Sports meeting at Divnl. H.Q.	
	23		C.O. & adjt. visited the line C & D Companies	
	24		- Do - ″ ″ ″ A & B ″	
	25		C.O. adjt. visited C Company	
	26		Strength of Battalion 56 Officers 752 O.R.	
	27		C.O. & 2/Lt Aitchph visited 'A' Company's Sports - Sports performance	
	28		C.O. visited Divisional Race Meeting	

Army Form C. 2118.

WAR DIARY
or
INTELLIGENCE SUMMARY.
(Erase heading not required.)

Instructions regarding War Diaries and Intelligence Summaries are contained in F. S. Regs., Part II. and the Staff Manual respectively. Title pages will be prepared in manuscript.

Place	Date	Hour	Summary of Events and Information	Remarks and references to Appendices
Cologne	April 29.		C.O. + C.C. "D" Company visited H.Q. 2nd Cavalry Bde. and arranged H.S. positions afterwards reconnoitering Cavalry Sector	Sd.
	30.		CO visited D Company in left Brigade Sector	Sd.

R. Lindsay
Lieut Colonel
Commanding 41/st Battalion
Machine Gun Corps.

Army Form C. 2118.

WAR DIARY
or
INTELLIGENCE SUMMARY.
(Erase heading not required.)

Instructions regarding War Diaries and Intelligence Summaries are contained in F. S. Regs., Part II. and the Staff Manual respectively. Title pages will be prepared in manuscript.

41st M.G.C.

Place	Date	Hour	Summary of Events and Information	Remarks and references to Appendices
COLOGNE.	May-1.		"A" Company's Sports postponed. Cwt. Cinema at M-Gladbach.	
	2.		Lieut. VICKERY reported to Battalion as Q.M. - C.O. visited "A" Company.	
	3.		"A" Company's Sports again postponed. = Lieut. MEEK proceeds on Leave.	
	4.		Meeting of Company Commanders to decide as to distribution of Canteen Funds with regard to Sport, also general points discussed.	
	5.		C.O., attended Conference at Division, re Demobilization = Draft of 148 men reported from Inf.	
	6.			
	7.		Major BARRY visits "B" Company, and inspects the section training for Divisional Sports, good progress reported.	
	8.			
	9.		Major BARRY proceeds to England on Leave. C.O., visits "A" and "C" Companies at HEUMAR re sites for Tennis Courts and Cricket Pitches.	
	10.		C.O., visits 32nd Bn. M.G.C. Draft of 68 O.R's., from Royal Fusiliers attached to this Bn. 24. O.R's., to "B" Company, 19.O.R's., to "D" Company, 25. O.R's., to "A" Company.	
	11.		C.O., visits 29th Bn. M.G.C. The Battalion holding positions on our left.	
	12.			
	13.		C.O., and Adjutant were to meet O.C. "A" and "D" Companies to go round the line. Owing to inclement weather it was postponed until the following day.	
	14.		C.O., and Adjutant and Os.C. "A" and "D" Companies went round the line.	
	15.		C.O., and Adjutant and Os. C. "A" and "B" Companies went round the line.	
	16.			
	17.		Draft of 40 O.R's., attached to this Battalion, and posted :- 25 O.R's., 9th East Surreys to "B" Company, 15. O.R's., 23rd Middlesex to "D" Company.	
	18.		"A" Company Sports held at HEUMAR. Strength of Battalion, 55 Officers, 892 Other Ranks.	
	19.		C.O., visits "C" and "D" Companies.	
	20.		C.O., and Adjutant visit 42nd Battalion M.G.C.	
	21.		Adjutant visits HEUMAR and arranges about position of tents etc.	
	22.		C.O., visits "A" and "B" Companies, and then went round the line.	
	23.		C.O., with Os. C., "A" and "B" Companies visit back areas of the line.	
	24.		"D" Company at IMMEKEPPEL, and Battalion Headquarters at MARIENBURG move to Camp at HEUMAR. Battalion Strength. 55 Officers, 826 Other Ranks.	
HEUMAR.	25.		Lieut. G.C. GRIMSHAW. Lieut. E.W. KAHN., Lieut. R.B. FERGUS., reported from England. Lieut. G.C. GRIMSHAW and Lieut. E.W. KAHN posted to "B" Company. Lieut. R.B. FERGUS to "C" Coy.	

Army Form C. 2118.

WAR DIARY
or
INTELLIGENCE SUMMARY.
(Erase heading not required.)

Instructions regarding War Diaries and Intelligence Summaries are contained in F.S. Regs., Part II. and the Staff Manual respectively. Title pages will be prepared in manuscript.

Place	Date	Hour	Summary of Events and Information	Remarks and references to Appendices
COLOGNE.	May.26.		Draft from 42nd Bn. M.G.C. - 6 Officers, 171 Other Ranks. 1 O.R. from the 46th Bn. M.G.C. Officers posted :- Lt. A.V. COATES to "A" Company. Lts. H.T. GOULD and T.C. BLACK to "C" Coy. Lt. H.P.S. WISE and 2/Lieuts. J.E. WEBB and L. JORDAN to "D" Company. - G.O.C. Division inspected the Camp during the morning.	9/8
	27.		Draft of 6 Officers from 42nd Bn. M.G.C. - Capt. A.S. DENNY, Lieut. W. SANDIFORD. posted to "A" Company. - Lieut. R.D. ROSS to "B" Company. Capt. E.J. BRETT and Lieut. G.E.T. SMITH to "C" Company. - Major J.F. NICHOLS to "D" Company. - Major A.G. BARRY reported from Leave.	9%
	28.		2 Officers proceeded for dispersal (one for repatriation and one for Demobilization).	9%
	29.		1 Officer proceeded for Dispersal.	9%
	30.		Draft of 37 O.R's., arrived from 42nd Bn. M.G.C.,	9%
	31.		Strength of Battn. 70 Officers. 1104. Other Ranks.	9%
HEUMAR.				

[signature]

Lieut-Colonel,
Commanding,
41st Battalion Machine Gun Corps.

WAR DIARY or INTELLIGENCE SUMMARY

Army Form C. 2118.

41st M.G.C

Place	Date	Hour	Summary of Events and Information	Remarks and references to Appendices
HEUNAR.	1/6/19.		G.O.C., visits Major. A.M. PRATT. M.G., Battalion Education Officer and arranges about Educational Classes, etc.,	
	2.			
	3.		Draft of 32 Other Ranks from 42nd Bn. M.G.C.	
	4.			
	5.		2 Officers for Demobilization.	
	6.		Lecture on War Savings by Major RAYNER. - 2 Officers for Demobilization.	
	7.		Strength of Battalion. 61 Officers, 1098 Other Ranks. 4 Officers for Demobilization.	
	8.		Cricket Match. Officers V Sergeants. Officers won by 34 Runs.	
	9.		do do Possibles V Probables. Possibles won by 60 Runs.	
	10.		Meeting of Executive Sports Committee. Capt. & Q.-M. WRIGHT reported for Duty from 30th Division.	
	11.		Capt. J.O.R. EVANS. M.C.; reported for Duty from 42nd Bn. M.G.C. Posted to "D" Company.	
	12.		1 Officer for Demobilization.	
	13.		G.O., and Adjutant visited "B" Company.	
	14.		Adjutant goes to "B" Company and visits part of the Line.	
	15.		Cricket Match 41st Bn. M.G.C. V 3rd Northern Bde. 41st Bn. M.G.C. won by 140 Runs.	
	16.		Strength of Battalion 62 Officers, 1084 Other Ranks. - G.O., goes on Leave to England.	
	17.		Received orders to prepare for going forward. 27 Candidates sat for 2nd Class Army Certificates.	
	18.		G.O.C. visits Camp. - Wire sent recalling Lieut- Colonel. Lindsay, returning from Leave.	
	19.		"A" Company move to OVERATH.	
	20.		"A" Company move forward to SUEINHAUS. "B" Company move forward to ENGELSKIRCHEN.	
	21.		Colonel. Lindsay returns to Battalion from Leave. 2/Lieut. J.G. HOUSIN. to Hospital.	
	22.		Strength of Battalion 62 Officers, 1083 Other Ranks. 2/Lieut. A.K. BROOKS. from Hospital.	
	23.		Training as per programme. i.e., Machine Gun Training Part I, Close Order Drill & Elementary training. - Capt. W.H. PARNIS. M.G., arrived from 11th Bn. M.G.C.	
	24.		C.O., visits L.G. Guards on Bridges -- Division, and then "A" & "B" Companies.	
	25.		Capt. W.H. PARNIS. M.G. takes over Duties of Adjutant.	

Army Form C. 2118.

WAR DIARY
or
INTELLIGENCE SUMMARY.
(Erase heading not required.)

Instructions regarding War Diaries and Intelligence Summaries are contained in F. S. Regs., Part II. and the Staff Manual respectively. Title pages will be prepared in manuscript.

Place	Date	Hour	Summary of Events and Information	Remarks and references to Appendices
HEUMAR.	1/8/19.		C.O., visits Major. A.M. PRATT. M.C., Battalion Education Officer and arranges about Educational Classes, etc.,	
	2.		Draft of 32 Other Ranks from 42nd Bn. M.G.C.	
	3.			
	4.		2 Officers for Demobilization.	
	5.		Lecture on War Savings by Major RAYNER. - 2 Officers for Demobilization.	
	6.		Strength of Battalion. 61 Officers, 1098 Other Ranks. 4 Officers for Demobilization.	
	7.		Cricket Match. Officers V Sergeants. Officers won by 84 Runs.	
	8.		do do Possibles V Probables. Possibles won by 80 Runs.	
	9.		Meeting of Executive Sports Committee.	
	10.		Capt. & Q.M. H. WRIGHT reported for Duty from 30th Division.	
	11.		Capt. J.O.R. EVANS. M.C., reported for Duty from 42nd Bn. M.G.C. Posted to "D" Company. 1 Officer for Demobilization.	
	12.		C.O., and Adjutant visited "B" Company.	
	13.		Adjutant goes to "B" Company and visits part of the Line.	
	14.		Cricket Match 41st Bn. M.G.C. V 3rd Northern Bde. 41st Bn. M.G.C. won by 140 Runs. Strength of Battalion 62 Officers, 1094 Other Ranks. - C.O., goes on Leave to England.	
	15.			
	16.			
	17.		Received orders to prepare for going forward. 27 Candidates sat for 2nd Class Army Certificates.	
	18.		G.O.C., visits Camp. - Wire sent recalling Lieut- Colonel. Lindsay, ~~Exercising~~ from Leave.	
	19.		"A" Company move to OVERATH. "B" Company move forward to ENGELSKIRCHEN.	
	20.		"A" Company move forward to STEINHAUS. 2/Lieut. J.C. HOWSIN. to Hospital. Colonel. Lindsey returns to Battalion from Leave. 2/Lieut. A.K. BROOKS. from Hospital.	
	21.		Strength of Battalion 62 Officers, 1083 Other Ranks.	
	22.			
	23.		Training as per programme. i.e., Machine Gun Training Part I. Close Order Drill & Elementary training. - Capt. W.H. PARNIS. M.C., arrived from 11th Bn. M.G.C.	
	24.		C.O., visits M.G. Guards on Bridges - Division, and then "A" & "B" Companies.	
	25.		Capt. W.H. PARNIS. M.C. takes over Duties of Adjutant.	

Army Form C. 2118.

WAR DIARY
or
INTELLIGENCE SUMMARY.

(Erase heading not required.)

Instructions regarding War Diaries and Intelligence Summaries are contained in F. S. Regs., Part II. and the Staff Manual respectively. Title pages will be prepared in manuscript.

Place	Date	Hour	Summary of Events and Information	Remarks and references to Appendices
HEUMAR.	June 26.			
	June 27.		2/Lieut. L. JORDAN proceeded to D. of S.& T., G.H.Q., Rhine Army.	
	" 28.		Lieut. A.J. SLADE proceeded to KREFELD,/for Duty. Auth. Rhine Army A.308/1473.	
	" 29.		Lieut. A.J. SLADE proceeded on leave to U.K.	
	" 30.		Lieut-Colonel. G.M. LINDSAY. C.M.G., D.S.O., relinquished Command of the Battalion. "A" Company moved from STEINHAUS to HEUMAR. "B" Company moved from ENGELSKIRCHEN to HEUMAR.	
HEUMAR. 5/7/19. G.H.				

A. Vivian Oakeshott 2/04
Lieut-Colonel.
Commanding,
41st Battalion Machine Gun Corps.

Army Form C. 2118.

WAR DIARY
or
INTELLIGENCE SUMMARY.
(Erase heading not required.)

Instructions regarding War Diaries and Intelligence Summaries are contained in F. S. Regs., Part II. and the Staff Manual respectively. Title pages will be prepared in manuscript.

Place	Date	Hour	Summary of Events and Information	Remarks and references to Appendices
HEUMAR.	June 26.			
	June 27.		2/Lieut. L. JORDAN proceeded to D of S.& T. G.H.Q. Rhine Army.	
	" 28.		Lieut. A.J. SLADE proceeded on Duty. Anth. Rhine Army A.308/1473.	
	" 29.		Lieut. A.J. SLADE proceeded on Leave to U.K.	
	" 30.		Lieut-Colonel. G.M. LINDSAY. C.M.G., D.S.O., relinquished Command of the Battalion. "A" Company moved from STEINHAUS to HEUMAR. "B" Company moved from ENGELSKIRCHEN to HEUMAR.	

HEUMAR.
3/7/19.
G.H.

A. Niven Cockerton Lt./jnr
a/jnr

Lieut-Colonel.
Commanding,
41st Battalion Machine Gun Corps.

Army Form C. 2118.

WAR DIARY
or
INTELLIGENCE SUMMARY.
(Erase heading not required.)

Instructions regarding War Diaries and Intelligence Summaries are contained in F. S. Regs., Part II. and the Staff Manual respectively. Title pages will be prepared in manuscript.

Place	Date	Hour	Summary of Events and Information	Remarks and references to Appendices
RATH CAMP.	1st July.		Lieut-Col. A.G. BARRY. D.S.O., M.C. assumed command of the Battn, vice Lieut-Col. G.M. LINDSAY. C.M.G., D.S.O., to U.K. for Duty.	
	2nd.		Lieut. E.A. PULLAN to U.K. on Leave. Lieut. H.P.S. WISE to duty at Army Technical College, Siegburg. Cricket Match. Battn. V 161 Bde R.F.A. Battn.128. R.F.A. 32.	
	3rd.		Cricket Match. Battn.(156) V 5th K.O.Y.L.I. (47).	
	4th.		2/Lieut. C.J. TOMKINS. ⎫ 2/Lieut. W.D. TREVOR. ⎬ To U.K. for Duty. 2/Lieut. A.K. BROOKS. ⎭ 2/Lieut. S.A. De Ste CROIX. DCM. MM. Draft of 29 O.R's., joined for Duty from 42nd Bn. M.G.C. Capt. A.C. DENNY. M.C. rejoined from Leave to U.K. Cricket Match Battn. (168 for 5) V 3rd Bn. M.G.C. (59).	
	5.		Athletic Meeting V. 15th Bn. Hampshire Regt. 1 O.R. joined for Duty from 42nd Bn. M.G.C. Major. J.W. GARDEN. D.S.O., M.C. to U.K. on Leave.	
	6.		4. O.R's to Paris for Victory March. Capt. H.C. WATKINS rejoined from Leave to U.K.	
	7.		Examination for 2nd and 3rd Class Army Certificates. Lieut. J.S. STOREY admitted to Hospital.	
	8.		Lieut. ASPINWALL to U.K. on Leave.	
	9.		Major. F.M. ARKLE. rejoined from Leave to U.K.	

Army Form C. 2118.

WAR DIARY
or
INTELLIGENCE SUMMARY.
(Erase heading not required.)

Instructions regarding War Diaries and Intelligence Summaries are contained in F. S. Regs., Part II. and the Staff Manual respectively. Title pages will be prepared in manuscript.

Place	Date	Hour	Summary of Events and Information	Remarks and references to Appendices
RATH CAMP.	10th July.		Lieut. E.J. BRETT. M.C. rejoined from Leave to U.K. 2/Lieut. R.A. DEEGAN.) To U.K. for Duty. Lieut. R.B. FERGUS.) H.Q., and Company Officers' messes Amalgamated into Battalion Officers' Mess. Major. F.M. ARKLE assumed duties of 2nd in Command. Capt. R.G. BACKRATH. appointed O.C. "A" Company.	
	11th.		Amalgamation of Company Canteens with Battalion Canteen. Institution of voluntary class in German for all ranks, under Major. A.M. PRATT. M.C.	
	12th.		Commanding Officers' Parade. Full Marching Order.	
	13th.		Ablution Huts completed and taken into use.	
	14th.		Lieut. A.J. SLADE rejoined from Leave to U.K. 1 O.R. joined from General Base Depot. for Duty.	
	15.		Cricket Match Battn. (127) V Northern Division R.E. (53).	
	16.		Lieut. J.L. ROGERS. M.C. to U.K to Leave. Rehearsal parade for G.O.O's inspection.	
	17.		Inspection of Battalion by Major-General Sir, S.T.B. LAWFORD. K.C.B. Commanding London Division Strength on Parade 40 Officers, 750 Other Ranks. 227 Animals. G.O.C. afterwards inspected Battalion Lines, Cook-houses, Dining Halls, and Transport Lines.	
	18th.		Lieut. L.A. PULLAN rejoined from Leave to U.K.	
	19th.		Lieut. A.V. COATES to U.K. on Leave. Competition for best kept and neatest tents. Prizes awarded by Commanding Officer as under :- 1st Prize. "D" Company. 210 Marks. 2nd Prize. "A" Coy. 200 Marks. 3rd Prize. Transport. 140 Marks. 4th Prize. "C" Company. 80 Marks. 5th Prize. "B" " 50 " Special H.Q. Saddlers. 150 " Cricket Match Battn. V Team from Rhine Army H.Q.	

Army Form C. 2118.

WAR DIARY
or
INTELLIGENCE SUMMARY.

(Erase heading not required.)

Instructions regarding War Diaries and Intelligence Summaries are contained in F.S. Regs., Part II. and the Staff Manual respectively. Title pages will be prepared in manuscript.

Place	Date	Hour	Summary of Events and Information	Remarks and references to Appendices
RATH CAMP.	20th July.		Cricket Match Battn. (62 for 2) V Wahn Survey Dept. (60)	
	21st.		Lieut. R. HOUGH M.C. and Lieut. K.L. FISHER. M.C. and Draft of 29 O.R's from 42nd Bn. M.G.C. joined for Duty, and posted to "B" Company.	
	22.		Lieut. H. BANDFORD joined for duty from 42nd Bn. M.G.C. and posted to "D" Company.	
	23rd.		Capt. F.L. CRANFIELD. to U.K. on Leave. Lieut. J.F. NICHOLS. M.C. Posted to 3rd Bn. M.G.C. and proceeded for duty. Lieut. J. TRAYLEN (employed VI Corps Officers Club) posted to 3rd Bn. M.G.C.	
	24.		Cricket Match Battn. (158) V 2nd Bn. M.G.C. (70).	
	25th.		Lieut. A. ASPINWALL rejoined from Leave to U.K.	
	26.		Lieut. E.F. KENNETT. to U.K. on Leave. Funeral of 170478. Pte C.R. PARKER, at SUBFRIEDHOS CEMETERY, COLOGNE.	
	27.			
	28.		Cricket Match Battn. (93 for 2) V 5th R. Irish Regt. (87).	
	29.		2/Lieut. L. HOUSTON. to U.K. on Leave.	
	30.			
	31.			
RATH CAMP. 2/8/19. G.H.				

Lieutenant Colonel,
Commanding,
41st Battalion Machine Gun Corps.

Army Form C. 2118.

WAR DIARY
or
INTELLIGENCE SUMMARY.
(Erase heading not required.)

Instructions regarding War Diaries and Intelligence Summaries are contained in F. S. Regs., Part II. and the Staff Manual respectively. Title pages will be prepared in manuscript.

41ST BATTALION MACHINE GUN

Place	Date	Hour	Summary of Events and Information	Remarks and references to Appendices
August	1		Lieut.J.O.R.Evans M.C. to U.K. on leave	
	2		2.Lieut.T.Brantingham M.M. to U.K. on leave	
	3		Lieut.H.M.Goold to U.K. on leave	
	4		"B" Company and 1 section of "C" Company to M.G.Musketry Camp, OVERATH, for General Musketry Course.	
	5		Lieut.A.Titley to U.K. on leave.	
	6		Lieut.W.Sandiford from leave to U.K.	
	7		Lieut.T.C.Black to U.K. on leave; Major J.W.Gordon D.S.O.,M.C., from leave.	
	8		Lieut.F.Smith to U.K. on leave.	
	9		2.Lieut.J.France M.C. to U.K. on leave; Lieut.A.V.Coates from leave.	
	10		2.Lieut.S.Darke } to U.K. on leave; Lieut.F.Kennett from leave.	
			Lieut.R.R.Foreman }	
			Capt.W.H.Parnis M.C. to France on leave; Lieut.P.F.Mird from leave.	
	11			
	12			
	13			
	14		"D" Company to EVERATH Musketry Camp for General Musketry Course. "B" Company withdrawn to Rath Camp on completion of course.	
	15		Capt.W.H.Parnis M.C. rejoined from leave to France.	
	16		Lieut.R.Fisher M.C. to U.K. on leave; 2.Lieut.L.Houston from leave.	
			Inter regimental Sports Meeting v 15th Hampshire Regiment at Vurmelskirchen. The Battalion won by 27 points.	
	17		Lieut.A.J.Dale joined for duty from 32nd Battalion M.G.Corps and posted to "D" Company.	
			2nd Lieut.G.T.Joslin posted from 32nd Battalion M.G.Corps (whilst on leave to U.K.)	
			Lieut.M.J.V.Harson to U.K. on leave.	
	18		Guard of Honour (50 O.Rs under Capt.W.H.Parnis M.C. & Lieut.J.L.Rogers M.C.) furnished by the Battalion to receive Army Council at VIth Corps Commander's House, Lindenthal, Cologne at 1330 hours.	
			First two Derby men proceeded for dispersal.	
			Lieut.W.Kahn to U.K. on leave.	

PTO

WAR DIARY
or
INTELLIGENCE SUMMARY.
(Erase heading not required.)

Army Form C. 2118.

Place	Date	Hour	Summary of Events and Information	Remarks and references to Appendices
	31st August 1919.	19	Lieut.J.S.Storey & 3rd Lieut.A.Duddin proceeded for duty with 52nd Battalion M.G.Corps.	
		20	Lieut.J.O.R.Evans M.C. from leave; Captain G.M.Christie M.C., R.A.M.C., to U.K. on leave. 400 yards Range at Rath Camp completed, and Board held in accordance with instructions from London Division.	
		21	Lieut.W.Thomas to U.K. on leave.	
		22	Lieut.A.J.Dale to U.K. on leave.	
		23	Lt.Colonel A.G.Barry D.S.O., M.C., runner-up in Rhine Army Golf Championship. Battalion inspected by Commanding Officer, with full transport.	
		24	Lieut.A.E.Walker to U.K. on leave; Lieut.J.E.France M.C. & Lieut.T.O.Black rejoined from leave.	
		25	Lieut.T.E.Andrews to U.K. on leave.	
		26	Lieut.R.Hough M.C. } from leave to U.K. Lieut.H.Goold }	
		27	Battalion with full transport inspected by Lieut.General Sir Aylmer Haldane K.C.B., D.S.O., Commanding VI Corps. After inspection, the Corps Commander inspected the lines, Dining Halls, Cookhouses &c, and addressed the troops. Lieut.E.A.Foreman & Lieut.L.Darke from leave to U.K. Lieut.E.S.Williams rejoined from Hospital. Battalion won 2 team events in London Divisional Rifle Meeting at OVERATH.	
		28	"D" Company withdrawn from Musketry Camp, Overath, to Rath Camp on completion of General Musketry Course. Musketry Camp at Overath struck, sanction having been granted for remaining Companies to use Rath Range for General Musketry Course. Lieut.E.S.Williams to U.K. on leave.	
		29	Captain & Q.M. H.Wright M.B.E. to U.K. on leave. Commanding Officer attended conference at London Divisional H.Qrs.	
		30		
		31	Guards furnished by 3rd London Infantry Brigade at Heumar Station and Nobels Dynamite Factory, Frankonfurst, taken over by this unit. Strength of unit on 31/8/19:- 54 Officers, 1102 O.Rs.	

Capt. & Adjt.,
1st. Bn. M.G. Corps.

Army Form C. 2118.

Sept 1919

41st BATTALION.
MACHINE GUN
CORPS.

WAR DIARY
or
INTELLIGENCE SUMMARY.
(Erase heading not required.)

Instructions regarding War Diaries and Intelligence Summaries are contained in F. S. Regs., Part II. and the Staff Manual respectively. Title pages will be prepared in manuscript.

Place	Date	Hour	Summary of Events and Information	Remarks and references to Appendices
	1.		London Divisional Sports Meeting. Battalion Team won the Divisional Championship, and a Silver Cup presented by the Divisional Commander.	
	2.			
	3.		"B" Coy. on WAHN Range. M.G. eliminating tests for selection of teams for Army Rifle Meeting. Major. D. BOUMPHREY. M.C. proceeded on leave to U.K.	
	4.		Major-General Sir.G.T.B.Lawford.K.C.B.Commanding London Division,visited the Battalion while at training. Lieut. R.F. KINNIMONT proceeded on leave.	
	5.			
	6.		VI Corps Sports. Battalion won the Corps Championship with 5 firsts and 2 seconds out of 10 events. Medals presented by Lieut.Gen.Sir Aylmer Haldane.K.C.B.	
	7.		Instructions received to reduce establishment of Officers from 52 to 34.	
	8.		4 Officers and 44 Other ranks proceeded to Army Rifle Meeting at DROVE. Lt.A.J.DALE rejoined from Leave to U.K.	
	9.		Semi-finals & Finals of VI Corps Tug-of-War and Basket Ball Competitions on Battalion Ground. Lieut.A.J.DALE admitted to Hospital. Lieut.A.HOLDING proceeded on leave to U.K.	
	10.		2/Lt.A.E.WALKER rejoined from leave to U.K. Lieut.J.E.FRANCE.M.C.proceeded for demobilization.	
	11.		Lt.Col.A.G.BARRY. D.S.O. M.C. proceeded on leave to U.K.and Major.F.MARKLE assumed temporary command of the Battalion.	
	12.		Major.A.H.PRATT. M.C. admitted to Hospital. 4 Officers and 44 Other ranks rejoined from Army Rifle Meeting.	
	13.		Lieut. E.S.WILLIAMS rejoined from Leave to U.K.	
	14.			
	15.		Capt. & Q.M.H.WRIGHT.M.B.M.rejoined from Leave to U.K.	
	16.		Lieut. F.R.LETTS.proceeded for demobilization.	
	17.		Army Athletic Championships.at RUHL. Battalion represented VI Corps. Lieut.R.HOUGH.M.C. & Lieut.F.SANDFORD granted 4 days leave to NAMUR,Belgium. 7 Officers proceeded for demobilization.	
	18.		Conclusion of Army Athletic Championships. Battalion won championship of Rhine Army. Major. D. BOUMPHREY.M.C.rejoined from leave to U.K.	
	19.		Captain Rev. E.MARRIOTT. arrived as C. of E. Chaplain to the Battalion. Lieut. R. F. KINNIMONT.rejoined from Leave to U.K.	
	20.		Captain.H.J.PICKERING.M.C. R.A.M.C.arrived and took over duties of M.O.to the Battalion.	

Army Form C.2118.

WAR DIARY
OF
INTELLIGENCE SUMMARY.

Place.	Date.	Hour.	Summary of Events and Information.	Remarks and references to appendices.
	21.		Lieut.R.HOUGH.M.G.and Lieut.H.SANDFORD rejoined from leave to Belgium.	
	22.		Battalion Sports held at RATH CAMP.	
	23.		Lieut.A.J.SLADE proceeded for demobilization. Lieut.(A/Capt) F.L.GRANFIELD	
	24.		Lieut.A.J.HAM rejoined from Hospital. Lieut.(A/Capt) F.L.GRANFIELD proceeded for duty with D.of S.& T.G.H.Q. Rhine Army, and struck off strength of Battalion.	
	25.			
	26.		Captain.E.G.WATKINS.M.G.proceeded on leave to U.K. 100 O.R's. proceeded for demobilization.	
	27.			
	28.		Major.A.M.PRATT.M.G.rejoined from Hospital.	
	29.			
	30.			
RATH CAMP. 4-10-19.			Strength of Battalion on 30/9/19. 41 Officers and 805 O.R's.	

Major,
Commanding 41st Battalion,
Machine Gun Corps.

Army Form W.3091.

Cover for Documents.

Nature of Enclosures.

41st Battalion M.G. Corps.

War Diary
October, 1919.

Notes, or Letters written.

Army Form C. 2118.

WAR DIARY
or
INTELLIGENCE SUMMARY.
(Erase heading not required.)

Instructions regarding War Diaries and Intelligence Summaries are contained in F. S. Regs., Part II. and the Staff Manual respectively. Title pages will be prepared in manuscript.

Place	Date	Hour	Summary of Events and Information	Remarks and references to Appendices
Cologne.	Oct.1.			
(Rath Camp.)	" 2.			
	" 3.		Lt. A.C. DENNY M.C. Proceeded on Leave to Weisbaden.	
	" 4.			
	" 5.		Capt. W. PARNIS M.C. Rejoined Battn. after leave from to Malta. resumed duties as Adjutant.	
(Wahn.)	" 6.		The Battalion moved from Rath Camp to No. 1. P.O.W. Camp. WAHN. Lt-Colonel A.G. BARRY D.S.O. M.C. resumed command of the Battn on his return from leave to U.K. Major. B. BOUMPHREY M.C. and Lt. L.S. DARK proceeded to 17th. Battn. Royal Fus. at Neunkirchen to assist in tactical schemes.	
	" 7.			
	" 8.		Lieut. R. HOUGH M.C. proceeded on Course to Lon. Div. Musketry School at Bruck.	
	" 9.		Capt. H.C. WATKINS M.C. rejoined from leave to U.K. Major D. BOUMPHREY M.C. and Lt. L.S. DARK return from Neunkirchen 10/10/19.	
	" 10.		Lieut. E.A. PULLAN and Lieut. T.E. ANDREWS proceeded on leave to Belgium Lieut. G. HOLDING rejoined from leave to U.K. 14. O.R. proceeded for Dispersal.	
	" 11.		15. O.R. proceeded for Dispersal.	
	" 12.		42. O.R. proceeded for Dispersal.	
	" 13.		Lieut. A. TITLEY proceeded to U.K. on D.C.D. and Leave in charge of 50 other ranks proceeding for Dispersal. The Battn. Rugby Team played the 53rd, Rifle Brigade at KALK.	

Army Form C. 2118.

WAR DIARY
or
INTELLIGENCE SUMMARY.
(*Erase heading not required.*)

* Instructions regarding War Diaries and Intelligence Summaries are contained in F. S. Regs., Part II. and the Staff Manual respectively. Title pages will be prepared in manuscript.

Place	Date	Hour	Summary of Events and Information	Remarks and references to Appendices
Cologne.	Oct.14.		Lieut. A.E. PULLAN and Lieut. T.E. ANDREWS rejoined from Leave to Belgium. 50 O.R. proceeded for Dispersal.	
	" 15.		20. O.R. proceeded for Dispersal.	
(Wahn.)	" 16.		Major. F.M. ARKLE proceeded on leave to U.K. Lieut. G. HOLDING admitted to Hospital. 40. O.R. proceeded for Dispersal.	
	" 17.		Lieut. A.C. DENNY M.C. rejoined from leave to Weisbaden. 52. O.R. proceeded for Dispersal.	
	" 18.		30. O.R. proceeded for Dispersal.	
	" 19.		40. O.R. proceeded for Dispersal.	
(Rhiel.)	" 20.		The Battalion moved from No. 1. P.O.W. Camp Wahn to Rhiel Barracks. Capt. Pickering M.C. R.A.M.C. ceased to be attached to the Battalion.	
	" 21.			
	" 22.		Lieut. W.A.S. HILL M.C. rejoined from Course at Army Science School Bonn.	
	" 23.		Lieut. L, HOUSTON proceeded on leave to U.K.	
	" 24.		9. O.R. proceeded for Dispersal.	
	" 25.		2/Lieut. T.E. BRANTINGHAM M.M. rejoined from Course at Army. General & Commercial College Cologne.	
	" 26.		4. O.R. proceeded for Dispersal.	
	" 27.		Capt. D.G.S. GARTSHORE R.A.M.C. joined the Battn. for Duty as M.O.	
	" 28.		A draft of 140 O.R. joined the Battn. for Duty from the 9th. Battn. M.G.C.	

Army Form C. 2118.

WAR DIARY
or
INTELLIGENCE SUMMARY.
(Erase heading not required.)

Instructions regarding War Diaries and Intelligence Summaries are contained in F.S. Regs., Part II. and the Staff Manual respectively. Title pages will be prepared in manuscript.

Place	Date	Hour	Summary of Events and Information	Remarks and references to Appendices
Cologne Rhiel	28	—	Battalion participated in Corps rehearsal of scheme for action in the event of civil disturbances. Shortage of personnel made up by commandeering all available men from the 3rd Batt. M.G.C. in Rhiel Barracks.	
	29	—	Drafts of 19 O.Rs from 2nd Batt.M.G.C. and 100 O.Rs from 3rd Batt.M.G.Corps reported for duty. Captain D.G.S.Gartshore R.A.M.C. ceased to be attached to the Battalion as M.O. Lieut.W.Sandiford & Lieut.H.Sandford rejoined from Draft Conducting Duty and Leave to U.K. 8 O.Rs proceeded for dispersal. Court of Enquiry held on fatal injury to a mule on 21st instant.	
	30	—	Lieut.F.Smith proceeded on leave to U.K. Lieut.A.Aspinwall rejoined from Draft Conducting Duty and Leave to U.K.	
	31	—	4 O.Rs proceeded for dispersal. Following Officers from 3rd Battalion M.G.Corps joined for duty:— Lieut.J.L.Piggin Lieut.J.Storey Lieut.N.V.Stephens Lieut.F.Hope Lieut.W.E.Beaumont Lieut.E.J.Hawkins Lieut.J.A.Roch M.C. Lieut.A.Duffey Strength of unit on 31st October 1919 Officers: 49 O.Ranks: 671 Total 720	

Lieut. Col.
Commdg. 4th Bn. M.G. Corps

Army Form C. 2118.

WAR DIARY
or
INTELLIGENCE SUMMARY.
(Erase heading not required.)

Instructions regarding War Diaries and Intelligence Summaries are contained in F. S. Regs., Part II. and the Staff Manual respectively. Title pages will be prepared in manuscript.

Place	Date	Hour	Summary of Events and Information	Remarks and references to Appendices
Cologne.	Oct.1.			
"	2.		Lt. A.C. DENNY M.C. Proceeded on Leave to Weisbaden.	
(Rath Camp.)				
"	3.		Capt. W. PARNIS M.C. Rejoined Battn. after leave from to Malta, resumed duties as Adjutant.	
"	4.			
"	5.			
"	6.		The Battalion moved from Rath Camp to No. 1. P.O.W. Camp. WAHN. Lt-Colonel A.G. BARRY D.S.O. M.C. resumed command of the Battn on his return from leave to U.K. Major. B. BOUMPHREY M.C. and Lt. L.S. DARK proceeded to 17th. Battn. Royal Fus. at Neunkirchen to assist in tactical schemes.	
(Wahn.)	7.			
"	8.		Lieut. R. HOUGH M.C. proceeded on Course to Lon. Div. Musketry school at Bruck.	
"	9.		Capt. H.O. WATKINS M.C. rejoined from leave to U.K. Major D. BOUMPHREY M.C. and Lt. L.S. DARK return from Neunkirchen 10/10/19.	
"	10.		Lieut. E.A. PULLAN and Lieut. T.E. ANDREWS proceeded on leave to Belgium Lieut. G. HOLDING rejoined from leave to U.K.	
"	11.		14. O.R. proceeded for Dispersal.	
"	12.		15. O.R. proceeded for Dispersal.	
"	13.		42. O.R. proceeded for Dispersal. Lieut. A. TITLEY proceeded to U.K. on D.C.D. and Leave in charge of 50 other ranks proceeding for Dispersal. The Battn. Rugby Team played the 53rd, Rifle Brigade At KALK.	

Army Form C. 2118.

WAR DIARY
or
INTELLIGENCE SUMMARY.

(Erase heading not required.)

Instructions regarding War Diaries and Intelligence Summaries are contained in F. S. Regs., Part II. and the Staff Manual respectively. Title pages will be prepared in manuscript.

Place	Date	Hour	Summary of Events and Information	Remarks and references to Appendices
Cologne.	Oct.14.		Lieut. A.E. PULLAN and Lieut. E. ANDREWS rejoined from Leave to Belgium.	
	" 15.		50. O.R. proceeded for Dispersal.	
	" 16.		Major. F.M. ARKLE proceeded on leave to U.K. Lieut. G. HOLDING admitted to Hospital. 40. O.R. proceeded for Dispersal.	
(Wahn.)	" 17.		Lieut. A.C. DENNY M.C. rejoined from leave to Weisbaden. 52. O.R. proceeded for Dispersal.	
	" 18.		30. O.R. proceeded for Dispersal.	
	" 19.		40. O.R. proceeded for Dispersal.	
(Rhiel.)	" 20.		The Battalion moved from No. 1. P.O.W. Camp Wahn to Rhiel Barracks. Capt. Pickering M.C. R.A.M.C. ceased to be attached to the Battalion.	
	" 21.			
	" 22.		Lieut. W.A.S. HILL M.C. rejoined from Course at Army Science School Bonn.	
	" 23.		Lieut. L. HOUSTON proceeded on leave to U.K.	
	" 24.		9. O.R. proceeded for Dispersal.	
	" 25.		2/Lieut. T.E. BRANTINGHAM M.M. rejoined from Course at Army. General & Commercial College Cologne.	
	" 26.		4. O.R. proceeded for Dispersal.	
	" 27.		Capt. D.G.S. GARTSHORE R.A.M.C. joined the Battn. for Duty as M.O.	
	" 28.		A draft of 140 O.R. joined the Battn. for Duty from the 9th. Battn. M.G.C.	

Army Form C. 2118.

WAR DIARY
or
INTELLIGENCE SUMMARY.
(Erase heading not required.)

Instructions regarding War Diaries and Intelligence Summaries are contained in F. S. Regs., Part II. and the Staff Manual respectively. Title pages will be prepared in manuscript.

Place	Date	Hour	Summary of Events and Information	Remarks and references to Appendices
Cologne Rhiel	28	-	Battalion participated in Corps rehearsal of scheme for action in the event of civil disturbances. Shortage of personnel made up by commandeering all available men from the 3rd Batt.M.G.C. in Rhiel Barracks.	
	29	-	Drafts of 19 O.Rs from 2nd Batt.M.G.C. and 100 O.Rs from 3rd Batt.M.G.Corps reported for duty. Captain D.G.S.Gartshore R.A.M.C. ceased to be attached to the Battalion as M.O. Lieut.W.Sandiford & Lieut.H.Sandford rejoined from Draft Conducting Duty and Leave to U.K, 8 O.Rs proceeded for dispersal. Court of Enquiry held on fatal injury to a mule on 21st instant.	
	30	-	Lieut.F.Smith proceeded on leave to U.K. Lieut.A.Aspinwall rejoined from Draft Conducting Duty and Leave to U.K.	
	31	-	4 O.Rs proceeded for dispersal. Following Officers from 3rd Battalion M.G.Corps joined for duty:- Lieut.J.L.Piggin Lieut.J.Storey Lieut.N.V.Stephens Lieut.F.Hope Lieut.W.E.Beaumont Lieut.E.J.Hawkins Lieut.J.A.Roch M.C. Lieut.A.Duffey	

Strength of unit on 31st October 1919
Officers:- 49
O.Ranks :- 671
Total 720

Commdg. 41st Bn. M. G. Corps.

www.ingramcontent.com/pod-product-compliance
Lightning Source LLC
Chambersburg PA
CBHW080846230426
43662CB00013B/2033